PLAS
PITT
LATIN
AMERICAN
SERIES

D0209795

RESTRUCTURING DOMINATION

Industrialists and the State in Ecuador

Catherine M. Conaghan

University of Pittsburgh Press

Published by the University of Pittsburgh Press,
Pittsburgh, Pa., 15260
Copyright © 1988, University of Pittsburgh Press
All rights reserved
Feffer and Simons, Inc., London
Manufactured in the United States of America

Library of Congress Cataloging in Publication Data

Conaghan, Catherine M.
  Restructuring domination.

  (Pitt Latin American series)
  Bibliography: p. 173.
  Includes index.
  1. Industry and state—Ecuador.   2. Industrialists—Ecuador—Political activity.
3. Elite (Social sciences)—Ecuador—Political activity.   4. Middle classes—Ecuador—
Political activity.   5. Capitalism—Political aspects—Ecuador.   I. Title.   II. Series.
HD3616.E23C65   1988   338.9866   88-1335
ISBN 0-8229-3826-X

To James F. Conaghan,
Helen Conaghan,
and James G. Conaghan

Contents

Tables

Acknowledgments

This book is a product of many journeys. And it is with pleasure that I thank my travelling companions.

My greatest debt is to the people of Ecuador, especially my informants in the private and public sectors. While many of my informants will disagree with the argument, I could not have formulated it without their help. A number of Ecuadorean institutions aided in the course of the research: the Faculty of Economics of the Pontificia Universidad Católica del Ecuador, Facultad Latinoamericana de Ciencias Sociales (Sede Quito), Centro de Planificación y Estudios Sociales, Consejo Nacional de Desarrollo (formerly JUNAPLA), the Banco Central del Ecuador, Comisión Fulbright, Superintendencia de Compañías, Corporación Financiera Nacional, Ministerio de Agricultura y Ganadería, and the Press Office of the Congreso Nacional. My thinking on Ecuador has been influenced by the work of a community of scholars both in and outside of Ecuador. I am grateful to César Verduga, Jorge León, Osvaldo Hurtado, Walter Spurrier, Rafael Quintero, Nick Mills, Peter Pyne, Howard Handelman, and James Levy for their insights and help over the years.

In many ways, this book began during my undergraduate years at the University of Pittsburgh. Pitt's Center for Latin American Studies funded my first field trip to Ecuador in 1975. At Pitt, I found friends and mentors in José Cisneros, Reid Reading, Bert Rockman, and Mark Rosenberg.

Later funding for field work was provided by the Yale Council on Latin American Studies, the Danforth Foundation, the Fulbright-Hays program for doctoral research, and the Simmons College Fund for Research.

Guidance and criticism from fine scholars, who I now happily count as friends, greatly improved the manuscript. As my dissertation adviser at Yale, David Cameron did heroic duties in supervising a thesis on Ecuador. The comparative approach reflects his prodding and the influence of his work on public policy. At every step of the way, James Scott lent a sympathetic ear. While we study domination at opposite ends of the spectrum, Jim's work has always been a rich source of ideas and inspiration. Thomas Biersteker, Marcelo Cavarozzi, and Joseph Love provided thought-provoking criticisms. So did Paul Drake whose enthusiasm and interest in the project came to mean a great deal. At a very early stage, Guillermo O'Donnell's endorsement helped me to get started. At a later stage, Deborah Miner and the supportive environment at Simmons College in Boston helped me to finish the dissertation. The Latin American Studies program at Ohio State University, under the direction of Douglas Graham, provided a stimulating setting as I worked on the final revisions of the book.

To my family, both nuclear and extended, I owe a special thanks. The Conaghan and Suprick families have long been a source of encouragement and entertainment. Their generosity and goodwill over the years allowed me to complete the education that led to this book.

Many friends made intellectual contributions to this book. Others contributed to the mental well-being of its author. They are: Richard Thypin, Angelo Messore, Michael Sabia, Ken Pittman, Gwynne Marstiller, Kemal Mericli, Mena Ubilla, Manuela Sanchez, Jorge "Coqui" Morandi, James Goodyear, the Aguilar family, Eanna O'Broin, Steve Nelson, and Joan Maclean. During the twists of the last year, Harold Mah's belief in the work and the author has bordered on awesome. I thank him.

I am grateful to the University of Pittsburgh Press, especially Cole Blasier for his interest in the book. Excellent copy-editing by Jane Flanders greatly improved the final product.

Finally, I thank two kindred Irish spirits who originally inspired the journeys—James Malloy and James Shanahan. It was Jim Malloy who introduced me to some of the most fascinating politics in the world, that of the central Andes. As a teacher and scholar, Jim Malloy taught lessons in courage and integrity. As a priest and activist, James Shanahan's commitment to social justice for the people of the Andes was an example to all who knew him. Father Shanahan did not live to see the conclusion of this work—but I hope some of his spirit is here.

Restructuring
Domination

Introduction

The intransigence and obstinacy of the bourgeoisie in the face of social change are by no means new themes in the study of Latin American politics. The "obstacles to reform" in Latin America are part of traditional terrain in the social science literature on the region.[1] And more recently, both the public and politicians in the United States have become intimately reacquainted with these themes in regard to Central America. The death squads of El Salvador stand as horrifying reminders of the extent to which dominant classes are willing to go to resist the intentions of even moderate reformers.

Certainly the privileged in every society seek to maintain the system from which they benefit. Yet the political and economic strategies employed by capitalist classes to ensure their domination vary dramatically at various times and in different countries. Sometimes the bourgeoisie gets its own way on its own terms, while at other moments the class may be forced into grudging accommodation or limited defeats. Pragmatism may push the class onto the bandwagon of reform. The revisionist interpretations of U.S. history by Gabriel Kolko and James Weinstein emphasize the leading role played by the monopoly fraction of the bourgeoisie in the reforms of the Progressive Era, which included the beginnings of business regulation and social welfare policies.[2] During the same period, Prime Minister Giovanni Giolitti managed a political coalition based on the support of northern industrialists and the emerging working class that brought about an

3

extension of the franchise in Italy. But reaction can swiftly follow such reformist interludes. Recent work by Theda Skocpol underscores the sharp resistance offered by the American business community to the New Deal reforms.[3] And there is no doubt that elements of the Italian and German bourgeoisie were key partners in the fascist coalitions of those countries.[4] Restraints on trade unionism, the expansion of the franchise, the repressive uses of the legal system, and the extension of social welfare are all part of the contradictory fabric of public policy under capitalism— the product of the interaction of classes and the state. Reform and repression blend together in endless variations.

The challenge for political theorists is to formulate explanations for such variations in dominant-class political strategies and such differences in the capacity of the upper classes to absorb reform. Why and under what conditions are reformist policies championed—or at a minimum, acquiesced to—by a bourgeoisie? And under what conditions does reform become unacceptable and even violently opposed? Recent debates in Marxist circles and among mainstream social scientists concerning the nature of the state under capitalism are relevant to these questions. Most of these debates focus on the issue of the relative autonomy of the state, that is, the degrees of independence the capitalist state can assume vis-à-vis the dominant classes and its capacity to impose policies contrary to the interests of those classes. The contributions of writers as diverse as Nicos Poulantzas, James O'Connor, Fred Block, David Vogel, and Charles Lindblom immediately come to mind.

Before looking at what these scholars tell us about the political behavior of capitalist classes, we should establish some definitions. The notion of *dominant classes* is used in the neo-Marxist sense; that is, it refers to those groups in the private sector that control and organize production and labor processes. Within this broad category, one can delineate subgroups or *fractions* that concentrate their activity in certain sectors of the economy. As we shall see, however, this concentration of investment in a particular area does not rule out the development of interests in other areas. Importers may acquire interests in industry and vice versa. The industrial bourgeoisie is composed of domestic owners and managers of both large modern manufacturing or agro-industrial plants.[5]

In this analysis, *reform* is broadly defined and refers to new and nonrepressive interventions by the state undertaken for the purpose of overcoming crises of accumulation and legitimation in capitalist systems. Reforms can involve the extension of new types of controls over the behavior of capital, or measures that incorporate the subordinate classes by responding to new economic or political claims. The essential quality of reformist policies is that while they often result in important adjustments in social and political relations in a particular system, these adjustments do not threaten the relations essential to maintaining the capitalist mode of production.[6] Thus, policies ranging from the regulation of business practices to social welfare measures can all be considered as varying types of reform policies.

To a large degree, reformism is the political grease of capitalist societies—the formula that allows for readjustments and the submergence of social conflict. In the absence of both symbolic and substantive attempts at reform, the state could not carry out its legitimating function. Popular support and loyalty would erode, threatening the viability of the capitalist order. Yet, with great frequency, the bourgeoisie does not perceive reform as the curative or preventive medicine that it is.

The notion that there are innate limitations on the political consciousness of the bourgeoisie is an old one. Marx's classic analysis in *The Eighteenth Brumaire* focuses on how the state takes up the task of political organization for a fragmented bourgeoisie. Georg Lukács discusses the inherent limitations on bourgeois consciousness in *History and Class Consciousness*. Recent restatements of the argument are found in the works of Poulantzas, Block, and Vogel.[7] They argue that capitalist classes are rarely advocates of progressive political and social policies that are often necessary for the reproduction of capitalism. This lack of insight stems from their own divided loyalties—they are concurrently individual capitalists as well as members of a class. The competitive tension within the class as a whole and between class fractions militates against the development of a unified class perspective on the social order.

It is precisely because of these conflicts within the bourgeoisie that the state takes up the transcendent role of organizing the society and economy. It is through the state that lower-class demands are filtered and processed. The state dampens social conflict through cooptation and channelling lower-class political energies into horse trading on discrete public policies. But the state's ability to process demands for reform is subject to serious constraints, given the state's reliance on overall economic performance. If capitalist classes judge reformism to be too costly, they can veto such policies through direct and indirect means. In liberal democratic systems, they may attempt to alter the composition of state personnel through elections. But, in addition, they have at their disposal a powerful and less overtly political tool—the investment strike. Capitalists can make the conscious decision to withold their capital from the economy. The investment strike depresses overall economic activity, endangers state revenues, and jeopardizes the electoral futures of politicians in power. The exercise of this veto power by capitalists can force state managers into a retreat on reform, or minimally, a renegotiation of the terms on which it will take place. In the words of Charles Lindblom, the business community has at its disposal an "automatic punishing recoil" that works to repress change.[8] Under certain circumstances, the economic and social demands for reform emanating from below and processed by the state may reach such levels that capitalists may seek to dismantle and restructure the prevailing political order in order to halt reform, substituting authoritarianism for liberal democracy.

Is the bourgeoisie's reaction to reform solely related to the extent to which such policies erode the margin for accumulation? Common sense would lead us to believe that the more capitalist classes are required by the state to bear the financial burden of lower-class cooptation and economic rationalization, the more likely they would be to resist such policies. But one of the recurrent paradoxes of the bourgeoisie's political history lies in its capacity to oppose even the most tepid reformism. Policies that do not directly damage dominant-class material interests are sometimes opposed with an intensity seemingly out of proportion to the issues at stake. These reactions can be explained, in part, as responses to the unpredictability of policy outcomes. Policy shift may replace the devil you know for one you don't know. With this principle in mind, the business community can be expected to oppose any sort of policy change that would upset the environment that they have already mastered. Uncertainties may combine with other factors to produce these outbursts of over-reactive behavior. Economic interpretations of class behavior that reduce class actions to pure demonstrations of structural position and the pursuit of material interests miss the other central components of class behavior. If other social classes operate with a "moral economy," as much historical and anthropological research suggests, there is no reason to believe that capitalists are bereft of similar impulses.[9] They too carry with them notions of how justice and equity are to be played out within the framework of capitalism. Ideological principles and psychological stakes are frequently part of the battle over reform on both sides. Perhaps, as John Merriman suggests, "it is time to put social classes on the couch" in order to understand the formation and internal logic of their collective consciousness.[10] Emotions and political memories can mix with calculations of profit and loss to produce what may often appear to be unnecessary or even bizarre behavior.

The political character of various fractions of the bourgeoisie is an important issue, in practice as well as in theory. To what extent the bourgeoisie is able to accept progressive public policies is a question that has long haunted theoreticians and politicians of the left. The Popular Front strategy of the 1930s was predicated on the prospects for a progressive alliance between bourgeois elements and the left. This issue was also at the heart of the controversies within the Unidad Popular government of Salvador Allende in Chile—debates that were tragically concluded on the streets of Santiago. The European left continues to struggle with issues surrounding reformist routes, as is evident in the ongoing permutations of Eurocommunist strategies.

So the question long debated on the left, "Why does the bourgeoisie act as it does?" underlies this study and will be posed in relation to the industrial bourgeoisie in Latin America.[11] Crucial to an explanation of the political behavior of this class is understanding the distinct conditions under which it has coalesced and operates. As both dependency and neo-Marxist theorists argue, the external conditions in which capitalism has developed in Latin America has produced distinct types of social formations and class configurations that are in no way analogous to those found in advanced capitalism. These are classes that must be understood on their own terms as the creatures of the dependent capitalist societies they inhabit, and not as some pale imitators of previous historical experiences.

Still, the notion of classes developing within the confines of dependent capitalism is only a point of departure for examining the structural and ideological roots of industrial class behavior. As Cardoso and Faletto so elegantly argue, the behavior of social classes can only be understood within the prism of concrete "situations of dependency."[12] Beginning with the colonial experience and continuing through independence, the economic linkages between countries at the center and on the periphery in

Latin American have differed dramatically. While all the countries of the region were being integrated into the world market as commodities producers, the different requirements of export production and styles of organization in each country produced dissimilar political economies. By the beginning of the twentieth century, the production of tin in Bolivia, beef in Argentina, and bananas in Honduras resulted in drastically different class structures. During the twentieth century, changes in the relationship between Latin America and the world economy introduced a nonuniform process of industrialization across the region. As it occurred from country to country at different points in time, industrialization took on distinct structural features depending upon the shape of the country's internal market, the role of foreign capital, the investment capabilities of local entrepreneurs and conditions in the international market. These variations in the timing, pace, and conditions of dependent industrialization further accentuated the differences in the class structures of the region.[13]

Emerging out of these variegated export economies was a new industrial bourgeoisie. But these industrial classes are distinguished by differences in their size, strength, strategic positions and political capacities. Just as the English entrepreneurs of the Industrial Revolution and the industrial barons of nineteenth-century Germany followed different political trajectories, the elite protagonists of industrial development in Latin America faced different political challenges en route to domination.

This study is an analysis of the different political paths chosen by the industrial bourgeoisie over the course of Latin American industrialization. It examines the linkages between political behavior, ideology, and material interests during the first phase of industrialization known as *horizontal import substitution*. Horizontal import substitution refers to the initial form of industrial expansion that revolved around the production of finished consumer goods for the domestic market. The next phase, *vertical import substitution*, is marked by the production of intermediate and capital goods along with more sophisticated consumer durables. Horizontal import substitution has been an elongated process throughout the region. The countries of the Southern Cone and Brazil led in the process, beginning their industrial development in the first three decades of the twentieth century. The rest of the region lagged considerably behind, with the smallest and poorest countries only initiating the process in the 1960s. Meanwhile, the industrial leaders moved into more sophisticated types of industrial production.

In Argentina, Chile, and Uruguay, horizontal import substitution coincided with classic populist regimes. The regimes of Perón in Argentina, Luis Batlle in Uruguay, and the Popular Front in Chile were all marked by policies promoting industrialization and various types of inclusionary policies vis-à-vis the working class.[14] Populism also marked the early stages of industrialization in Brazil and Mexico. The political base of these regimes was to be found in the multiclass coalitions of urban groups—the working and middle classes along with the emerging industrial bourgeoisie. Reformism was at the heart of these populist regimes and the industrial class was a part of the populist constituency. In sharp contrast to this coincidence of classic populism and horizontal import substitution is the experience of recent import-substituting countries, where reformist regimes have been actively opposed by the emergent industrial class. By the 1970s, the reformist role played by civilian politicians in the Southern Cone had been taken up by the military in the central Andean countries. Yet these regimes were plagued by their inability to construct multiclass coalitions around programs of national industrial development and social welfare. In Bolivia, the brief governments of Generals Ovando and Torres (1969–1971) were isolated and unable to form a coalition with any other social sectors, either from above or below. Much more successful was the Peruvian experiment under General Juan Velasco Alvarado (1968–1975). During this period, the state was able to assume a high degree of relative autonomy and enacted reforms over the heads of a recalcitrant dominant class. Ultimately, the experiment did succumb to an opposition which included the industrial class.

Like its Andean neighbors, Ecuador also underwent an interlude of military reformism. In 1972, the military overthrew President José María Velasco Ibarra in a bloodless coup. The new regime, under the leadership of General Guillermo Rodríguez Lara, proclaimed itself to be "nationalist," "popular," "antifeudal," and "antioligarchic." Like its Peruvian counterpart, the Rodríguez Lara government set its sights on modernizing reforms—the implementation of agrarian reform, the extension of social services and the acceleration of industrialization. But, just as in Peru, the reformist initatives of the regime were gradually eroded and eventually defeated by opposition from the dominant class. The antireform movement received across-the-board support from the emerging industrial bourgeoisie. In 1976, Rodríguez Lara was forced to resign and was replaced by more orthodox members of the armed forces who immediately announced their intention to return Ecuador to constitutional rule.

This study uses the case of failed reformism in Ecuador as the centerpiece for a comparative analysis of industrial-class politics in Latin America. The response of the industrial bourgeoisie to reformism in Ecuador is examined in the light of the behavior of the early industrial bourgeoisie of the Southern Cone countries: Argentina, Chile, and Uruguay. The purpose of this comparative analysis is to generate theoretical propositions concerning the economic interests, ideological imperatives, and political conditions that have shaped the bourgeoisie's reactions to reformism across Latin America.

The Ecuadorean bourgeoisie became the focus of this study for a number of reasons. Just as there is no one country that is typical of the region as a whole, given the variations in situations of dependency, no one country typifies the group of newly industrializing countries. Nonetheless, certain dimensions of Ecuadorean society and its economy do parallel those found in other small and poor countries of the region, including those of Central America and the Caribbean. Like those countries, Ecuador faces constraints on its industrialization posed by a small internal market made even more narrow because of extraordinary inequalities in the distribution of income. Moreover, class formation has been contorted by the enclave-style organization of export agriculture. Because of these structural similarities, an examination of the political behavior of the industrial bourgeoisie can both contribute to our knowledge of this neglected case and at the same time suggest the types of structural changes and political dilemmas that emerging industrial classes may be subject to in other "most like" cases.

As will be elaborated in later chapters, the major thrust of the argument is that in the 1940s the structural features of horizontal import substitution and the political threats contained in classic populism created conditions conducive to the industrial class's accommodation to reformism in Argentina, Chile, and Uruguay. The central structural reality of early import substitution in those countries was that production was concentrated in basic consumer goods; hence, industrialists maintained an interest in the popular internal market. Conversely, in the very late import-substituting countries such as those of the central Andes, horizontal import substitution has taken on new and distinctive structural features that reduce the bourgeoisie's margin of toleration for reform. In Ecuador's extraordinarily truncated internal market, horizontal import substitution is not linked to popular market expansion. This detachment from the market reduces the local bourgeoisie's direct material interest in reform. At the same time, the dissociation between the military and the popular classes that character- ized the reformist interludes in the Andean countries reduced the level of threat from below available to coerce the industrial class into accommoda- tion. Moreover, ideological elements came into play. In the thirty-year interim separating the import substitution of the Southern Cone from that of the central Andes, an important ideological reshaping had taken place. Early populism and the more radical initiatives represented by the revolu- tionary Cuba, Allende's Chile, Sandinista Nicaragua, and other assorted liberation movements exerted a negative demonstration effect on the newly emerging industrial classes of the region. A siege mentality took hold of these new capitalists. Holding the line against communism became an all enveloping strategy, allowing no room for even the mildest adjustments. This attitude was reinforced, of course, by the United States' foreign policy postures in the region.

As a prelude to examining the causes underlying the rejection of the reformist program by the industrial bourgeoisie in Ecuador, chapter 1 discusses the relationship of industrialists to reformist initiatives in the early industrializing countries of the region. The focus is on three impor- tant cases in which an industrial class did accommodate itself to a reformist project: Peronism in Argentina (1946–1955), the initial Popular Front governments in Chile (1938–1946), and the populist phase of Batllismo in Uruguay (1946–1950). While all these cases are divergent in certain re- spects, all are instances of "reactive participation" by the industrial class in a reform process. Peronism, Radicalism, and Batllismo are used to illus- trate how, at certain moments in the capital accumulation process, the structural position of an industrial class and the political mobilization of other social groups create conditions favorable to multiclass alliance with reformist objectives.

Chapter 2 traces the evolution of the structural position of the Ecuador- ean industrial bourgeoisie in the twentieth century. By the end of the 1970s, the conditions under which industrialization took place in Ecuador gave birth to an industrial class that was highly dependent on the state and foreign capital while becomingly increasingly dissociated from the impoverished masses within Ecuador.

The ideological position of the industrial bourgeoisie is discussed in chapter 3. The analysis of bourgeois ideology is based on interviews conducted by the author with the heads of the country's largest industrial firms in 1979–1980. The ideological portrait that emerged from these conversations is one of a class that rigidly adheres to antistatist and antipopular rhetoric with no disposition toward reformist politics.

Chapters 4 analyzes the reactions and manueverings of this highly conservative industrial bourgeoisie in the face of the reform policies proposed by the government of General Rodríguez Lara from 1972 to 1975. Specifically, the discussion focuses on the strategy and tactics adopted by industrial-class organizations to defeat the proposals aimed at agrarian reform, the regulation of foreign investment, and the "democratization" of firms. The bourgeoisie's mobilization against these policies is understood as a response structured by both economic and ideological considerations; the reforms threatened to reshape the behavior of private-sector actors in the accumulation process as well as to legitimate and strengthen the state's ability to regulate that behavior. Both the effects and principles of the policies were unacceptable to the industrial bourgeoisie and they joined with agrarian and commercial leaders in mobilizing against them.

Chapter 5 discusses the dilemmas of bourgeois representation within the reformist regime and how the tensions over representation created a consensus within Ecuador's dominant classes that set the forces in motion for democratization. The culmination of the bourgeoisie's frustration at being denied access to the state came with the tariff controversy of August 1975. This provoked a coup attempt and forced the resignation of Rodríguez Lara in 1976. Under the succeeding military government headed by Admiral Alfredo Poveda Burbano, the industrial bourgeoisie joined with other class fractions in attempting to shape a democratic state sympathetic to their demands for access and preferential policies. Chapter 6 describes this campaign to regain control over the state. During the process of regime transition and consolidation, the political revitalization of the forces on the right coincided with economic pressures to effectively eliminate reform as a viable political option in Ecuador.

Chapter 7 concludes with reflections on the factors that shape the industrial bourgeoisie's political responses to reformism. In comparison with the Southern Cone nations that mixed populist reformism with horizontal import substitution, the Ecuadorean case points to how economic structure and the immediate political conjuncture can heighten the bourgeoisie's capacity to resist reform and restructure the political system so as to remove reform from the public agenda.

1

Industrialists
and Reform
in Comparative
Perspective

Metaphors of illness dominate the analyses of the industrial bourgeoisie in Latin America. Adjectives such as "mutilated," "crippled," and "feeble" are frequently used to describe this portion of the dominant class.[1] Perhaps no capitalist group since the French bourgeoisie of Marx's *Eighteenth Brumaire* has been portrayed as so incompetent and lackluster in its exercise of domination.

Underlying the imagery of illness in Marxist analyses is an implicit comparison between Latin American socioeconomic development with that of Western Europe. The historical role of the Latin American bourgeoisie takes on pathological qualities when laid side by side with the accomplishments of the supposedly confident and conquering bourgeoisie of Western Europe. In Western Europe, the emergence and ascendancy of the industrial bourgeoisie is associated with the dismantling of precapitalist relations and the extension of political rights. The crowning achievement of this bourgeoisie was its construction of what Antonio Gramsci termed hegemony—an ideological acceptance of the established order by the masses that reduced the bourgeoisie's need to resort to repression to maintain social control. In contrast, the industrial bourgeoisie of Latin America is charged with complicity in maintaining backward agrarian structures, promoting exclusionary politics, and denationalizing their economies through alliances with foreign capital. Rather than orchestrat-

14

ing popular consent, the bourgeoisie of Latin America is portrayed as staggering from one hegemonic crisis to another.

The problems with these generalizations is not that they unfairly blame the Latin American bourgeoisie for economic dependence and authoritarianism. Rather, because they are overly generous toward that group's European counterparts, this may distort our thinking about the political behavior of capitalists in general. One only needs to think about the reactionary consequences of the alliance between industrialists and powerful landed aristocrats in nineteenth-century Germany to dull the notion of a heroic and democratic bourgeoisie. Even the much-lauded English bourgeoisie can be accused of a certain timidity regarding the political revolution they needed to assure their domination.[2] More often than not, both in Europe and the Latin America, it is the conservative spirit of the bourgeoisie, not its clever foresight or reform-minded rationality, that dominates its political history.

Capitalist classes everywhere are always subject to normal doses of conservatism based on their interest in maintaining a capitalist system once it is in place. But this is where the similarities end, both among different national bourgeoisies and within a particular bourgeoisie. Classes and class fractions can be distinguished in their political behavior by the expansion or retraction of their conservatism in the face of changing circumstances. In his essay on social classes, Joseph Schumpeter underscored the importance of and variations in class adaptability.

> There is the aristocrat, for example, who hurls himself into an election campaign as his ancestors rode into battle; and then there is the aristocrat who says to himself, "I can't very well ask my valet to vote for me." Here, in fact, is the measure of two radically different types of European aristocrat. The class situation may so specialize members of the class that adaptation to new situations becomes all but impossible.[3]

What are the determinants of upper-class flexibility or rigidity? Under what circumstances are they likely to engage in political alliances with subordinate classes? In an insightful essay, Guillermo O'Donnell suggests a framework for analyzing the bourgeoisie that is useful for delineating the variables at play in the decision to veto or tolerate reform.[4] O'Donnell points to three interrelated planes within classes—the structural, corporative, and politico-ideological planes. *Structural* position encompasses material interests and economic relations. The structural position of industrialists includes their sectoral specialization, market orientations, use of technology, relationships with labor, dependence on the state and other fractions within the same class. How these material interests and relations are aggregated and organized into institutional entities such as interest groups constitute the *corporative* plane. The *politico-ideological* plane is defined by how these class interests are formulated programmatically and articulated through corporate entities and political parties. These interest groups and parties forge concrete alliances with other fractions, classes, and segments of the state bureaucracy. O'Donnell's framework is useful because it does not focus exclusively on material interests in explaining the behavior of class fractions. It incorporates noneconomic variables such as organizational capacity and patterns of ideological development and alliance. In other words, we can look at capitalists' opposition to or acceptance of reform as the product of complex and historically rooted calculations that encompass material interests, ideological predispositions, and speculations as to future outcomes and effects.

In Latin America, the structural positions and political capabilities of the industrial bourgeoisie that emerged in the twentieth century have been conditioned by the incorporation of these economies into the world market. One can point to two historic "pacts" distinguishing the development of this class that reinforced and expanded its propensity to conservatism. First, the industrial bourgeoisie was closely aligned with both agroexport and traditional landowning fractions in most countries during the early stages of industrial development. The commodities boom in the international market at the end of the nineteenth century produced a new agrarian elite that was integrated into the power structure. In some countries, they became part of a stratum that included traditional landholders attached to hacienda system. With the appearance of industry, a new substratum of industrialists was layered into this dominant class. Friction between these groups, however, tended to be minimal. The low level of antagonism between fractions was due to the overlapping character of agrarian, commercial, and industrial capital as well as the class cohesion built around their ideological identification as members of the "propertied classes."

Close relationships existed between the traditional agrarian sector and industrial capitalists throughout the region during the early stages of industrialization. This overlapping of interests is evident in the analyses of Warren Dean and Joseph Love on the early twentieth-century industrialization of São Paulo and in Henry Kirsch's discussion of entrepreneurs in nineteenth-century Chile.[5] Maurice Zeitlin's work reaffirms the continued importance of this overlap in the Chilean case.[6] The early industrialization of Argentina was undertaken by agrarian producers as they moved into the processing of export goods.[7] These groups were composed of familial and friendship cliques of investors whose diversified portfolios spanned all sectors of the economy.

All this is not to say that the overlap between industrial and agricultural capital has been so complete that it is impossible to point to the existence of identifiable fractions within the capitalist class. In the case of Uruguay, for example, analysts have argued that the ties between agriculture and industry were more indirect; the transfer of agricultural capital to industrial activities occurred through the banking system rather than directly through diversification by the *estancieros* themselves.[8] Analyses of Argentina point to the emergence of a new wing of industrialists by the 1920s composed of immigrant entrepreneurs who manufactured goods for the internal market and lacked ties to agro-exporters.[9] Under certain circumstances, this differentiation of capital was expressed in sectoral clashes between industrialists and other dominant-class fractions. Battles over fiscal and monetary policies were the terrain of sectoral disputes. Yet, these clashes rarely assumed the character of direct frontal attacks by the industrial bourgeoisie on commercial or agrarian groups. Landowners, exporters, and importers were never definitively pushed from the inner circles of political power by industrialists.

Instead, as Florestan Fernandes argues, a horizontal integration took place at the upper levels of society and a consensus was forged around property holding. So significant segments of the emergent industrial bourgeoisie were melded into an amorphous upper class that included the most reactionary elements of the traditional landed oligarchies. For the most part, this alliance pattern effectively prevented any political alliance between industrialists and the lower classes. As will be discussed later in this chapter, it was only during some aberrant populist interludes that momentary breaks occurred in the relationship between the traditional elites and the newer industrial fractions. Fernandes describes the effects of this upper-class modus vivendi.

Divergent material interests pass through the filter of mutual concessions and mutual adjustments that cancel out or drastically reduce the revolutionary impacts of shifts in dominant bourgeois interests. Thus bourgeois domination interposes itself between bourgeois class antagonisms and the ferment they cause in economic, sociocultural, and political spheres. Class unity takes on an ultraconservative tone that is easily polarized around reactionary, even profoundly reactionary, values and behavior.[10]

The second decisive pact—the one between foreign capital and the industrial bourgeoisie—began crystallizing during the post–World War II period as multinational corporations (MNCs) entered the Latin American market to set up local production facilities. This shift toward direct foreign investment in manufacturing had far-reaching implications for the development of the local industrial bourgeoisie. As Peter Evans demonstrates in his important work on Brazil, the penetration of multinationals introduced new differentiations within the industrial class.[11] In certain sectors, they displaced local entrepreneurs or marginalized them as competitors in the market. In other industries, the local bourgeoisie became partners with MNCs in joint-venture arrangements. In addition to direct partnerships, local industrialists extended their ties to MNCs through transfer-of-technology, licensing, and subcontracting agreements. With the proliferation of these linkages, a new internationalized sector of the industrial bourgeoisie was forged whose interests were now intimately tied to those of foreign capital. Within the political sphere, this internationalized sector was in a position to act as a national advocate for MNC interests. But the "conservatizing" effect of this alliance was not just that it linked local and international capitalist classes per se; clearly such linkages between the center and periphery had been present since Latin America's incorporation into the world market. The phenomenon of a comprador bourgeoisie was certainly nothing new. What did distinguish this alliance and reinforce the political conservatism of industrialists was how it coincided with and promoted the restructuring of industrial production and the creation of new constellations of market orientations. It is in this alliance that Guillermo O'Donnell, Fernando Henrique Cardoso, and others locate the origins of the fiercely oppressive authoritarian regimes that surfaced in Brazil and the Southern Cone countries during the 1960s and 1970s.[12]

The entrance of MNCs after World War II was accompanied by changes in the structure of industrial production, particularly in the more advanced countries of Latin America. Industrialization had, until that point, still revolved largely around the production of simple consumer goods. By the late 1940s, however, this first phase of horizontal import substitution began to generate new structural problems. Horizontal import substitution was an import-intensive activity, exerting serious pressures on the balance of payments of these countries. A push toward vertical industrialization (that is, moving industrial production into intermediate and capital goods and extending into new lines of consumer durables) was one strategy for relieving import requirements. However, the prospects for undertaking more sophisticated industrial production was, given internal conditions in many countries and the nature of the international market, highly contingent upon access to technology and capital from abroad. According to O'Donnell, the central task faced by the state was to create a "stable" investment climate capable of attracting multinational investors. The construction of such a stable investment climate translated into policies aimed at disciplining the labor force both at the economic and the political levels. Because new industrial production was now focused on capital and luxury consumer goods, the changes in the mass internal market caused by wage compression policies was of little concern to the internationalized bourgeoisie and the multinational corporations. Thus, this new relationship with foreign capital altered the structural position of the local industrial bourgeoisie by detaching it from the internal market and by tying industrial expansion to the purchasing power of upscale consumers. This new position sharpened the bourgeoisie's preference for reactionary political formulas in response to continuing economic demands from the working classes.

It is important to underscore that this alliance between the local bourgeoisie and multinationals in the postwar period differed from one country to another and had different political implications in each. Only in the Southern Cone and Brazil did the alliance find its political expression in highly repressive regimes. In the rest of the region, the new relationships between foreign and local capitalists coincided with the first phase of import substitution. The involvement of multinationals in simple consumer-goods industrialization meant that, to a great extent, the very late industrialization of these countries mimicked the later stages of industrialization in the Southern Cone and Brazil, insofar as both processes were characterized by the employment of capital-intensive technology and the introduction of products targeted for affluent consumers. Nevertheless, systematic authoritarianism was not the political quid pro quo of the new alliance between MNCs and local capitalists in the laggard industrializing nations of Latin America. Lack of political mobilization by the popular classes in these countries and the weakness of trade union organizations made the introduction of new forms of repression unnecessary. Old modes of domination were still effective in maintaining a desirable investment climate for prospective investors with interests in these smaller and poorer markets. The new relationships between industrialists and multinationals jelled under both military and civilian regimes.

These pacts with traditional agrarian powerholders and foreign capital decisively shaped the political character of the emergent industrial bourgeoisie in Latin America. Both alliances worked to reduce the industrial bourgeoisie's direct material stakes in reforms aimed at expanding the internal mass market through redistribution. As interests among these actors overlapped, a political and ideological consensus was forged around their status as owners and property holders. Their antidemocratic and antiegalitarian convictions, so prevalent in the ideology of business executives everywhere, were reinforced in Latin America by these patterns of alliance.[13]

While antireformist political postures have been the rule rather than the exception for the Latin American bourgeoisie, important breaks in this mode of behavior did occur during the populist interludes of the 1940s. These populist interruptions occurred prior to the deepening of the alliance between multinational corporations and local industrialists. During the 1940s, populist regimes welded together heterogeneous coalitions that included the industrial bourgeoisie and the urban working classes. To varying degrees, all these regimes pursued redistributive policies that brought real economic gains to the urban working and middle classes. In addition to redistribution, these populist regimes undertook important symbolic and legal reforms that legitimized trade unionism. What role did the industrial bourgeoisie play in these populist alliances? How were industrialists integrated into reformist regimes pursuing redistributive objectives? To understand the factors that interrupted the normal patterns of business conservatism, we turn to a comparative analysis of populist regimes in Argentina, Chile, and Uruguay.

Industrialists and Populism

The waves of populism that rolled through Latin America during the 1940s signaled the end of traditional oligarchical politics. Populism represented the final rupture in the conduct of politics as a clash of notables. The old power struggles—between hacendados and exporters, ranchers and merchants, bishops and bureaucrats—were supplanted by new players and new issues. For the first time, under the banner of populist movements, subordinated classes entered the public arena as a force to be reckoned with, as legitimate claimants to participation in the political system.[14]

The sources of the demise of oligarchic politics are to be found in the dynamism of the export sector. In the late nineteenth and early twentieth centuries, export booms generated spinoff effects in these economies that set the wheels in motion for the emergence of populist movements. In Argentina, Chile, and Uruguay, the growth and development of exports were the prime movers behind the early acceleration of urbanization and industrialization. In Argentina, beef exports gave birth to a processing industry centered in Buenos Aires; the meat industry in turn created demand for subsidiary industries and services. Uruguay also developed a meat-packing industry. In Chile because the upper class was able to extract a portion of the surplus from the largely foreign-controlled mining sector through their control over the state, some capital was channeled into Chilean industry. The technological and organizational features of export production, combined with the dominant class's acumen in retaining control over a portion of the export surplus, accounts for the early spurt of industrialization in these countries. Elsewhere in the region, the spinoff effects of export booms were dissipated by the minimal production requirements of certain types of exports, the absolute limitations of the domestic market, and the weak entrepreneurial impulses of the comprador elite.

Horizontal import substitution, revolving around the production of simple consumer goods, received a further boost during the Great Depression, which reduced the import capacity of these countries. As a result, local demand for manufactures was channelled into the domestic market to be satisfied by local entrepreneurs. Uruguay, Chile, and Argentina registered manufacturing growth rates between 3 percent and 5 percent in 1929–1939. Industrial production increased along with the number of factories and the size of the industrial labor force.[15]

By the mid-1930s, the dual processes of urbanization and industrialization significantly altered the class structures in the Southern Cone countries. Urban middle classes, working classes, and an embryonic industrial bourgeoisie began to develop and were layered into the old social pyramid populated by rural lower classes and agrarian and commercial elites.

Populism reflected the ascendancy of these new social groups. Regimes with political bases in these new groups emerged in Argentina under Perón, in Chile under the Radical party, and in Uruguay under Luis Batlle Berres. Each of these populist governments was based on a limited and tactical alliance between the urban industrial bourgeoisie and urban popular classes that was managed, sometimes with great difficulty, by these populist politicians.[16] All of these regimes pursued policies that combined state support for import-substitution industrialization with social and economic concessions to the urban middle and working classes. Policies of redistribution stood side by side with policies favoring accelerated accumulation in the industrial sector.

In Chile, populist policies were initiated during the presidency of Pedro Aguirre Cerda in 1938 and continued through the succeeding Radical governments. Aguirre Cerda, who represented the Radical party, was the candidate of the Popular Front coalition, which included the socialist and communist parties. The populist state became the engine behind industrial expansion that channelled credit to the industrial sector. Not surprisingly, given the ties between the trade union movement and the parties of the Popular Front, the state adopted prounion labor legislation. Wage increases were also a central component of the Popular Front program in Chile.

In Argentina, industrial workers saw real increases in their wage share during the first phase of the Peronist government (1946–1949). At the same time, the state subsidized an accelerated import-substitution process. The 1947–1950 presidency of Luis Batlle Berres in Uruguay represented a renewed commitment of the Colorado party to the reformist initiatives first undertaken during the administrations of José Batlle y Ordóñez earlier in the century. Protectionism for industry was the first priority of the government and was pursued through manipulating controls over trade and exchange. At the same time, the expansion of the internal market in Uruguay was achieved by wage increases. From 1948 to 1954, wages in thirty-one trade unions rose by 110 percent, while the cost of living rose 58 percent.[17]

This intense pursuit of accelerated accumulation in the industrial sector, income redistribution, and labor reforms by populist governments was the political cement that held together industrialists and the middle and working classes in these alliances. At the same time, the pursuit of these often contradictory imperatives generated tensions within the alliance. Redistribution enforced by the state—and all that implies in terms of interrupted market principles and expanded state authority vis-à-vis business—is never favored by the private sector. Yet, while business leaders in Argentina, Chile, and Uruguay were not enthusiastic about wage increases, social welfare expenditures, and stricter labor codes, they came to terms with and tolerated the heterodox economic policies of populist regimes. That business confidence in the investment climate was not eroded by populist policies is reflected in the economic statistics of the period. Increases in the number of new industrial establishments, industrial production, and new investment demonstrate the continued interest in investment opportunities in these countries. Capital flight and investment strikes, which were to undermine later attempts at reform such as those undertaken by Allende in Chile and Velasco Alvarado in Peru, did not plague classic populism. The industrial bourgeoisie's accommodation to the redistributivist side of populism was a product of: (1) internal structural characteristics of the class that expanded its "margin of toleration" for redistribution and (2) the political features of populist regimes that guaranteed the industrial bourgeoisie access to decision making, created mechanisms for regulating class conflict, and enabled a portion of the economic surplus to be extracted and transferred to the industrial sector. In other words, both political and economic incentives were at work in securing the participation of the industrial bourgeoisie in populist alliances.

When the industrialists of Argentina, Chile and Uruguay entered into populist alliances, they all occupied similar structural positions in relation to the market. These classes as a whole were still dedicated to producing consumer nondurables and simple durables for the domestic market. In Uruguay, "traditional" industries (food products, beverages, tobacco, textiles, clothing, wood, furniture, and leather products) accounted for 62.3 percent of the total industrial product in 1945.[18] Traditional product lines similarly dominated the industrial structure of Chile and Argentina, although some shifting to more sophisticated goods took off in the 1930s. But given the overall structure of industrial production, most industrialists depended on the internal market and relied (albeit in varying degrees) on the expansion of popular purchasing power. For Uruguayan industrialists, the issue of market size was particularly acute; with a population of just one million in the 1940s, industrial growth was contingent upon an expansion of purchasing power across social classes. This reliance on the domestic market created the basis for accepting the reform initiatives of populist governments. Limited economic gains for urban groups could be tolerated for the purposes of market expansion.

The structural position of the Southern Cone industrial bourgeoisie, defined by production for the domestic market, was important in the sense that it reduced the economic obstacles in the path of populist alliances. Yet we should keep market considerations in perspective when explaining the behavior of the industrial bourgeoisie. While some may have seen the link between wage increases, expanded government expenditures, and a broadening of the internal market, many did not. As Eldon Kenworthy argues, "With regard to the role increased wages play in expanding the internal market [in Argentina], one must beware of the fallacy of thinking that businessmen, with the interest of one company foremost in mind, will take a macro view of the economy."[19] Not all individual firms and branches within the industrial sector were in positions to benefit equally from market expansion through wage increases. For many, increased wages were not offset by increased sales. In the Argentine case, Judith Teichman's research on business interest groups during the Perón period indicates that those groups which directly felt the effects of market expansion, such as producers of consumer durables and textiles, were more likely to espouse pro-Peronist positions than heavy metallurgical producers who had little to gain from increases in popular purchasing power and much to lose from Perón's liberal import policy for capital goods.[20] The overall threat posed by wage increases, however, was mitigated by the state's mediation of the bargaining between capital and labor. As William Ascher points out, in Argentina wage increases were negotiated and applied differently across industries and sectors, so that the entire industrial class never confronted across-the-board increases at the same time.[21] This method of managing wage adjustments reduced the prospects for the industrial bourgeoisie's unified mobilization against them.

Market considerations created some propopulist industrialists, but the market alone does not account for the accommodation to populism by the industrial bourgeoisie as a whole. What really reduced the likelihood of retaliatory investment strikes by industrialists to protest populist redistributivism was the populist state's ability to offset the costs of reform by providing pro–import substitution policies to the private sector along with labor policies that, although they promoted unionization, rationalized labor relations and defused working-class demands through institutional bargaining. While access to populist policymakers was not always smooth (especially in Argentina under Perón), the industrial bourgeoisie's access was never in jeopardy and the penetrability of the populist state assured industrialists that political maneuvering, rather than economic resistance, was the best tool for negotiating the terms of reform.[22]

The increased demand for Latin American commodities exports during and immediately after World War II set the stage for the adoption of proindustrial policies by populist regimes. The surplus generated by the export boom was used to underwrite the extension of cheap credit and subsidies to the industrial sector. Together with protectionist trade policies, this transfer of resources to the industrial sector rapidly accelerated import substitution. In all three cases, the populist state either created, or already had at its disposal, institutions through which to extract the surplus from the export sector. In Argentina, Perón created the Instituto para la Promoción del Intercambio (IAPI) to act as a state monopoly over agricultural commodities. Artificially low prices imposed on producers by IAPI allowed for a state-enforced transfer of surplus from agriculture to industry.[23] The Aguirre Cerda government in Chile created the Corporación de Fomento de la Producción (CORFO) as the agency to channel resources into the industrial sector. In Chile, the transfer of the surplus did not affect agriculture, but was financed by a combination of taxes on foreign-owned mining interests, external credits, and reallocations within the government budget. When the Batlle Berres administration came into power in Uruguay, the bureaucratic machinery for the state's proindustrial manipulations of the economy was already in place; the Office of the Controller of Exchange, Exports, and Imports was created in 1941.[24] An elaborate system of multiple exchange rates that gave preferential treatment to industry by lowering the costs of raw materials and capital goods imports was constructed and was the principal policy tool for promoting industrialization.

Studies of dominant-class structure in Argentina and Uruguay suggest that penalizing the agricultural sector was acceptable to industrialists because there was little direct connection between agricultural and industrial capital. During the Depression in Argentina, a differentiation took place between the old pampean bourgeoisie and new industrial entrepreneurs. The older group, the landholders who controlled the export trade in beef and cereals, had invested in the first processing and consumer goods industries. By the 1930s, however, as industrial investment became more profitable, new immigrant entrepreneurs emerged. The previous overlap between industrial and agrocommercial capital attenuated as the new entrepreneurs moved to take advantage of new investment opportunities.

Given the lack of social and economic ties between these two groups, the new entrepreneurs were not threatened by the populist policies that drained the surplus from the agricultural sector. A similar breach between newly arrived industrialists and traditional landholding families developed in Uruguay during this period. In Chile, where there were stronger ties between elite groups, agriculture was not the target for surplus extraction. Instead, the Aguirre Cerda government turned to the foreign-owned mining sector. Thus, in the cases of Uruguay and Chile, pronounced differentiations within the upper classes and the resulting political estrangement between dominant-class groups made it possible to finance both consumption and investment policies. Moreover, even the agrarian interests in these countries had the blow softened because extraction took place within the context of general economic prosperity. In Chile, where the interests of industrialists and landholders were more closely linked, the question of who would bear the costs of populist redistribution was avoided by imposing the burden on a politically less sensitive sector, foreign capital in mining.

Finally, it is important to understand the direction of the road *not taken* by the populist leadership. In all three Southern Cone countries, land reform was deleted from the political agenda; it was a nonissue. This freezing of the agrarian structure was the quid pro quo the Chilean dominant classes exacted from the Popular Front in exchange for their seeming flexibility on other issues. Under populism, private property remained sacrosanct in industry as well as agriculture. Despite industrialists' constant fears to the contrary, these regimes made no serious attempt to intervene into the day-to-day operations of firms. The issue of workers' control did not surface as part of the populist program. None of the regimes attacked the principle of private property and accumulation. These reformist projects represented an effort to accelerate the type of capitalist development already under way—one centered around national industrialization and internal market expansion. No restructuring of capital or redefining the style of development was intended or attempted. For the industrial bourgeoisie, populism did not pose either substantive or ideological threats.[25]

Along with these economic considerations, a political rationale propelled industrialists into populist coalitions. Underpinning the industrial bourgeoisie's accommodationist stance was their fear of the special relationships forged between populist politicians and the urban working classes. The participation of industrialists represented an attempt to moderate the socioeconomic demands on the state from the newly mobilized working class.

Before the emergence of the populist movements, the working classes in all three countries were relatively marginal in the political process. Legal restrictions on the franchise and union organization limited working-class integration into political life. The political impotence of the working class was perhaps more pronounced in Argentina where political parties were lax in their attempts to mobilize workers' support.[26] Instead, working-class activity was channelled into the embryonic trade union organizations. Economic claims (such as demands for higher wages) were the focus of union activity. Until the advent of Peronism, union membership among the Argentine proletariat remained low. Only 13.5 percent of the total urban labor force was organized in 1940. Political rivalries between Communists, Socialists, and Syndicalists fragmented the organized segment. The ten years preceding Perón's tenure in the Secretariat of Labor was marked by wage compression and political repression. Within this context Perón launched his campaign to organize and harness working-class support. Through a combination of strategies, including creating new union organizations, co-opting union leadership, and solving labor disputes through state intervention, Perón was able to create the political base he sought. Capitalizing on that base, Perón captured 54 percent of the vote in the elections of Februrary 1946 despite the opposition mounted by traditional political parties and dominant-class organizations.

In Chile, the circumscription of popular participation in elections notwithstanding, a leftward trend in voting behavior became evident as early as the 1912 presidential elections, which brought Arturo Alessandri to power.[27] Although the Chilean labor force was just as unorganized as its Argentine counterpart, the unions in existence maintained strong ties to left-wing political parties. Formed through a consolidation of several of these parties in 1932 and capitalizing on the popular appeal of Marmaduke Grove, the Socialist party quickly became the chief political representative of the working class in the 1930s. The new party was the major beneficiary of the growth in union organization during this period, winning the affiliations of both new and old unions. The Popular Front coalition of 1938 was able to mobilize this working-class vote and launch the reformist project under President Pedro Aguirre Cerda.

In Uruguay, the populist policies of Luis Batlle Berres did not initiate, but reinforced, the close ties between the working class and the Colorado party. This clientelistic relationship had been forged earlier during the reformist governments of José Batlle y Ordóñez. This relatively early spurt of reformism in Uruguay was made possible because of the political weakness of the country's dominant classes and the concomitant rise of a relatively insulated political elite within the Colorado party.[28] Given the immigrant character of the industrial class and the extremely small market in the early decades of the century, Uruguayan industrialists lacked both the desire and the political power to block the early reforms.

Previous historical experiences played an important role in shaping the industrial bourgeoisie's stance toward populism. As Paul Drake convincingly argues, the Chilean upper classes were already schooled in the politics of accommodation and conciliation prior to Popular Front reforms, having faced the persistent claims of an organized working class since World War I.[29] The dominant classes of Uruguay also underwent a similar learning process starting with José Batlle y Ordóñez. In Argentina, however, this learning process was more equivocal and eventually aborted. Under the government of Radical party leader Hipólito Yrigoyen, political reforms occurred (such as a limited extension of the franchise) and social change (the expansion of white-collar employment in the public sector), but were aimed entirely at incorporating the middle classes into the political system. With the overthrow of Yrigoyen in 1930s, the Argentine upper classes drew a line to guard against further reform.[30] Nonetheless, across these three societies, the upper classes had already confronted the specter of reform prior to the coming of populism and had experience in developing conciliatory tactics. On the politico-ideological plane, these classes were already familiar with the notion of alliance and compromise across classes.

Argentina, Chile, and Uruguay are all cases in which the industrial bourgeoisie engaged in "reactive participation" in these multiclass populist alliances. Their participation was reactive insofar as it was not the product of an autonomous initiative on their part, but rather a response to pressures from below.[31] In all three cases, such an alliance came about only *after* a populist leadership came to power through elections. The electoral victories were by no means the fruits of dominant-class maneuverings. Once the regimes were in power, however, industrialists yielded to the inevitable, preferring pragmatic compromise to all-out confrontaton with the the state. Fernando Henrique Cardoso characterizes this relationship between the industrial bourgeoisie and these regimes as follows:

> Confronting the consummate fact of the new relation of forces, industrialists always knew how to react with shrewd realism. They aligned themselves with the populist schemes, eventually creating concrete obstacles to the distributivist excesses, and proposing political and ideological alternatives to the idea of the "social conquest of the rights of workers" which they preferred replaced by the idea of the collaboration of all in the effort of national reconstruction.[32]

From the popular point of view, the postelectoral modus vivendi established between the populist leadership and the industrial sector proved to be double-edged. On one hand, as Guillermo O'Donnell points out, the presence of a wing of the bourgeoisie in the Peronist camp cloaked the populist movement of Argentina with a legitimacy that few others Latin America have enjoyed.[33] In Chile, the accommodationist position adopted by the bourgeoisie was important in the maintenance and expansion of a competitive electoral system. On the other hand, as Cardoso notes, the inclusion of the industrial bourgeoisie in this new alignment of political forces muted the more radical elements within these regimes. This was particularly true in Chile where a close relationship developed between the state technocrats of the Popular Front in CORFO and the industrial class. As a result, Chilean industrialists were highly successful (more so than their Argentine counterparts) in holding the line on wage concessions to the working class.[34] For the most part, the gains of Chilean workers under the Popular Front were largely institutional, involving the recognition and promotion of the trade union movement. Under the Popular Front from 1938 to 1942, both public- and private-sector white-collar employees registered substantially higher wage increases than industrial workers. For industrial laborers in Chile, the wage concessions granted under the Front did not keep pace with inflation.

The crucial point here is that the populist state was relatively penetrable; the industrial bourgeoisie's access to policymaking institutions was never ruptured by populism. While populism's dangerous flirtation with working-class demands worried the industrial bourgeoisie, these regimes remained responsive to dominant-class interests.

The Politics of Closure

The populist experiences of Argentina, Chile, and Uruguay represent moments in which the interests of the new industrial and working classes converged. The reconciliation of consumption and investment policies was facilitated not only by economic prosperity but also because the popular internal market constituted the axis of import substitution in its initial phase. Within this context, reforms could be tolerated especially when populist politicians revealed their willingness to compensate the industrial class through preferential state policies. Moreover, the success of the populist leadership in capturing and articulating the aspirations of the lower classes for political and economic inclusion raised the costs of opposition for industrialists.

Industrialists began their retreat from reformism as the model of accumulation upon which it was built suffered a severe crisis. The onset of economic stagnation prevented the populist leadership from juggling the contradictory imperatives of consumption and investment. In Argentina, industry's dependence on imports and a lag in agricultural exports led to serious problems in the balance of payments situation by 1950. In addition to the foreign exchange crisis, increases in consumption generated by Perón's wage policies fueled inflation and further aggravated economic difficulties. The economic contraction seriously undermined the stability of populism built around the dual objectives of distribution and industrialization. According to David Rock, the economic crisis meant that "the state's adjudicatory role in the economy ceased to be a matter of allocating relatively higher rates of return to one group or another in the midst of an expanding surplus."[35] If redistribution was still to be pursued, it would be "coercive," with the costs borne by the industrial class. With the painlessness stripped from reform, industrialists were prepared to participate in a new anti-Peronist alliance which overthrew him in 1955.

In the same manner, the demise of the Radical regime in Chile coincided with the exhaustion of easy import substitution and the beginning of economic crisis in that country. Inflation and stagnation quickly eroded the margin of toleration that had made populism palatable to the industrial class. The demise of Chilean populism was a gradual process, beginning with the election of Juan Antonio Ríos to the presidency in 1942. The Radical veer to the right accelerated under President González Videla from 1946 through 1952. Tensions among the Popular Front parties and divisions within the Socialist party led to a steady electoral decline and the Radicals' loss of the 1952 presidential elections.

Uruguay experienced the same syndrome of stagnation, inflation, and chronic balance-of-payments problems beginning in the mid-1950s. With changes in the demand and price structure of the international commodities market, the Batllista program of consumption and industrial protectionism faltered. After the defeat of the Colorado party in the 1958 elections, the victorious Blanco party imposed an economic stabilization favored by the International Monetary Fund and discarded populist policies.

With the economic basis of populism eroded by the crises associated with horizontal import substitution, the industrial bourgeoisie of the Southern Cone began its search for new economic models and political formulas. It was within this context that the critical "pact" described earlier between segments of the industrial bourgeoisie and foreign capital was forged, initiating the attempt to change development policies. These new forms of economic association between industrialists and foreign capital altered the structural position of the industrial bourgeosie—shifting their market orientation to industrial and high-income consumers and heightened their interest in disciplining the labor force both economically and politically. In other words, the industrial bourgeoisie ceased to tolerate reformist political projects once economic strategy was shifted away from traditional horizontal import substitution.

This closure thesis regarding the political behavior of the industrial bourgeoisie has been argued by a number of writers such as Cardoso,

O'Donnell, Cavarozzi, Faria, and Martins.[36] Its underlying economic determinism has also been subject to extensive criticism. Whether or not authoritarianism was the inevitable quid pro quo of the exhaustion of horizontal import substitution, that is, whether or not it was objectively necessary to the transition from one stage of industrialization to another, is certainly not clear. Moreover, critics have convincingly argued that economic stabilization, not vertical import substitution, was the first priority of these authoritarian regimes.[37] Nonetheless, what is clear is that the industrial bourgeoisie of the Southern Cone and Brazil shared with the military the perception that economic crisis had to be resolved by breaking with the old populism and this break was compatible with the new directions in which their economic interests were evolving.

What are the implications of the closure thesis for countries currently undergoing the first phase of industrialization? A mechanistic reading of the history of the Southern Cone might suggest that other countries of the region would experience the same cycle of populism and bureaucratic authoritarianism as they became industrialized. Nonetheless, Central America and the central Andean countries have not replicated the political patterns of the Southern Cone. The persistence of business conservatism suggests that the industrial bourgeoisie of these newly industrializing countries is not subject to the same economic incentives and political pressures that characterized the early industrializing countries of Latin America. Instead, the new industrial bourgeoisie is in a fundamentally different structural position and faces different political imperatives. Horizontal import substitution in recently industrializing countries reinforces, rather than cracks, the old patterns of dominant-class conservatism. To understand this process and how reform options are being limited in our own time, we turn to an examination of recent horizontal import-substitution industrialization and failed reform in Ecuador.

2

The Making
of the
Industrial
Bourgeoisie

Every process of industrialization produces legendary heroes. In Brazil, Francisco Matarazzo Conde presided over a grand industrial empire that began with the founding of a small lard factory. In Argentina, an Italian immigrant, Torcuato di Tella, made a fortune in the metallurgical industry producing bakery equipment and home appliances. The biographies of these well-known entrepreneurs reveal much about the structural characteristics of the first three decades of import-substitution industrialization in Latin America. Both men turned from commerce to industry. Both created industries that were based on an expanding internal demand for consumer goods. And both were examples of the essentially national character of early industrialization and the marginal role played by foreign capital in the first phases of the process.[1]

The late-starting industrializing countries have also produced their own breed of industrial entrepreneur whose personal odyssey mirrors the structure and the logic of the capitalist development taking place in these small and poor countries. In Ecuador, there is no better example than that of Luis Noboa Naranjo.

Noboa began his career in the 1940s as a rice exporter with the financial backing of the well-known *guayaquileño* financier, Juan X. Marcos. As demand in the international commodities market changed, so did Noboa's business activities. In the 1950s, Noboa moved into banana and cocoa exports and quickly became one of the most important independent banana

33

traders in a market dominated by two multinational corporations. With demand for Ecuadorean bananas stagnating in the 1960s, Noboa began to diversify his investments. He converted an old rice mill into a flour mill, Industrial Molinera, that quickly became a giant in local food processing. By the 1970s, Noboa was building coffee and cocoa processing plants along with operating a carton plant and chocolate factory. His links to foreign capital deepened through partnerships and transfer-of-technology agreements. At the same time, he expanded his investments in finance and banking. By the end of the 1970s, the *grupo económico* created by Noboa was an important network of firms deeply enmeshed in international trade as well as serving diverse groups of consumers in the internal market.[2]

The growth and development of the Noboa group enterprises was part of a larger process of portfolio diversification by dominant-class fractions that brought horizontal import substitution and export-oriented industrialization to Ecuador. Importers, exporters, and landowners turned industrialist in the 1960s and 1970s in response to new incentives created by the state, foreign capital, and changes in the international commodities market.

But the economic transformation of Ecuador, given the conditions created by the timing of the industrialization process and the extremely circumscribed internal market, was marked by twists on earlier historical experiences and exaggerations of structural tendencies present in the more advanced industrialized countries of the region. In short, as Alexander Gerschenkron so elegantly argued, the replaying of industrialization across different settings and in different eras produces new variations on the process as countries mimic and combine technologies and organizational arrangements.[3] As industrialization itself undergoes transformations through time, so do its social and political consequences. Torcuato di Tella and Luis Noboa, both central figures in the capitalist development of their respective countries, faced very different circumstances in the world economy and their own internal markets and made very different political choices.

To understand the choices made by Noboa and other industrial entrepreneurs in Ecuador, we begin with an examination of the structural position of this new class fraction. The relationships that evolved between the emergent industrial bourgeoisie and the state, foreign capital, markets, and other dominant-class groups created the material boundaries within which their political consciousness and capabilities were formed. And this combination of structure and ideology explains the industrial bourgeoisie's total rejection of the military reformist project of the 1970s and its search for an alternative political formula.

The Legacy of Cacao: Constituting the Limited Market

Luis Noboa launched his business empire in 1941 when he leased several small rice mills and set up export operations in Guayaquil. Noboa's success in his initial venture coincided with a long-awaited recovery of the Ecuadorean economy. Like other countries of the region that were incorporated into the world market as agricultural producers, Ecuador was subject to the boom-bust patterns of the international commodities market. From the 1890s through the 1920s, the Ecuadorean economy pivoted on the export of cocoa. At the turn of the century, Ecuador was the leading producer of the commodity, supplying one-third to one-half of world demand. But plant diseases, plantation neglect, competition from new African producers, and finally the Depression took their toll and brought economic stagnation. The recuperation of the Ecuadorean economy began during World War II as international demand for rice, rubber, balsa, and other commodities grew.

The heyday of the millionaire "Cacao kings" was long over as the young Noboa began his export business, but the boom left its definitive imprint on the structure of social classes. At the upper reaches of Ecuadorean society was a heterogeneous stratum of agro-exporters, financiers, importers, and traditional hacienda owners. The coastal agro-exporters and key financial groups were based in the port city of Guayaquil. In the interior provinces where the Andes changed the climate and the terrain, landowners presided over a traditional hacienda system with its center in the capital, Quito.[4] Importers and merchants were part of the economic elite of both cities.

As one moved down the social ladder, the effects of the cacao prosperity were increasingly limited. In contrast to the beef export boom of Argentina in the same period, cacao exports had only minimal spinoff effects on society and economy in Ecuador. Cacao production was relatively undemanding in relation to two factors of production—capital and labor. With a perfect climate for cultivation and easy river transportation from the coastal plantations to Guayaquil, cacao did not require major investments in its cultivation or accompanying infrastructure for the export trade. Except for drying the product prior to shipping, no processing was necessary. Because of the peculiarities of the crop, the economic boom generated by the trade did not result in a dramatic expansion in the urban middle classes or working classes. Along with some growth in the tertiary sector in Guayaquil, the only significant nonagricultural work directly generated by the cacao boom was found on the docks where the *cacahueros* packed and loaded the product on ships.[5]

The economic effects of this export boom were not confined to coastal Ecuador where the trade was located but reverberated within the society as a whole, affecting the relations between dominant and subordinate classes. Because of the minimal labor requirements of cacao plantations, the development of commercial agriculture on the coast did not come into conflict with the precapitalist hacienda system of the sierra. No significant tensions developed between the agro-export bourgeoisie of Guayaquil and traditional landowners over the question of labor. While each fraction struggled for control over the state apparatus, state power was never definitely used by one to destroy the other. Instead, underneath the personal power struggles and sectoral clashes that were the stuff of oligarchic politics, a modus vivendi was forged that was buttressed by social ties and often overlapping economic interests. As a result, the indigenous population of the sierra remained trapped within the hacienda system and subject to the precapitalist relationships they had known since the Conquest. They could look to no elite allies to champion the cause of free labor.

The constrictive economic and social character of Ecuador's export boom of the early twentieth century contrasts starkly with the transformative effects of export-led growth in other countries of the region. Beef, wool, and wheat exports in Argentina and the rapid urbanization that accompanied those industries produced middle and working classes that formed the base of the modern consumer market for the first stages of horizontal import-substitution industrialization. By contrast, cacao export contributed only slightly to forming a domestic market for industrial products. The use of wage labor in coastal agriculture and the expansion in employment in the public and tertiary sectors in Guayaquil and the public sector did create a small mass market for such basic items as food, beverages, textiles, and cigarettes. Nonetheless, it is important to underscore the restricted and regional character of this market expansion. For the most part, the precapitalist organization of *serrano* agriculture was untouched by the economic windfall on the coast. The indigenous agricultural laborers of the sierra still stood outside the money economy. As late as 1950, nearly 72 percent of the population remained in the countryside.[6]

The extremely limited industrialization that did occur in the wake of the cacao export boom was concentrated in the production of simple wage goods. During the first two decades of the century, the capital necessary for industrialization came from investors from the landowning and mercantile classes. Likewise, industrialists maintained investments in other sectors. On the coast, the major source of industrial capital was the commercial bourgeoisie linked to importing activities.[7] In the sierra, the textile industry developed as an offshoot of sheep raising on the haciendas. The top agro-export families played only a small role in the creation of new industrial firms. Most of the profits of the trade were not reinvested in the local economy; some were remitted to foreign stockholders, while the rest was used to support the sumptuous life styles of the absentee plantation owners in Paris.[8]

Despite the absence of direct industrial investment by agro-exporters, the pace of industrialization was clearly linked to the performance of the export sector. Capital goods imports surged and declined in relation to cacao exports, affecting the rhythms of import substitution.[9] In contrast to the Southern Cone countries and Brazil where an important domestic market was already formed by the 1930s, the trade hiatus created by the Depression did not stimulate local import substitution in Ecuador. Instead, further import substitution in this small and impoverished market awaited the recuperation of the export economy.

The Political Economy of Bananas: Demand and Diversification

Rice export turned out to be a minor prelude in the making of the Noboa fortune and the revitalization of the Ecuadorean economy. World War II initiated the recovery, but the real resurgence of the economy did not get under way until 1948 when the economy was consciously redirected by the efforts of the state and interested multinational corporations toward the production of a new agricultural product—bananas. Bananas became the basis of the new agro-export wealth of coastal Ecuador, with Luis

Noboa as its leading figure. In turn, the economic expansion generated by banana export led to the first sustained process of horizontal import substitution as it enlarged the internal market and turned the attentions of individuals like Noboa to major industrial investments.

By the late 1940s, an increase in the consumption of bananas along with an outbreak of labor unrest and plant diseases in the banana plantations of Central America created a serious crisis in production. It was under these circumstances that the United Fruit Company, the multinational firm that dominated world trade, looked to Ecuador as an alternative site for production. In 1947, United Fruit technicians traveled to Ecuador and met with the recently elected president, Galo Plaza Lasso.[10] Plaza, himself a member of an important *serrano* landholding family, came to power espousing a development program based primarily on the promotion of agricultural production. Subsequent to these discussions with United Fruit, the Plaza government embarked on an active program to encourage banana production on the coast. In 1948, Plaza created the Comisión de Orientación y Crédito para el Banano, a lending agency dedicated to dispensing 15 million sucres in credit to banana producers. In addition to these loans to farmers, banana production was facilitated by a road-building project financed by the U.S. government and international lending agencies.[11]

The banana promotion program and the attentions of multinationals had immediate effects. The rapid gestation time of banana plants allowed for a quick adjustment of production in response to the lucrative prices and new credit incentives. From 1947 to 1953, the dollar value of exports increased from $5 million to $44 million.[12] The number of bunches exported in the same period rose from 2.6 to 16.7 million.[13] The growth of exports continued to be impressive throughout the 1950s. By the early 1960s, Ecuador was the world's largest single producer of bananas.

But in contrast to the Central American experience, banana production in Ecuador did not develop around vertically integrated operations owned by multinational firms. Rather than sink substantial capital into the creation of a plantation system, the multinationals chose to rely upon purchases of the product from local farmers in the open market. The near hegemonic control of United Fruit and Standard Fruit over the shipping and sales of the product allowed them to profit from Ecuador's shift into banana production without becoming involved in a politically sensitive investment at the production end itself. Instead, production was left in the hands of a heterogeneous mix of farmers with small, medium, and large operations. Farms of less than twenty-five hectares accounted for 48 percent of all banana-producing units. Approximately 49 percent of all land under banana cultivation belonged to farms composed of less than one hundred hectares.[14]

The significant participation by small and medium-sized farmers in export production had important effects in other economic sectors, especially industry and domestic agriculture. The direct involvement of farmers of modest means in the export boom triggered a wave of expansion in the internal market both because of increased profits to middle-class landowners on the coast and expanded agricultural employment. White-collar employees and small businessmen rushed to take advantage of the government's extension of credit. They acquired small properties, became absentee owners, and hired wage laborers to work the farms.[15]

The expansion of popular purchasing power that accompanied banana exports accelerated industrialization in two ways. First, it encouraged a steady increase in the use of the production capabilities of existing plants such as those in beer, textiles, and cement. Second, it provided new incentives to the dominant class to diversify their investments through import-substitution activities. As during the cacao boom, commercial fractions of the bourgeoisie were at the forefront of industrial investment. But in contrast to the cacao period, the pursuit of industrial investments began to threaten the position of importers, and tensions between the new entrepreneurs and traditional importers began to emerge.

This new differentiation within the dominant classes was reflected in policy clashes over import substitution beginning in the 1950s. A number of such sectoral conflicts occurred in relation to the development of the food processing industry. In the late 1940s, Francisco Yllescas, a political figure and lawyer with interests in oil exploration and real estate, borrowed money from a British grain company to build a flour mill on his riverfront property in Guayaquil. Subsequently, Yllescas spearheaded a fierce campaign to ban flour imports and lift import restrictions on wheat. Yllescas artfully used the idea of developing a national wheat crop as the basis for his public relations campaign against flour importers. By 1951, the political battle was won and Yllescas monopolized flour production on the coast. Yllescas went on to expand his investment to include forty-three bakeries, a textile mill, and a power plant.[16] Similarly, a small core of industrialists in the edible oils industry lobbied successfully for measures that included prohibiting the export of vegetable fats, banning the import of animal fats, and special tax breaks on the import of capital goods. As a result, edible oils production rose throughout the 1950s.[17]

The antagonism between importers and new industrialists as reflected in the battles over protectionism became recurrent. In the mid-1950s, local investors in the southern province of Azuay decided to mount the first tire factory in the country. Coastal importers virulently opposed the decision. Otto Arosemena, a leading political figure with ties to commercial and financial groups in Guayaquil, led the attack in Congress. The attempts to stop the project failed and the Compañía Ecutatoriana de Caucho opened its doors in 1963.[18] In another attack on import substitution, the Orrantia family with investments in importing led the opposition to the installation of the Ecasa assembly plant. Ecasa, S.A., was the first firm in Ecuador to assemble home appliances such as refrigerators and washers. Failing in their attempt to stop the plant and faced with local competition, the Orrantia group retreated from its anti-industrial rhetoric and later founded a competing appliance firm, Electrodomésticos Durex.

Just as commercial fractions were turning to industry, the traditional agricultural system of the sierra felt the impact of growth in demand due to banana prosperity. The increase in the demand for agricultural products, coupled with the insecurities created by peasant agitation in the countryside, moved a number of landholders to advocate agricultural modernization.[19] One of their leaders was ex-President Galo Plaza. The linchpin of the modernization program was abolishing the precapitalist relations of production and establishing a wage labor system in the sierra. With the agrarian reform of 1964, hacendados were relieved of their traditional obligations to their peons. Hacendados introduced capital-intensive production. Milk production replaced the cultivation of such labor-intensive crops as wheat and corn. These modernizing landholders also invested in processing plants. Pasteurizadora Quito was formed in 1961 by a group of *serrano* landholders in association with the municipality of Quito. In 1963, the Plaza family founded a dairy, La Avelina. By 1968, these two firms accounted for the production of 44 percent of all the pasteurized milk in the country.[20]

With the two gigantic multinationals—Standard Fruit and United Fruit—dominating world trade in bananas, most of the traditional agro-exporting firms of Guayaquil did not participate directly in banana export. The exception was Luis Noboa, who first acted as an agent for Standard Fruit but broke away to form his own Exportadora Noboa in 1954. Despite their marginalization from the banana trade, agro-exporters of cacao and coffee prospered during the 1950s and took advantage of the new opportunities for investment. Two of the major exporters, Victor Maspons and Jorge Salcedo, made major industrial investments in the 1960s. Maspons headed one of the largest and oldest cacao and coffee exporting firms, Intercambio y Crédito. In 1964, he joined with Salcedo to establish Inedeca, S.A., a chocolate factory. By the 1970s, the Maspons group holdings included a cacao processing plant and a fish cannery. Salcedo established the first coffee processing plant, Solubles Instántaneos, C.A., and a convenience food processing firm.[21] The diversification of the Maspons and Salcedo operations closely paralleled the expansion of the Noboa group.

The portfolio diversification by dominant-class groups that accelerated during the 1960s was not solely a response to the market expansion triggered by the banana boom. It was also part of a strategy to minimize risk. Faced with a renewed round of price stagnation in the international commodities markets in the early 1960s, domestic capitalists sought a more balanced approach to investment by extending investments across economic sectors. The development of conglomerates under the direction of a family or a clique of investors is a classic mechanism for coping with the risks and uncertainties of a dependent economy.[22] The *grupos económicos* of Ecuador have their counterparts all over Latin America. In addition to the motivations provided by market forces, both the state and multinational corporations played a pivotal role in making industrialization an attractive economic alternative.

The State, Multinationals, and Intentional Industrialization

The transition from a laissez-faire to an interventionist state in Ecuador began with the July Revolution (Revolución Juliana) of 1925. The coup, led by young military officers and supported by broad coalition including the middle and upper classes, toppled the Liberal government and ended the political hegemony enjoyed by agro-exporting fractions since the Liberal Revolution of 1895. The July Revolution brought the first systematic attempt to modernize the state bureaucracy and extend state power.[23] The major accomplishment of the modernization drive was to remove monetary policy from the purview of the private banks of the coast and to assert state control over economic policy through the establishment of the Banco Central del Ecuador. While the state's takeover of the monetary system did represent an important move toward increasing state power over the economy, it is important to note that the manipulation of exchange rates by the state constituted a relatively passive and indirect tool of influence, albeit one highly compatible with an agro-export economy.[24] Apart from the initial protectionist measures dictated by the Industrial Laws of 1905 and 1925, the exchange rate continued to be the vehicle through which the state attempted to direct the economy throughout the 1930s and 1940s.

More direct modes of state intervention came with the banana promotion program of the Plaza government in 1948 and continued through the period known as the "democratic parenthesis"—the string of elected civilian governments that succeeded each other without military interventions from 1948 to 1963.[25] The establishment of a national planning board, the Junta Nacional de Planificación (JUNAPLA), embodied this new commitment to direct state participation in the management of the economy.[26]

The creation of JUNAPLA in the 1950s and its diagnosis of Ecuador's economic ills reflected the sociostructural changes of the period as well as the ideological influences from the external sources, particularly the United Nations Economic Commission for Latin America (ECLA). Beginning with the July Revolution, middle-class elements assumed positions within the expanding state bureaucracy. With the foundation of JUNAPLA, the presence of the middle class within the public bureaucracy was even more pronounced. JUNAPLA became the province of young professionals trained as economists, engineers, and sociologists. The international institution that shaped the ideological outlook of this first generation of Ecuadorean technocrats was ECLA. An ECLA team wrote the first thorough analysis of the Ecuadorean economy in 1953.[27] Shortly thereafter, three ECLA functionaries were directly involved as consultants in forming the first development plan of 1958.[28]

The ECLA influence is evident in the first economic analyses published by JUNAPLA. The thrust of the arguments in these documents is in keeping with the ECLA orthodoxy of the time—namely, the Prebisch thesis regarding the deteriorating terms of trade for Third World commodities producers. JUNAPLA looked to import-substitution industrialization as the only alternative to agro-export dependence. Pessimistic forecasts concerning the future of agricultural exports permeated JUNAPLA's thinking on Ecuadorean development problems. Although import substitution was viewed as secondary to increasing internal domestic agricultural production, both were recommended as cushions against the chronic instabilities generated by the international commodities market.[29]

The conservative government of President Camilo Ponce responded to JUNAPLA's suggestions on the promotion of import substitution by enacting the first comprehensive Industrial Development Law in 1957. The law created packages of tax breaks for industrial firms with eligibility determined by their contribution to the substitution of imports, use of local raw materials, and export capability. Amendments in the 1960s allowed for liberal interpretations of the eligibility requirements and the law was broadly applied. Along with this legal framework promoting import substitution, the Centro de Desarrollo Industrial (CENDES) was created in 1960 as a state agency charged with carrying out feasibility studies for new industrial projects.

At the same time the technocrats of JUNAPLA were advocating developmentalist projects, the embryonic industrial bourgeoisie was acquiring more direct representation within the government through cabinet appointments.[30] This was especially evident in the government of Camilo Ponce in which industrialists occupied seven key cabinet posts. Thus, middle-class technocats and industrialists formed a proindustrial lobby inside the state apparatus.

By 1961, it was painfully evident that JUNAPLA's predictions concerning the exhaustion of export-led growth were correct. The terms of trade steadily deteriorated as the price of the two major exports, bananas and coffee, failed to keep pace with the price of industrial goods.[31] This deterioration in the export sector provoked a serious exchange crisis for the government of President Velasco Ibarra, bringing a wave of unemployment and price increases.

The export crisis of the early 1960s underscored the desirability of pursuing the economic diversification strategy posed by the technocrats of JUNAPLA. This strategy was incorporated into the program of the 1963 military junta that had forced the resignations of the preceding civilian government of Velasco Ibarra and Carlos Julio Arosemena, bringing the "democratic parenthesis" to a close. The military junta headed by Castro Jijón continued the drive for economic modernization and diversification already under way. Regarding industrial policy, the junta provided new incentives for industries through a 1965 amendment to the Industrial Development Law and the establishment of the public finance corporation, Corporación Financiera Nacional (CFN). The Corporación Financiera was modeled after such agencies as Chile's CORFO and the Mexico's Nacional Financiera that had been established during the first phase of those countries' import-substitution process. The Corporación was to act as a passive investor and financier of top-priority industrial projects. The state, through the Corporación, took responsibility for underwriting accumulation in the industrial sector by providing seed capital for the initial industrial project and then returning these enterprises to the private-sector partners.

As the state adopted protectionist measures to stimulate industrialization, a few multinational corporations began to abandon export and set up local production facilities. Prior to the 1960s, foreign investment was concentrated in extractive industries such as gold mining and petroleum, in addition to its role in shipping and the international marketing of agricultural commodities. With a few important exceptions, resident foreigners, rather than multinationals, accounted for most of the "foreign" investment in manufacturing. In 1947, Fleischmann began producing yeast and gelatins in Guayaquil. Foreign firms were important in manufacturing pharmaceuticals. Dow Chemical, Schering, and Sterling Drugs opened local production facilities in 1940, 1950, and 1956, respectively. But the real takeoff in foreign investment in manufacturing began after 1963. Between 1963 and 1969, aggregate foreign investment more than doubled from $24 million to $57 million.[32] Among the most important international firms to begin some type of product elaboration during the sixties were City Investing, Continental Grain, W. R. Grace, International Multifoods, Morton International, Phelps-Dodge, St. Regis Paper, Seaboard Allied Milling, Thomas Built Buses, Union Carbide, Warner-Lambert, and Crown Cork.[33]

With the industrialization process still in its infancy, the entrance of these multinationals during the 1960s did not pose a threat to Ecuador's existing industries. For the most part, these multinationals did not buy out or compete with local producers, but mounted their own plants and initiated the first local factory production of many items. The multinationals differed in their relationships to local capital. Grace, Morton, and Thomas sought out local capitalists as partners while Continental, Seaboard Allied, Crown Cork, Union Carbide, St. Regis, and City Investing created wholly owned subsidiaries.

By 1969, the skeletal industrialization of Ecuador was marked by a distinctive style of development and contradictions that would deepen during the economic growth generated by the advent of oil exports in the 1970s. Central to the process was the tutelary role assumed by the state and its creation of a legal framework and public institutions that facilitated capital accumulation in the industrial sector. The elaborate protectionism created by the Industrial Development Laws and tariff structures awakened the interest of both local capitalists and multinationals in the industrial investment.

In addition to the incentives provided by the state, industrialization accelerated as a result of dominant-class interest in portfolio diversification in the wake of export stagnation. The transfer of resources from commerce and agriculture to industry took place as wealthy merchants and landowners sought to protect themselves from the vagaries of the international commodities market and to enjoy the generous tax benefits provided by the state. But as they became industrialists, they did not abandon their investments in other sectors. Rather, *grupos económicos* such as the one headed by Luis Noboa emerged with investment portfolios that spanned industry, agriculture, and commerce. Evidence of these intersectoral linkages can be found in the survey data in tables 1 and 2 on the family background and the investment activities of forty-three major industrialists. As table 1 indicates, a shift in economic activity took place as older agrarian and commercial classes moved their younger members into industrial occupations. Intersectoral overlap continues through stockholding. As seen in table 2, industrialists reported their involvement in commercial, financial, and agricultural enterprises as well as extended investments in more than one industrial firm.[34]

Notwithstanding the influx of multinational and new local capital into industry, traditional consumer nondurables continued to dominate of industrial production. Food, textiles, beverages, and cigarettes accounted

Table 1   Social Origins of Ecuadorean Industrialists:
Occupation of
Grandfathers and Fathers

	Grandfather		Father	
	N	%	N	%
Industry	6	14	15	35
Commerce	9	21	13	30
Liberal professions	5	11	9	21
Agriculture	12	28	2	5
Artisan/tradesman	2	5	1	2
Other	2	5	3	7
No information	7	16	0	0
Total	43		43	

Source: See appendix.

Table 2   Additional Business Interests of Ecuadorean Industrialists

	N	% of Informants
Other industrial firm(s)	29	67
Commerce	7	16
Finance	13	30
Agriculture	8	19
Construction	3	7
Other	5	12
None reported	7	16

Source: See appendix.

Note: Of the forty-three respondents, twenty-three reported interests in at least two outside activities.

for 55 percent of the total value of industrial production and 75 percent of all industrial investment in 1969. In the same year, these branches employed 57 percent of the total industrial work force.[35]

The continuing specialization of Ecuadorean industry in basic consumer goods was rooted in the extremely truncated character of the internal market. Despite the market expansion created by the banana boom, the growth of the state bureaucracy, and the elimination of precapitalist economic relations in the sierra, industrialization was superimposed on one of the smallest and poorest markets in Latin America. In 1950, the total population of the country was just a little over 3 million. According to the 1960 JUNAPLA study of social classes, approximately 78 percent of the total population was classified as "lower/popular" classes, with per capita annual incomes averaging approximately $52. Only 22 percent of the population was described as middle- or upper-class.[36]

The extreme inequality in income distribution remained virtually unchanged during the 1960s. The statistics that most dramatically illustrate the concentration of demand, even for simple products, are found in the ECIEL study of consumer behavior. In Quito and Guayaquil, between 43 and 45 percent of all expenditures for food products were made by consumers falling into the top income quartile. The share of expenditures accounted for by this top quartile was even higher in other categories such as clothing, housing, and furnishings.[37] So, even at this early stage, industrialists were operating within the confines of an extremely limited internal market in which a small number of middle- and upper-class consumers generated the lion's share of demand for many products.

By the end of the 1960s, the making of the industrial bourgeoisie remained unfinished. The state was still a feeble ally for industrialists, hampered in its promotion of industrialization by sagging export revenues. The underdevelopment of the nexus between the state and industrial capital was paralleled by the weak relationship between multinational corporations and local capital. Although some partnerships had been struck between international firms and local entrepreneurs, the attempted alliances were tentative and not widespread. Only a few strategic individuals such as Noboa took part in joint ventures with multinationals. The small size of the internal market, the legacy of agro-export and the class relationships that accompanied it, remained the key obstacles to further industrial development.

Oil and the Market in the 1970s

The initiation of major oil exports in 1972 brought significant alterations in the shape of the internal market. In contrast to previous export booms where the state was only a passive beneficiary, the state directly captured a large portion of the surplus generated by oil export through its legal monopoly over exploitation rights and the creation of a state-owned oil company in 1972, the Corporación Estatal Petrolera Ecuatoriana (CEPE). Government revenues soared, more than tripling from 1970 to 1975.[38]

The fiscal character of the Ecuadorean state was rapidly transformed; with oil revenues at its disposal, the state occupied an unprecedented dominant position in the economy. With the state cast in the role of arbiter of the new oil wealth, the locus of decisions on the distribution of the surplus shifted from the market into the heart of the state bureaucracy. The conflicts between industrialists and the state over the distribution of these resources and the role to be assumed by this fiscally rejuvenated state are described at length in chapter 4. For the moment, let us examine the impact of the oil-generated economic expansion on the internal market.

Public-sector growth was substantial during the 1970s. The ratio of public expenditures to gross domestic product climbed steadily during the decade.[39] The state used these new resources in a number of ways—but one immediate use was to expand the state apparatus itself. Public employment swelled as new bureaucracies proliferated. From 1970 to 1975, the number of public employees grew from 61,277 to 103,911.[40] The most dramatic increases in public-sector employment occurred in the education, labor, social welfare, and health ministeries. Increased support to education, and the job opportunities created by the expanding public sector, swelled university enrollments. Students entering institutions of higher education grew from 40,000 in 1970 to 70,000 by 1976. Among the urban employed, 8.7 percent held university degrees in 1975 in contrast to 5.1 percent in 1968.[41]

While public employment was increasing, the adoption of capital-intensive techniques in the agricultural sector and the elimination of traditional tenancy arrangements displaced rural laborers and increased the pace of migration to cities. Urban areas increased their share of the population from 36 percent in 1968 to 41 percent in 1974.[42] The most common types of employment available to these new migrants were found in the informal sector; migrants poured into Quito and Guayaquil working as construction laborers and street vendors.[43]

State-sponsored expansion in white-collar employment and accelerated urbanization enlarged the ranks of the urban middle and lower classes. These developments are reflected in the changing distribution of income from 1968 to 1975. In this period, there was a significant reduction in the percentage of the urban population earning S/10,500 or less; only 27 percent of the urban population fell in this category in 1974 as opposed to the 42 percent in 1968. The number of urban residents earning between S/ 10,500 and S/40,000 rose from 45 to 56 percent. The percentage earning between S/40,000 and S/90,000 rose from 8.5 to 14.5. A World Bank study characterized the new middle- or lower-middle classes as the "winners" in a substantial change in the income structure between 1968 and 1975.[44]

As the number of middle- and lower-middle-class consumers increased, overall levels of consumption increased. Ecuador was rated as one of the fastest growing markets in Latin America during the 1970s, ranking second to Brazil. Per capita annual income increased from $303 in 1972 to $547 by 1975. Per capita private consumption expenditures increased during the same period from $194 to $335.[45]

Despite these adjustments in the share of the national income absorbed by urban middle and lower classes, income distribution as a whole remained severely skewed. The proportion of the national income received by the lower 20 percent of the urban population actually declined from 3.4 to 3 percent between 1968 and 1975. The percentage of income held by the top 10 percent of the urban population decreased, but the decline still left this group in control of 34 percent of all income. The situation in the countryside remained grim. At least 65 percent of the rural population was judged by the World Bank to be living below the absolute poverty level in 1975. Even with the alterations in income distribution, about three-fourths of the entire population absorbed only 30 percent of the country's wealth, while a fourth controlled 70 percent. Approximately 59 percent of the total population fell below the absolute poverty line in 1975.[46]

Given this income distribution, the surge in demand for industrial products was generated almost exclusively in urban areas. A study of the food processing industry estimated that 90 percent of all canned food products was consumed in Quito, Guayaquil, and Cuenca.[47] Moreover, even within the urban population, the demand for industrial products was constrained by inelasticities in the expenditures of the urban poor. As the ECIEL study of consumer behavior reports, the poor spend most of their meager incomes on basic necessities, primarily food. And even the purchase of processed items such as dairy products lags behind nonprocessed foods. Outside of the food industry, demand for industrial goods was even more concentrated among the rich.

By the mid-1970s, the internal market was populated by a small core of the very affluent surrounded by urban middle and lower-middle groups with expanding purchasing power. Outside of these privileged rings of consumers stood the majority of the population struggling for survival in the countryside and in the urban slums.

In this market situation, industrial firms pursued growth strategies that further attentuated their already weak ties to low-income consumers. Firms introduced new product lines specifically designed to appeal to upscale consumers. This type of product diversification was especially evident in the food processing industry and the manufacture of personal care products. Notwithstanding a crisis in milk production and chronic shortages, the milk industry undertook the production of high-priced cheeses, ice cream, and yogurt. In Guayaquil, the Vallarino group, owners of Fábrica de Aceites La Favorita and Jaboneria Nacional, introduced new product lines that included Signal toothpaste and Lux soap under an agreement with the international firm, Unilever. The largest brewery, Compañía de Cervezas Nacionales, signed a transfer of technology agreement that allowed them to introduce Löwenbrau as their top-of-the-line product. Three Guayaquil businessmen linked up with the Colgate-Palmolive Company in a joint venture to manufacture Colgate detergents, toothpastes, and soaps. Johnson and Johnson opened its first plant in Guayaquil in 1977 in order to enter the lucrative new market for personal care products among high-income consumers. This process of rapid product diversification—or "industrial development in breadth"—was given further impetus by Ecuador's participation in the common market arrangements of the Andean Pact.[48] At least potentially, the proposed reduction in trade barriers among pact members would make the middle and upper classes of the entire region available as consumers for Ecuadorean industry.[49]

As the examples above indicate, this quest for the upscale consumer brought more extensive linkages between local entrepreneurs and multinational capital. For the first time, multinationals began to look at Ecuador as a market that could justify direct investment. Imported and locally produced foreign brands presented the greatest threat to domestic industrialists seeking to capture these new consumers. Rather than face multinational competition and its sophisticated advertising, many domestic industrialists sought to achieve a modus vivendi through joint ventures and transfer-of-technology agreements. The agreements between Vallarino and

Unilever as well as the introduction of Löwenbrau beer by Cervezas Nacionales were conceived of by management as unavoidable "preemptive" strikes—made to ensure that direct competition from these multinationals would not occur.

The dramatic increase in foreign investment in manufacturing in this period is indicative of the new attractiveness of the Ecuadorean market. From 1970 to 1976, foreign participation in manufacturing increased from $60 million to $220 million.[50] But a key feature of this new foreign investment was the forms it assumed. Approximately 48 percent of all direct foreign investment from 1973 to 1977 was channelled into *compañías mixtas*, joint-venture arrangements in which foreign capital controls less that 51 percent of the shares.[51] Transfer-of-technology agreements also linked the two. In my 1979–1980 survey of forty-three of the largest industrial firms, 42 percent of the respondents reported current transfer-of-technology agreements. Aulestia and Ayora report a near-doubling of transfer-of-technology payments from 1976 to 1977, rising from $6,897,500 to $11,840,110. While there are no comparable statistics from earlier periods about the rates of association between local and multinational capital over time, the fragmentary evidence suggests that they became increasingly intertwined during the 1970s as they pursued the new breed of Ecuadorean consumer.

The style of industrialization described above was reinforced by certain aspects of state policy that encouraged industrial investment. Provisions within the Industrial Development Law, especially the tariff exemptions on capital goods, encouraged capital-intensive industry. The result was the development of an industrial sector characterized by oversized plants, much excess capacity, and low employment growth. Factory employment grew at rates substantially lower than the increases in the economically active urban population. Thus industry contributed only minimally incorporating the marginalized masses into the market by providing jobs. The capital intensity of Ecuadorean industry itself restricted market expansion.[52]

To a great extent, industrialists were able to compensate for the small consumer base by a lack of competition and the power this gave them to control prices. Protectionist trade policies maintained monopolies and oligopolies in a number of industries. On the national level, the production of beer, cigarettes, sugar, salt, and confections was highly concentrated among a few firms. Across twenty-nine categories, three firms or fewer captured 50 percent of the sales in all but five product categories.[53] The persistent market domination by a small number of firms allowed industrialists to impose prices that compensated for the low volume of sales. A World Bank study pointing to the presence of oligopolies fueled by tax rebates and facing no competition from imports concluded that the "benefits to firms resulting from fiscal incentives were hardly ever passed on to consumers."[54]

This tendency toward oligopolistic pricing practices did not proceed completely unchecked. The military government of General Rodríguez Lara attempted to curb the power of the oligopolies, particularly in the food industry. In 1973, the Rodríguez Lara government established the Superintendencia de Precios for the purposes of controlling the prices of basic foodstuffs. The agency controlled the price of edible oils, sugar, cigarettes, flour, soft drinks, milk, meat, and medicines. But this attempt at price control generated two unintended consequences that reinforced the upscale market orientation of industrialists. First, this system of "political" prices forced industrialists into bargaining with the state bureaucracy over price issues. With the establishment of this new relationship, profit levels became directly contingent on the ability of firms to lobby effectively for price increases or subsidies. Politics replaced performance in the market as the key to profitability. Once again, the narrowness of the market was irrelevant to determining profits and losses. Second, the extension of price controls over those industries producing *artículos de la primera necesidad* encouraged industrialists to move investments into the production of other items not covered by price controls. As one executive in the flour milling industry explained during an interview, his decision to invest in a television assembly plant was based on a desire to avoid price controls and the recognition that the demand among high-income consumers for consumer durables was growing.

The economic growth generated by oil revenues did not so much change the structural characteristics of Ecuadorean industrialization as it reinforced and deepened the tendencies already present in the process. The market remained limited by the enormous income inequalities in Ecuador. Yet, the compensations created by new middle-class consumption and the collection of subsidies from the state allowed accumulation in the industrial sector to proceed unperturbed in the face of widespread poverty.[55] At the same time, new opportunities prompted investors to look outward rather than inward as they contemplated future industrial development.

The Rise of Export Industries

With investments made in import-substitution industries, Luis Noboa and other major coastal entrepreneurs turned their attention during the 1970s to external markets as a basis for further industrialization. It was only natural for coastal capitalists to look abroad—Luis Noboa, Victor Maspons, and Jorge Salcedo had all founded their business empires on their success as agro-exporters. Attuned to the rhythms of the international commodities markets, these entrepreneurs were well prepared to take advantage of new opportunities to engage in the semi-elaboration of agricultural products.

The most attractive new external market of the 1970s was the one for cacao semi-elaborates. Traditionally, cacao was exported from Ecuador in its raw state. The grinding and processing of cacao into the semi-elaborates required for chocolate manufacture (such as paste, liquor, and butter) remained under the control of the leading manufacturing firms in Europe and the United States. But a rise in energy prices and labor costs in the 1970s encouraged chocolate manufacturers to phase out first-stage grinding operations and to purchase the intermediate cacao products from other sources. The movement to phase out grinding operations coincided with enormous disparities between the prices for raw beans and semi-elaborates on the international market. In the early 1970s, the average price of a ton of cacao semi-elaborates was 54 percent higher than the price of a ton of raw cacao.[56] The dramatic price differences and the willingness of chocolate manufacturers to surrender their monopoly enabled a cacao semi-elaborates industry to develop in Ecuador.

The shift from the export of the raw material to the semiprocessed product was swift. Leading coastal exporters such as Jorge Salcedo, Victor Maspons, and Raúl Balda were joined by importers like José Carvajal and Werner Moeller in the rush to mount semi-elaborates plants. The result was a dramatic growth in the export of semi-elaborates; from 1970 to 1975, exports jumped from $2.6 million to $29.8 million.[57]

As was the case with import-substitution enterprises, the rise of the cacao semi-elaborates industry was heavily stimulated by active state intervention. After intense lobbying by the Salcedo group, the government of President Velasco Ibarra passed measures in 1970 exempting the semi-elaborates industry from the 25 percent export tax and granting them a 15 percent subsidy on exports. With the availability of oil revenues after 1972, the government opened generous lines of credit to the incipient industry. From 1972 to 1975, the Corporación Financiera Nacional increased its credit to the semi-elaborates industry from S/63 million to S/352.4 million.[58]

The blatant state subsidization of the semi-elaborates industry was not without its opponents. A number of exporters resisted the conversion to semi-elaboration and adamantly opposed the 40 percent price differential created by the state's pro-elaboration policies. Diehard exporters accused the state of engaging in a fiscal sacrifice by forgoing taxes on semi-elaborates and fabricating a "false industry" that benefited only a handful of local monopolists and the foreign firms that purchased the subsidized product. The semi-elaborators countered by portraying themselves as the vanguard of national industrialization. They argued that the semi-elaborates industry was "authentically Ecuadorean," "obviously nationalist," and "real."[59] Their campaign was successful and the military governments from 1972 to 1979 maintained the tax rebates and subsidies.

The expansion of the cacao semi-elaborates industry was matched by the development of other export-oriented industries. The Salcedo group, owners of Solubles Instantáneos, C.A., monopolized the export of coffee semi-elaborates during the first half of the decade with financing from the Corporación Financiera Nacional. Late in the decade, the Noboa group also entered the coffee semi-elaborates market. Foreign firms as well as the Maspons and Balda groups founded firms to produce canned tuna and sardines, primarily for export. Shrimp farming also began to attract the attention of many of the same investors.

This expansion in nontraditional exports added another layer onto an already complex web of market orientations held by the emerging industrial bourgeoisie, especially that of Guayaquil. Agro-exporters turned to industry without altering their longstanding dependence on external markets; cacao and coffee semi-elaboration was but an extension of existing export businesses. As a result, these industrialists did not have to rely on growth in the internal market.

But one must keep in mind that these new export-oriented industrialists were not completely devoid of ties to the internal market. The *grupos económicos* involved in export also invested in production for local consumption. For example, in addition to coffee and cacao semi-elaborates, the Salcedo group produced instant coffee (under the brand name, Si Café) for the internal market, and manufactured convenience foods for local sales through Sopas, S.A. Inedeca, S.A. (jointly owned by Nestlé and the Maspons group), produced cacao semi-elaborates as well as chocolate, dairy products, and convenience foods for the internal market. La Universal, S.A., also involved in the semi-elaborates trade, was the major national producer of cookies, crackers, and candy for local consumption. But the key point is that with the exception of La Universal, which sold more than three-quarters of its products in Ecuador, exports constituted the major concern for this wing of coastal industrialists. In the case of the Salcedo group, 70 percent of their coffee production was destined for foreign markets.[60] The combined sales of the Salcedo operations in coffee and cacao semi-elaborates was three times greater than the sales registered by Salcedo's convenience food firm.[61] Similarly, the export operation of Inedeca, S.A., was the firm's major activity even though it also produced a range of food products for local sale. As table 3 demonstrates, production for the local market was a related activity for economic groups involved in cacao semi-elaborates. Local purchases of fish products constituted a tiny percentage of the total sales of the Maspons' group, Industrial Pesquera Monteverde, as it did for other fish canning firms.

The development of these export operations during the 1970s cushioned the industrial bourgeoisie against the problems of pursuing industrialization despite a limited market. The limitations posed by the unequal distribution of income were canceled out by the opportunities in external markets, state subsidies, and the oil-induced expansion in middle-class purchasing power. At the close of the decade, the Junta Nacional de Planificación grimly summarized the characteristics of Ecuador's industrialization:

> The growth of industrial establishments did not provoke nor did it translate into a substantive modification either of the productive process or the forms of organization of the national economy. New companies continued producing for either the richest strata of the population or the external market. Meanwhile, the consumption of the masses whose income borders on the level of subsistence remains unsatisfied. They do not produce simple goods for the great national majority because the interests of the poorest groups of the country do not constitute a significant market either to sustain the installation of industries or to broaden the production of already existing industries.[62]

Table 3   Related Business Activities of Major Stockholders
in Cacao Semi-elaborates Firms

	Related Activities	Market Orientation of Related Firm(s)
SALCO	Manufacture of coffee semi-elaborates	Internal/External
	Manufacture of convenience foods	Internal
	Real estate brokerage	—
PROCOA	Manufacture of paper products	Internal
	Import of office equipment	Internal
CAFIESA	Import of liquor	Internal
INCACAO	Manufacture of fish products	External
	Manufacture of milk/food products	Internal
	Export of coffee beans.	External
	Import of air conditioners	Internal
	Management of steamship agency	—
INEDECA	Same as INCACAO	
CACOS DEL ECUADOR	Export of coffee beans	External
	Manufacture of fish products	External
EXPELCA	Export of coffee beans	External
COLCACAO	Export of bananas	External
	Manufacture of coffee semi-elaborates	Internal/External
	Milling of flour	Internal
	Import of liquor	Internal
	Management of financial/insurance agencies	—
MANACOA	Export of coffee beans	External
LA UNIVERSAL	No information available	

Source: See appendix.

Conclusion: The Structural Position of Industrialists

Timing and the market context combined to produce a baroque form of industrialization in Ecuador—an extremely late-starting process layered with exaggerations, twists, and departures from the experiences of the early industrialization countries of the Southern Cone. In a generic sense, many of the structural characteristics of the early phase of import substitution in the Southern Cone that spanned the 1920s, 1930s and 1940s were recreated in Ecuador from the 1950s through the 1970s. At the same time, there were important divergences between them in the processes that altered the dominant class's material interests in each case.

There were important differences in the relationships between sectors of the dominant class. Certainly, the emergence of economic groups during industrialization is a phenomenon not confined to contemporary Ecuador. Successful entrepreneurs in Chile, Argentina, and Uruguay diversified their portfolios and invested in other sectors of the economy. In this sense, the story of the development of the Noboa group enterprises in Ecuador is not much different from that of the di Tella industrial empire in Argentina. Notwithstanding the general process of portfolio diversification, there appear to be important differences in the extent of crossover investments in agriculture and the extent to which industrial entrepreneurs were socially integrated into the ranks of the traditional landowners. Because many of the import-substituting industrialists in Argentina and Uruguay were immigrants, there were some social rifts in the upper ranks of these societies. In the case of Chile, Henry Kirsch suggests that a much closer social integration occurred between industrialists and old landed fractions to produce a homogenous and completely overlapping economic elite. Survey results concerning past family occupations and the histories of the leading economic groups indicate that relationships between upper-class groups in Ecuador more closely resemble the Chilean pattern.[63]

In the case of Ecuador, the takeoff of import-substitution industrialization was concomitant with the investment of foreign capital in manufacturing. There was an immediate internationalization of some important local industrialists through joint-venture arrangements and transfer-of-technology agreements. The interests of industrialists rapidly became interlocked with those of multinational corporations. Given the lack of comparable statistical evidence, it is impossible to measure the extent of the relationships between foreign capital and industrialists across cases. But the historians of the early industrialization of Argentina, Chile, and Uruguay present a more mixed and less encompassing view of the position of foreign firms in manufacturing. In Argentina and Uruguay, British and American firms invested in the meat packing industry, but most other manufacturing activities were in the hands of local or recently arrived entrepreneurs. Entrepreneurs like Torcuato di Tella did seek out licensing and contracting agreements with foreign firms when necessary, but joint ventures were not common. The hiatus in the inflow of foreign capital and imports that accompanied the Depression gave industrialists in the Southern Cone the opportunity to develop national industries without fear of foreign competition. It is important to keep in mind that the bulk of multinational investment in the region for the first half of the century remained concentrated in mining, agriculture, railways, and public utilities.[64] As such, the industrial bourgeoisie of the Southern Cone was able to carve out economic niches of their own in the spaces not occupied by foreign capital. For Ecuadorean industrialists, no such space for autonomy was available.

The immediate association of the Ecuadorean industrial bourgeoisie with international capital had important implications for the technical and organizational features of industrialization. The purchase of advanced technology made Ecuadorean industry highly capital-intensive. The employment-generating capabilities of this kind of industrialization proved to be minimal. Industrial employment virtually stagnated; in 1978, 12.6 percent of the economically active population were employed in manufacturing as compared to 11.8 percent in 1970.[65] As such, industry was incapable of expanding the consumer market by expanding the pool of wage earners. Apart from the market effects of this style of industrialization, there were also considerable effects at the political level. The labor movement remained dwarfed by the small size of the proletariat and its marginal position in the economy.

In contrast, the import substitution of the Southern Cone was labor-intensive and contributed to rapid increases in the ranks of the working classes.[66] But even more important to the creation of a modern mass market was the rapid and intense urbanization that took place in these systems. Urban middle classes and the wage-earning working class formed the base for the development of manufacturing. By 1914, 20 percent of the Argentine population resided in Buenos Aires and 30 percent of the Uruguayan population in Montevideo.[67] In Argentina and Uruguay, massive European immigration brought skilled laborers and entrepreneurs. Moreover, the development of wheat and beef production did not depend upon precapitalist labor relations that tied a large part of the population to the countryside. Hence, the rural population was available for internal migration. In Uruguay, the hyperexpansion of the public bureaucracy that began with the first *batllista* government became a permanent feature of political life, one that ensured the existence of a critical core of middle-class consumers. In Chile, the causes of early urbanization were diverse. Unlike Argentina and Uruguay, almost half of the rural labor force were tied to haciendas as *inquilinos* and immigration was less important as a source of population growth. Nevertheless, the mass mobilization for the War of the Pacific, the development of mining industry and the expansion of railroads, and an increase in the number of landless rural laborers at the end of the nineteenth century produced important population shifts.[68] By the 1920s, 46 percent of the Chilean population was urban.[69]

In contrast to the Southern Cone, the shift from country to city in Ecuador was a slower process. Urbanization was slowed by the minimal spinoff effects of the cacao trade and by the relatively late expansion of the state bureaucracy. But perhaps the greatest obstacle to rapid urbanization and the formation of a mass market was the persistence into the 1960s of precapitalist relations of agricultural production. Even after the Junker commercialization of *serrano* agriculture in the 1960s, the agricultural labor force was still marginalized in the economy—suffering from unemployment and underemployment. Desperately poor, the rural population remains effectively outside the market for industrial products.

The Southern Cone industrialists of the 1930s and 1940s looked out on internal markets that both resembled and diverged from the one Ecuadoreans confronted in the 1960s and 1970s. For all, the market was certainly growing. Increases in the size and purchasing power of urban classes were central to industrial expansion in all cases, but the pace of Southern Cone urbanization by the 1930s outstripped that of contemporary Ecuador. Even by the late 1970s, over 53 percent of Ecuador's population of 7 million lived in the countryside. With consumption levels so low in rural areas, industrial growth was found only in the expanded purchasing power of the middle and lower-middle classes that was the aftereffect of the oil-induced state expansion. Moreover, Ecuadorean industrialists could look beyond the boundaries of the internal market as a consequence of the Andean Pact arrangements and the demand in the international market for nontraditional products such as cacao semi-elaborates. By the 1970s, export-oriented strategies emerged as a "safety valve" for the industrial bourgeoisie that allowed for continued industrial growth without wrestling with income distribution problems.

The character of the state as well as the market carved out different structural positions for the Ecuadorean and Southern Cone bourgeoisie. In Chile, Uruguay, and Argentina, middle-class demands for political participation and the emergence of militant trade unions provided the ammunition for the rupture of oligarchic politics. The breakdown in oligarchic state power coincided with the development of the industrial bourgeoisie. So even before the implantation of the populist projects of the 1940s, popular class pressures had already altered the character of the state in the Southern Cone, albeit to varying degrees. The state was no longer seen as a reliable and always malleable instrument for dominant-class interests. In Ecuador, the disintegration of the oligarchic state was not nearly as advanced as import substitution proceeded. A slow integration of the middle classes into the state bureaucracy began with the 1925 July Revolution, but demands from below were effectively contained by sporadic repression, the tenacity of precapitalist forms of domination in the sierra, and limitations on the franchise that were in force until 1979. The industrial bourgeoise that emerged during the 1950s and 1960s was nurtured by a string of civilian governments clearly linked to dominant-class fractions through their traditional parties. The smallness and the factionalization of the trade union movement diluted any serious threat from labor. In short, the Southern Cone bourgeoisie developed within an atmosphere of highly fluid relations between state and civil society. In comparison, the advance of pluralism in Ecuador was painfully slow. Ecuadorean industrialists took their place alongside traditional economic elites in political institutions that restricted contestation and competition.

Within these very different material worlds, the industrial bourgeoisie of the Southern Cone and Ecuador forged ideological constructs and honed their political capabilities. With an aborted market as a backdrop, Ecuadorean industrialists looked to exports, product diversification for middle-class consumers, and collusion with the state. At their service was a malleable state that created the institutional framework and incentives that gave life to the process. In the earlier Southern Cone experience, the demand starvation of the economies was not so acute and national industries had the opportunity to meet local demand, especially as the Depression dried up the competition from foreign imports. But, for Southern Cone industrialists, the state was no longer an inviolate instrument of dominant-class interests. By the 1920s, middle-class reformist governments headed by

Yrigoyen, Alessandri, and Batlle Ordóñez had placed the social question clearly on the national agenda. While the 1930s saw attempts at political retrenchment by the traditional oligarchies, old-style politics was definitely fractured. These unlike historical experiences shaped the very different political responses of industrialists in the Southern Cone and the Andes to the subsequent challenge of developmentalist reformers.

3

The Conservative Class: Ideology, Alliances, and State Power

A remarkable quality of the bourgeois ideology lies in its tenacious traditionalism and uniformity across time and in different settings. While the structural features of industrialization change as the process is repeated in various countries, industrialists everywhere cling to familiar normative visions that revolve around a fear of the state and the masses. At the rhetorical level, there is very little that separates the American robber barons of the nineteenth century from Ecuadorean industrialists of the 1970s. The leitmotif of the political discourse of both groups has been the same—the inviolability of property rights and managerial autonomy within the firm. The state, with the capacity to violate those principles, always looms as the enemy in the mind of the bourgeoisie.

While bonded by common values, industrial classes have been forced to employ a wide variety of political strategies and tactics in their defense. The maneuvering and lobbying of the bourgeoisie in the face of political challenges is the subject of following chapters. My purpose here is to map out the contours of conservatism within the Ecuadorean bourgeoisie. The findings do not break new ground so much as they confirm the findings of other empirical work of the same genre—that the industrial bourgeoisie in Latin America is not the "progressive" class that so many analysts and institutions had hoped for in the 1950s and 1960s.[1] Instead, the new industrialists of Ecuador are deeply conservative and steadfastly reject the notion of a linkage between social reform, market expansion, and economic growth.

The Social Lives of Industrialists

Before examining the ideological positions of the industrial class, let us consider the backgrounds and social characteristics of the group as a whole. The following discussion is based on interviews conducted by the author in Quito and Guayaquil during 1979–1980 with executives heading the country's largest industrial firms.[2] The interviews involved both open- and closed-ended questions about their views concerning the state, economic development, and public policy. The forty-three executives interviewed were all top executive officers in their respective firms; thirty-nine held the title of president or general manager. With one exception, the remaining four informants were sons of the firms' presidents holding assistant manager titles.

As I have noted, family control over ownership and management continues to be the organizing principle of Ecuadorean firms. Among those interviewed, at least 63 percent of the individuals were either the founders of the firms or close relatives of the founders, usually sons. Yet this figure probably underrepresents the fusion between management and stockholding, since information concerning kinship ties among stockholders and management was not available in a number of cases. This absence of a separation between ownership and control removes a number of the standard methodological problems that typically plague the study of dominant classes in advanced capitalist societies.[3] The chief executives of these major firms clearly constitute the upper stratum of the Ecuadorean industrial bourgeoisie; they are not neutral "hired guns" who worked their way up from middle-management positions.

On the average, the executives had worked in their respective firms for over ten years at the time of the interview. The average age of the informants was forty-five years. Only one of the forty-three executives was female and just one was a naturalized citizen. The firms produced a range of consumer nondurables, durables, and intermediate goods for the internal market as well as semiprocessed and processed goods for export. These firms maintained a variety of relationships with foreign capital that included partnerships and transfer-of-technology agreements.

As one would expect, Ecuadorean industrialists move within a closed and homogeneous social world. More than three-fourths of the executives were born in the two major cities, Quito and Guayaquil. The regional concentration of industry in these two cities insures a large measure of professional and social interaction among industrialists. Elite social clubs function as an important conduit for interaction among businessmen of all sorts.[4] Of the industrialists interviewed, 88 percent reported at least one or more memberships in the following organizations: Quito Tennis Club, Salinas Yacht Club, Guayaquil Yacht Club, Club de la Unión, Guayaquil Tennis Club, Guayaquil Country Club, and the Polo Club.

Along with activity in social settings, business associations are important sites for interaction among the industrial bourgeoisie. Corporate membership in the sectoral producers' associations (the Chambers of Industry, Agriculture, or Commerce) is required by law. As later chapters will show, these chambers are the most powerful and visible corporate representatives of the private sector. All of those interviewed were members of their regional Industrial Chambers of Quito or Guayaquil. In addition to the chambers, an array of voluntary membership organizations represent general, sectoral, and regional interests within the industrial bourgeoisie. The Ecuadorean–North American Chamber of Commerce, the Asociación Nacional de Empresarios, the Centro de Ejecutivos, and the International Chamber of Commerce were among the organizations cited by the 74 percent of the interviewees reporting such voluntary affiliations.

The homogeneity of the industrialists' social world is not surprising. Perhaps the most striking indicator of the similarities in their experiences is found in the data on education. Over 70 percent of the thirty-seven executives who attended institutions of higher education did so outside of Ecuador, primarily in U.S. colleges and universities. Schools attended included Notre Dame, the University of Texas, the University of California at Berkeley, the University of Southern California, and Louisiana State University, as well as a number of small colleges and technical institutes. In their studies industrialists gravitated toward technical and managerial fields. Close to 60 percent of the industrialists with university educations reported that they studied engineering or business. This tendency was even more pronounced among those attending universities abroad; 86 percent of those who studied abroad specialized in those two fields. The data on education is summarized in table 4.

The technocratic/managerial character of the bourgeoisie's education is an important sociological factor, as it may work to homogenize and reinforce the conservative predispositions of class members. In his study of

Table 4 Educational Background of Ecuadorean Industrialists

	National		Foreign	
	N	%	N	%
High school	2	5	—	—
Vocational school	2	5	1	2
University, undergraduate	8	19	19	44
University, graduate	3	7	7	16

Source: See appendix.
Note: Total N = 43. There was no information about one respondent (2%).

the origins of bureaucratic-authoritarian regimes, Guillermo O'Donnell points to the effects of a professional socialization that stresses the values of rationality and efficiency. He argues that it produces "brutally simplified" maps of social reality in the minds of technocrats—a mentality in which bargaining and politics are seen as hindrances to the rational solution of socioeconomic problems.[5] As the following survey findings on political beliefs show, the hostile attitudes of industrialists toward the extension of the suffrage and the participation of labor unions in economic decision making indicate such an antipolitical mentality among this technocratic bourgeoisie.

The social statistics on the industrial bourgeoisie in Ecuador suggest that the class inhabits a structured and exclusive social world whose members share common cultural forms and educational experiences. The resort homes in Salinas, ritual trips to Miami, Sunday polo games, and the frequent luncheon meetings in the exclusive hotels of Quito and Guayaquil are all part of the social web within which industrialists live and form attitudes about politics and the social hierarchy.

Visions of State and Society

Students of dominant-class ideology will find that my conversations with Ecuadorean industrialists covered familiar terrain. Antistatism, elitism, and antipopulism were important elements in the thinking of most of the industrialists interviewed. Perhaps the concept that best describes their constellation of political beliefs is productivism—the idea that increased production under the leadership of the private sector is the best answer to the problems of economic development and that, by extension, the state and lower classes should be subordinated to that goal.[6]

Industrialists clearly perceive themselves as occupying leading positions in Ecuadorean society. When asked to identify the most powerful groups in society, 63 percent mentioned their own group. The commercial (export-import) bourgeoisie was cited by 47 percent of the respondents as being powerful. As seen in table 5, the power attributed to other groups such as the state, labor, and the middle classes drops off significantly in comparison to that of the bourgeoisie.

While they viewed themselves as dominant, industrialists demonstrated a sharp sense of their interconnection with other class fractions. In many of their comments, industrialists underscored the fact that they were not a fundamentally new group. Rather, they depicted industrial capitalists as individuals with strong economic and social ties to traditional landowners, merchants, and bankers. Some spoke of industrialists as "people with money from Guayaquil" who wished to diversify investments. Their recognition of the overlap between industrial and other types of economic interests dovetailed neatly with their view of the harmony within the dominant class. In response to a question concerning conflicts of interests between agrarian and industrial elites, 58 percent of the respondents denied any such conflict. And even among the 37 percent who acknowledged the existence of conflict, half argued that the friction was due to erroneous government policies or the machinations of other groups and *not* to a fundamental antagonism between agricultural and industrial capital.

Counterpoised against the industrial bourgeoisie's sanguine attitude toward their own position and relationships at the top of social hierarchy is their deep distrust of the working classes and their desire to limit their economic and political autonomy. This exclusionary mentality vis-à-vis the working classes is particularly evident in responses to questions related to specific policy issues. Commitment to the economic and political inclusion of the lower classes tended to break down when respondents were confronted with choices on specific policies rather than asked to comment on the desirability of popular-class participation in the abstract.[7] When asked to choose between increasing rationality in the political system or expanding popular participation, 56 percent of the industrialists opted for greater

Table 5   Industrialists' Identification of Most Powerful
Socioeconomic Groups in Ecuador

	No. of Responses	% of Total	% of Informants
Industrialists	27	38	63
Commercial groups	20	28	47
Financial groups	6	8	14
State politicians	8	11	19
Middle class	2	3	5
Laborers	2	3	5
Agricultural producers	3	4	7
Other	2	3	5
No information	1	1	2
Total	71		

Source: See appendix.

Note: Table reflects responses to open-ended responses by forty-three informants, who were permitted to register more than one response.

participation. In the follow-up question dealing with the enfranchisement of illiterates, 51 percent of the respondents opposed the extension of suffrage arguing that illiterates were incapable of making competent electoral decisions. The restrictive attitude toward participation was further evident in their conception of who should be included in economic policymaking. Over 50 percent reported that economic policy should be left solely in the hands of the private sector and the state; only 26 percent mentioned labor representatives as possible participants in policymaking. Just 19 percent of the industrialists made any positive comments on the role of trade unions in general. Most thought of unions as incompetent, permeated by communist ideology, and reflective of the low educational and cultural level of workers. Unions were commonly described as corrupt, manipulated, contaminated; their members immature, selfish, egoistic, and emotional.

The political restrictions on popular-class participation envisioned by the industrial bourgeoisie were paralleled by their tight-fisted approach to allocating resources to the lower classes. While 63 percent of the industrialists agreed that an income redistribution would have positive effects on the economy, 58 percent believed that the minimum wage increase of 1979 had negative effects. Only 7 percent of the informants mentioned measures to expand the internal consumer market as part of their preferred development strategy.

In discussing their visions of how the state should promote economic development, industrialists constantly reverted to measures to increase overall production levels. To achieve this, industrialists on the whole tended to favor the creation of large-scale production units. The single most popular development strategy was the promotion of agriculture; 49 percent of these interviewed cited this as a top priority. When asked about the best way to organize agricultural production, 51 percent of the industrialists said that they preferred giving incentives to the development of large agro-industrial operations rather than to smaller farming units. Similarly, when asked if large or small industry should be encouraged, their first choice was to favor large-scale units.

Industrialists clearly recognize the obstacles to growth created by the restricted internal market. The limited market, marginalization of the poor, and high unemployment were cited by 23 percent as important economic problems. Yet industrialists generally avoided incorporating improved distribution in their formula for achieving economic development. Table 6 summarizes their preferred development strategies. Instead of looking to the internal market, industrialists pinpointed the sources of growth outside it, favoring the pursuit of exports over import substitution. When asked to choose between the two, only 14 percent gave first priority to import substitution.

In the minds of Ecuadorean industrialists, the problems of underdevelopment are not so much rooted in an unequal distribution of economic resources, but the absolute scarcity of wealth itself. They consistently stress that wealth creation must precede any attempts at redistribution. One industrialist summed up the feelings of his peers by commenting, "Development does not consist in making rich people poor and poor people rich." Wealth and poverty are not related phenomena in their conceptual world.

This fixation on the scarcity of supply in the economy rather than demand-starvation is evident in the industrialists' discussions of the "human resource" problem. The lack of skilled personnel in both industry and government was cited as the second most important economic problem facing the country. Industrialists were divided, however, on the underly-

Table 6   Industrialists' Preferences for State Development Strategies

	No. of Responses	% of Total	% of Informants
Increase agricultural production	21	30	49
Reform macroeconomic policies	14	20	33
Improve the educational system	11	16	26
Develop clear policy to improve the investment climate	8	11	19
Develop the nation's infrastructure	7	10	16
Develop exports	4	6	9
Expand the internal market	3	4	7
Other	2	3	5
Total	70		

Source: See appendix.

Note: Table reflects responses to open-ended questions by forty-three informants, who were permitted to make more than one response.

ing causes of the situation. Some saw the problem in cultural and moral terms. They attributed deficiencies in the quality of labor to certain innate aspects of national character. There were numerous references to "ignorance," "lack of honesty," and the nation's "low cultural level," as the key causes of Ecuador's developmental problems. In contrast, other industrialists focused their comments more explicitly on the lack of technical education for the masses. They expressed a desire to see more vocational training in order to increase the efficiency of the work force and a depoliticization of university education.

The core of the industrial bourgeoisie's economic critique was reserved for the state. According to industrialists, the single most important problem in the economy was inadequate and inefficient management by the state. Thirty-three percent listed excessive public expenditures, insufficient state credits to industry, and the government's inability to control inflation as examples of poor state administration of the economy. The state was also assailed by 19 percent for its lack of policies in some areas and the creation of an uncertain investment climate.

No other single subject achieved a greater consensus among industrialists than the proper role of the state. A recurrent phrase was that the "state is a bad administrator." Across the board, industrialists rejected the notion of an aggressive state taking on an entrepreneurial role in the economy as the owner of firms. Rather, they envisioned the ideal state as completely complementary to business—a state dedicated to creating the conditions for capital accumulation and imposing minimal claims on the private sector. As one of the top industrial financiers of Guayaquil put it, the state's main task was simply that of maintaining "order and vigilance." These industrialists believe that state that should provide the necessary infrastructure, create a stable investment climate, and stimulate the private sector through tax breaks and credits. For industrialists, accumulation rather than legitimation should be the state's paramount concern.

Despite the political and social changes that have taken place in Ecuadorean society in the post–World War II period, dominant-class conservatism remained intact at the end of the 1970s. But the ongoing transformation of Ecuadorean society had turned traditional conservatism into a normative vision increasingly at odds with the reality surrounding it.[8] While highly dependent on the state for subsidized development, industrialists espouse laissez-faire principles. Confronted with popular demands for political participation and economic equality, capitalists call for more production and exclusion of the people from its benefits. As they demand preferential access to and security from the state, they deny the legitimacy of similar claims by other social actors.

Bourgeois Ideologies in Comparative Perspective

These conversations failed to uncover much reformist sentiment in the thinking of the Ecuadorean bourgeoisie. Numbers alone do not adequately convey the depth of this business conservatism. Even among those industrialists who favored alliances with the working class, the comments that accompanied their prolabor responses revealed an essentially corporatist approach to capital-labor relations. With few exceptions, industrialists that spoke of the development of a *pacto social* envisioned it as a means to increase efficiency by taming the labor movement. In a similar survey of Peruvian industrialists, Frits Wils also voiced skepticism regarding the authenticity of industrialists' verbal commitment to cooperation with the working class, particularly given their explicit antagonism toward labor unions. Wils suggests that prolabor responses made during interviews represents "more tokenism than genuine interest in a mutual political front" between labor and industry.[9]

Much of the literature on the industrial bourgeoisie in Latin America is preoccupied with linking support for or opposition to reformism with the structural position of class fractions. Fernando Henrique Cardoso, Luciano Martins, and Vilmar Faria are among the analysts who have attempted to map out these specific relations between interests and ideology in Latin American settings.[10]

Using interview data from Argentina and Brazil, Cardoso argues that the maturation of the industrialization process and the penetration of multinational corporations have resulted in a structural differentiation within the local bourgeoisie that is reflected in divergent ideological positions.[11] As industrial production becomes more sophisticated, a segment of the bourgeoisie is "internationalized"—that is, it becomes linked to multinational corporations through joint ventures, transfers of technology, or financial dependence. This internationalized sector tends to be concentrated in the more dynamic sectors of industry in consumer durables, and intermediate and capital goods. In contrast, the remainder of the bourgeoisie remains concentrated in the production of simple consumer nondurables such as beverages, processed food, and textiles.

According to Cardoso, these divergences in the specialization and market orientations of these two groups translate into different ideological positions. Because the noninternationalized bourgeoisie specializes in the production of relatively simple consumer goods, these industrialists maintain a pragmatic interest in the expansion of the consumer market and are more likely to favor political alliances and policies that include the working classes in politics and the economy. In contrast, Cardoso argues, the internationalized bourgeoisie is less likely to favor policies that benefit the popular classes because they do not depend on their consumption capabilities.

While Cardoso's argument is thought-provoking, his empirical evidence of ideological divergences between the two fractions is scant. But even apart from the methodological problems that flaw this study, the historical case studies of industrialists in Latin America also undermine the idea that there is a straightforward correspondence between political ideas and economic interests. Discussions of the political behavior of the early import-substituting industrialists of the Southern Cone suggest that reform-mindedness did not necessarily coincide with production for the internal market. In his study of industrialization in São Paulo, Warren Dean makes the point that

> industrialists along with merchants and large landowners often referred to themselves as the "conservative classes," an interesting definition because it acknowledges an attitude common to industrialists' ruthlessness toward workers, their admiration for hierarchy, and their indifference toward social development; once their factories were built, they were concerned not with enterprise but hanging onto their property.[12]

Similarly, Eldon Kenworthy argues that industrialists did not view Perón's policies of wage increases as beneficial to them even if it did result in expanding the internal market. He argues that industrialists are more likely to evaluate policies in light of their immediate effects on their firms rather than from a broad macroeconomic perspective.[13]

Under what conditions and to what extent can the political consciousness of the bourgeoisie advance to the point of espousing reform? Considerable controversy rages around this point regarding the development of the industrial elite in the United States. The revisionist historians of the Progressive Era, especially Gabriel Kolko and James Weinstein, have taken up the "class consciousness" interpretation of the reforms of that period. Both argue that the movement toward state regulation of business and social reforms were led by a progressive element within the monopoly fraction of the industrial bourgeoisie who realized that such reforms would stabilize and rationalize the capitalist system.[14] This "class consciousness" position, which attributes to the bourgeoisie a sophisticated understanding of social problems and the capacity to solve them through reform, is echoed in the "power elite" arguments that have prevailed in North American sociology.[15]

Powerful criticisms of the "class consciousness" theory are found in recent work by Fred Block, Theda Skocpol, and David Vogel. Block maintains that capitalists on the whole are "not conscious of what is necessary to reproduce the social order."[16] Vogel, in turn, argues that the appearance of a reformist wing of the American bourgeoisie during the Progressive Era was highly aberrant, the product of a unique set of structural conditions. According to Vogel, the centralization of corporate power in the hands of a few entrepreneurs at the turn of the century created a small and highly cohesive group of capitalists within the monopoly sector. Their combined control over industry gave them a unique overview of the workings of capitalism and put them in a position to realize the rationalizing effect of reform. With the decline in the domination of these personal empires and the rise of managerialism, the myopia of immediate profit maximization once again took hold and reformist ideology vanished.[17]

If Progressivism was an almost pathological moment for the American bourgeoisie, what is its "normal" ideological state? The abundant literature on this topic leaves little room for doubt; ranging from Kirkland's and McCloskey's treatments of the nineteenth century to Sutton's *The American Business Creed*, the persistent theme is the "historic negativism" of the business community regarding social reform and state intervention. Antipopular strains blend with fear of democracy and antistatism.[18]

From both a comparative and historical perspective, it is clear that reformism lies outside the bourgeois ideology. Left to its own devices, the bourgeoisie remains caught in the ideology of classical liberalism with little sympathy for the legitimation functions of the modern capitalist state.[19] It is no wonder that Joseph Schumpeter's reflections on the "rationalist and unheroic" character of the bourgeoisie still ring so true.[20] How then does the bourgeoisie periodically emerge from its normal ideological enclosure to become enmeshed in reform processes? In her analysis of the New Deal, Theda Skocpol interprets the reforms of the era as a product of multiple interactions and calculations among state managers and dominant and subordinate classes. The New Deal was not determined by the superior rationality of a single actor, but reflected class pressures mediated by self-interested state managers.[21] In a similar vein, Angela Maria de Castro Gomes's study of the politics of early labor legislation in Brazil concludes that the bourgeoisie's acceptance of protective labor laws was the result working-class pressures and a "new" state apparatus that emerged in the 1930s. That conclusion coincides with an earlier study by James Malloy of the expansion of the social security system in Brazil that points to the leading role played by politicians and government bureaucrats in the process.[22]

In short, two interrelated phenomena are central to reform. First, reform occurs when there is heightened state autonomy. What this means concretely is that the state must be under the control of a cohesive political-administrative elite that is capable of defining its interests in terms that do not coincide with any single class interest. Second, the bourgeoisie must not be able to veto the reform process. In its weakened state, the bourgeoisie's ideological resolve gives way to pragmatism.

State Autonomy and Class Veto

This brings us back to a consideration of the key factors that explain the industrial bourgeoisie's "reactive participation" in the populist projects of the Southern Cone. These industrialists were not part of a reformist project by choice, but by necessity. Hard political and economic calculations intersected with increased state autonomy to produce a guarded accommodation between the populist state and the industrial bourgeoisie.

In her analysis of Mexico during the Cárdenas period, Nora Hamilton delineates three conditions that are conducive to heightened state autonomy and are relevant to understanding the classic populism of the Southern Cone. The state will be more able to assume high levels of autonomy vis-à-vis the dominant classes when: (1) those dominant classes have been weakened by internal or external crises, (2) the state is able to command the support of subordinate classes, and (3) there is unity and consensus within the state apparatus on policy decisions.[23]

Populism succeeded in the Southern Cone countries because the power of the dominant class was undermined by multiple weaknesses. In Argentina and Uruguay, sectoral clashes between agricultural and industrial capital were overlaid with ethnic and status discrimination against immigrant entrepreneurs. This allowed populist politicians to impose some of the burden of redistribution on agriculture without alienating industrial capitalists. In Chile, however, these divisions within the dominant-class ranks were much less pronounced. The weakness of the Chilean bourgeoisie had more to do with the crisis in the mining sector during the 1930s, which reduced their capabilities for social control. In all three cases, oligarchic politics was ruptured prior to the installation of populism by the middle-class regimes of Alessandri, Yrigoyen, and Batlle Ordóñez. The exclusivity of the state and upper-class psychological claims to that state were severed. In Uruguay, the attenuation of the relations between dominant classes and the state was deepened by the rise of a separate "political class" in the Colorado party that managed the party system.

The classic populist experience was defined by the success of populist leaders in creating alliances with subordinate classes who could force the bourgeoisie into at least a partial acceptance of their claims. These alliances were based on the state's ability to create a clientele within the ranks of the labor movement. Yet, it is important to keep in mind the quality of the threat posed by the state-union nexus in these cases. For the most part, populist politicians championed the economic demands of workers (that is, demands for higher wages) rather than making an ideological assault on market principles. The alliance between populist state managers and the working classes, while certainly worrisome to the bourgeoisie, did not constitute a direct ideological violation of the bourgeoisie's view of the world. Moreover, the maintenance of preexisting parliamentary and interest-group politics allowed the bourgeoisie to adopt cooptive strategies rather than directly confronting these regimes.

In a paradoxical way, the cohesiveness and unity in the populist state was rooted in its own heterodoxy as a policymaker and arranger of across-class alliances. The favorable conditions in the international market enabled populist state managers to pursue simultaneously the often mutually exclusive goals of distribution and accumulation. Given these favorable economic circumstances and the structural position of the bourgeoisie at that point in the industrialization process, there was a painless quality to populist reformism.

History would not reproduce the conditions leading to heightened state autonomy and a weakened veto power of the bourgeoisie in contemporary Ecuador. Uninterested in the development of a mass market, industrialists in the 1970s shared with other fractions a rigid ideology that had not been tempered by struggles with militant subordinate classes or a forceful state. Unschooled in the subtleties of cooptation and compromise, they confronted the military reformers with the aggression and confidence of a class unacquainted with defeat.

4

Policy Wars: Indstrialists versus the State, 1972–1975

Louis Noboa rarely gives interviews. But in 1979 he broke with custom to give an interview in one of Ecuador's leading magazines, *Vistazo*. During the discussion Noboa was asked to identify the best government of the last twenty years. Noboa chose that of Dr. Camilo Ponce. President between 1956 and 1960, Ponce was the founder of the Partido Social Cristiano (PSC) in the 1950s and came from one of the leading landowning families of the sierra. It was under the Ponce government that the first industrial development laws were enacted. The interviewer then asked Noboa to identify the worst government of the same period. He replied, "Without a doubt the worst government was that of General Rodríguez Lara, but the petroleum boom drew a dark curtain around government action undertaken by dreamers, ingenues, incompetents, and Bolsheviks who were on a romp to ruin the country."[1]

Noboa's views reflect the deep hostilities and tensions that marked the relationship between the industrial class and the reformist military regime between 1972 and 1976. Joining in the industrial bourgeoisie's fierce opposition to the regime were the traditional landowning and commercial groups of the dominant classes. This unified coalition was primarily responsible for the demise of reformism and the replacement of Rodríguez Lara by a more conservative military triumvirate in January 1976.

This consolidation of dominant-class opposition to Rodríguez Lara was the result of a serious miscalculation by the reformist policymakers within the regime concerning the industrial bourgeoisie and its relationships with other fractions and foreign capital. Believing that "progressive" elements within the bourgeoisie would support limited economic reforms to modernize the economy, the reformers attempted to mount a "national capitalist" model that gave generous incentives to the private sector while allowing for some state intervention in critical areas of the economy. Notwithstanding the very circumscribed nature of these reforms, they were rejected by all segments of the private sector. Instead of casting a wedge between segments of the privileged, the proposed reforms created a broad consensus within the business community on the need to hold the line against the state. Before examining the reactions and responses of industrialists to specific reforms, let us look at the conditions that gave birth to this feeble reformist regime that was unable to stake out for itself sufficient autonomy to achieve its goals.

Origins and Content of the "Nationalist Revolution"

The discovery of major oil reserves in the eastern jungles of Ecuador in 1967 saved the state from yet another fiscal crisis emanating from the traditional export sector. A combination of circumstances in the international commodities market which included the recovery of Central American banana production and the slow growth in world demand for the commodity depressed the Ecuadorean banana trade in the 1960s. This in turn decreased government revenues. With the initiation of major oil exports in 1972, rapid economic recovery brought a dramatic reversal in the state's finanical position. Between 1970 and 1974, the economy enjoyed one of the highest rates of growth in Latin America. Revenues from petroleum tripled the government's budget.[2]

The sudden rejuvenation of the state's fiscal position due to petroleum export drew all relevant political actors into serious reconsiderations of how this change could affect their relationships to the state and the appropriate form that this newly wealthy state should assume. In contrast to previous agricultural export booms which created opportunities for local entrepreneurs, the organization and character of petroleum export guaranteed that only two actors could directly participate in the trade—the state and multinational corporations. Multinationals possessed the technical and financial capabilities to invest in exploration. The state, through its monopoly over concessions, stood as the sole agent controlling these investments and the direct recipient of a large portion of the profits. In short, the state was suddenly cast in the role of arbiter of the new oil wealth. The locus of decisions concerning both the internal and external distribution of this income was not to found in the machinations of the market and private actors, as was the case in previous booms, but within the heart of the state bureaucracy.

Given the character of petroleum boom and magnitude of the resources at stake, forces within civil society and the state mobilized to redefine the policy direction and the form of the Ecuadorean state in the early 1970s. One thing was certainly clear—all social sectors rejected the existing political formula that combined a limited formal democracy and a party system composed of oligarchic electoral cliques and populist vehicles.

The corruption of past civilian regimes, especially in natural resource policy, and their dismal performance in other policy areas was an affront to the nationalist and developmentalist aspirations of the armed forces. The military's frustration with civilian regimes was nothing new; reformist currents were evident in three previous military interventions. The July Revolution of 1925, in which a core of junior officers participated, wrested fiscal and monetary policy from the manipulation of coastal bankers through the establishment of the Banco Central. The brief military regime of Alberto Enríquez in 1937–1938 continued the modernizing thrust of the July Revolution by granting legal recognition to the trade union movement, striking down restrictions on leftist political activity, and regulating the business practices of foreign companies. The military government of 1963–1966 terminated the embarrassing civilian administration of Carlos Julio Arosemena and attempted to initiate some structural reforms. The commitment of members of the armed forces to the pursuit of economic development deepened as they were exposed to a new model of civil-military relations during the 1960s. The new concept legitimated military intervention on the grounds that the military should act as an agent of "structural reforms" for "national security" purposes. Professional training abroad increased the officers' susceptibility to this developmentalist perspective. According to John Fitch's study of the Ecuadorean military, the number of officers holding either "developmentalist" or "arbiter" role definitions (that is, the belief that the military should act as arbiter in periods of national crisis) increased from 21 to 86 percent from 1954 to 1966.[3]

From the perspective of the military, the conduct of civilian regimes from 1966 to 1972 underscored not only the corruption of the traditional political leadership, but also its inability to systematically address the need for structural reforms and economic modernization. Nowhere was the mismanagement more glaring than in natural resources. The most notorious incident, known as the ADA scandal, occurred during the interim civilian administration of Otto Arosemena Gómez when important offshore oil concessions were granted to a group of Ecuadorean investors who immediately sold their rights to an North American consortium.[4] The military feared that the type of official misconduct evident in the ADA scandal and other lucrative concessions ceded to foreign oil companies would become the norm with the new petroleum boom. The military's concern with the future direction of petroleum policy was a key factor motivating the coup of 1972. According to Fitch, by 1972 "there was a consensus that it would be hard for a military government to do any worse than the civilians had."[5]

While the military's fears were focused on the spectre of civilian politicians pillaging these windfall revenues pouring into the state, dominant-class groups feared the possibility of appropriation of these revenues by the masses through a populist program. Presidential elections were scheduled for 1972 and an expansion of the electorate heightened the prospect of Assad Bucaram assuming the presidency. Bucaram headed the Concentración de Fuerzas Populares (CFP), a party founded in Guayaquil in the 1940s that mobilized lower-class voters around antioligarchic appeals and clientelist networks.[6] Though successful in capturing local and city offices in Guayaquil, the CFP had been unable to expand its electoral base beyond the coast. But with the rise of Bucaram within the party, the possibility of a CFP candidate capturing nationwide office seemed real for the first time. His demagogic style as mayor of Guayaquil proved popular, but also alienated that city's establishment. Given the lackluster presidential contenders nominated by the conservative oligarchic parties, Bucaram seemed a likely winner. Dominant-class groups viewed Bucaram as an obnoxious and unstable personality. Populism, as previously practiced by José María Velasco Ibarra since the the 1930s, was unusually tame in tone and substance. Velasco Ibarra always maintained close ties with dominant-class groups; his deep conservatism was reflected in everything from his cabinet appointments to his political discourse.[7] In contrast, Bucaram looked like a potentially unreliable occupant of the executive office. Although Bucaram did not hold firmly to any radical ideology, the vagaries of his political position and the possibility that his popular base might push him to the left made him appear to the private sector a possibly irresponsible steward for the new oil economy.

By 1972, a coup coalition formed that included the military, dominant-class groups, and middle-class technocrats in the state bureaucracy. Yet, the motivations of the military and the technocrats diverged greatly from those of their dominant-class allies. For the officers and the bureaucrats, the coup was not so much a rejection of Bucaram in particular as an expression of their complete dissatisfaction with traditional political arrangements. In contrast, the willingness of the dominant class to veto the electoral process stemmed from their deep distrust of Bucaram and their anxieties about his support among the people. From their point of view, any of the old guard politicians stood as acceptable alternatives. Those candidates could be counted on to give them access to the key policymaking centers within the state bureaucracy.

Given these profoundly different perspectives on Ecuador's political problems, the original coup coalition quickly disintegrated after the overthrow of President Velasco Ibarra in February 1972 and the installation of the commander of the army, General Guillermo Rodríguez Lara, as the new head of government. With the short-run goal of the suspension of presidential elections achieved, the controversy over the direction of the new regime got under way.

The disjunction between the armed forces and their dominant-class allies became immediately apparent when the military issued their first statement of goals, *Filosofía y plan de acción,* and declared themselves to be "antifeudal," "antioligarchic," "popular," and "nationalist." These aspirations were translated into policy guidelines in the July publication of the tentative economic plan; this was followed by the release of the completed *Plan integral* in December 1972.[8] These documents provided the first comprehensive statements of the ideological objective of Rodríguez Lara's self-proclaimed "nationalist revolution." The principal institutional collaborator in the formulation of the plan was the Junta Nacional de

Planificación, well known as the home base of the modernizing and socially concerned technocracy.

According to the analyses of the civilian and military bureaucrats in these documents, Ecuador's economic problems could be explained by its place in the international division of labor as a producer of agricultural commodities. The planners described what they termed the "radical heterogeneity" of the economy—the coexistence of a backward, stagnant productive structure in the interior and a dynamic capitalist one on the coast. In addition to the inequitable distribution of resources generated by agroexport, the economy's reliance on international market prices meant recurring fiscal crises and political instability. In short, the judgment rendered by the bureaucrats and officers was that continuing the traditional style of economic growth was inadequate to solve the country's grave socioeconomic problems and would only induce further political instability.

The alternative was spelled out in the *Plan integral*. The primary objectives in the new developmental model were nationalist, moderately redistributive, and modernizing. The plan set forth the government's commitment to bettering the living conditions for the poor, raising employment, using natural resources efficiently, and spreading economic growth more equitably across regions. Comprehensive agrarian reform and direct participation by the state in certain sectors were the key policies through which these objectives would be achieved.

According to the *Plan integral*, a thoroughgoing agrarian reform was pivotal, not only for the purpose of redressing social injustices in the countryside, but also because such a reform would create the modern consumer market necessary for further industrialization. Because industrialization was envisioned as contingent on agrarian reform, a major portion of the industrial production projected in the plan was directed toward simple consumer goods industries. Of the 210 top-priority industrial projects outlined in the plan, the food industry alone accounted for 60 of the projects. Taken together, basic consumer goods accounted for 100 of the priority investments.

Yet, perhaps more dramatic than the regime's commitment to agrarian reform was its assertion of the state's obligation to intervene actively in the economy as a shareholder in enterprises, particularly in basic industries. In a country with a weak tradition of direct state intervention, the *Plan integral* proposed extending state control over petroleum refining and outlined future projects for state enterprises in steel, chemicals, and fishing. Mixed public- and private-sector participation was slated for such projects as cement, petrochemicals, tractors, diesel motors, and insecticides.

As depicted in the plan, this new and more aggressive role of the state in the economy was not meant to circumscribe the private sector, but to compensate for the lack of investment in key areas of industry and the national infrastructure. The plan repeatedly assured the private sector of its right to continue operating existing firms in the areas targeted for public investment. In reference to the treatment of foreign capital, the plan underscored the important role assigned to foreign capital and technology in the development scheme and stressed the state's obligation to channel foreign capital into areas of the economy not adequately served by national capital. The plan consistently emphasized the complementary, not competitive, character of state and private-sector relations.

In short, the *Plan integral* posed a "national-capitalist" rather than a "state-capitalist" developmental model.[9] The restructuring of Ecuadorean capitalism was to be a process reliant upon inducements by the state rather than direct coercion. National and foreign capital, while more closely monitored by the state, would continue to be the key agents of economic growth; the state, through the efficient deployment of petroleum revenues, was cast in the role of supportive guide and partner to the private sector. The cautious character of the Ecuadorean plan is evident when compared with the Peruvian plan issued by the military regime of Velasco Alvarado during the same period. Peru's plan mandated sweeping changes that included nationalizations of certain types of enterprises as well as introducing workers' self-management in some sectors of the economy.[10] The bold economic interventionism of the Peruvian plan and its subordination of certain capital groups to the state brought it much closer to a state-capitalist model. In comparison, Ecuador's plan was notable for its studied moderation.

Why did the planners at the Junta believe that their national-capitalist model was politically viable? Why were they unable to anticipate the intensity of the policy battles that were to follow the unveiling of the model? High-ranking technocrats in JUNAPLA and other state agencies thought that the plan was viable because they believed that it played on existing antagonisms within the dominant classes; as such, the plan would be a vehicle of a multiclass alliance. Their dualist vision of the economy (the "radical heterogeneity" thesis) translated into a dualist perspective on the social structure, especially regarding upper-class interests. Planners at the junta believed that there were modernizing elements within the dominant classes, especially industrialists, who would support the regime's attempt to rationalize Ecuadorean capitalism. Writing in 1976, one of the top architects of the junta's industrial policies expressed its point of view on progressive tendencies of the industrial bourgeoisie:

> The idea of industrial planning in Ecuador has been to create another powerful group capable of facing other important sectors that have controlled the Ecuadorean economy, the [neo-feudal] agrarian sector and the commercial sector. The country traditionally has been run by agrarian and commercial sectors—and through this industrial planning we have been trying to create a new power to act as a counterweight to these two traditional powers and so that when the industrial sector encounters tremendous limitations in the socio-economic apparatus of this society, they can undertake the structural changes necessary . . . that is, we think the industrial sector can propose changes such as agrarian reform, tax reform etc., and that they can make the search for a better panorama of economic development in the country possible.[11]

What was lost in the Junta's dualist perspective on the dominant classes was an appreciation of the industrial bourgeoisie's structural position as well as the depth of its ideological commitment to the symbols and images of the market. As we have seen, the upper reaches of the industrial bourgeosie was clearly tied to other dominant-class fractions, in terms of social origins and investment connections, and foreign capital. Moreover, the peculiar twists in Ecuadorean industrialization—the deepening of middle- and upper-class purchasing power rooted in the oil boom, the rise of semiprocessing industries—had reduced the obstacles to continued growth created by mass poverty. As such, the "reforms" that the Junta had hoped would be championed by the industrial bourgeoisie were of little real interest to them. Rather than worrying about internal market expansion, industrialists closed ranks with the rest of the private sector against what they perceived to be a threatening new assertion of power by the state.

Autonomy Affirmed: Industrialists versus Estatismo

Compared with other Latin American countries, Ecuador had not traditionally played an obtrusive role in the direction of its economy, particularly in the form of state enterprises. Prior to 1970, the only state enterprises included two fertilizer plants, the national railway, a utility, and a distillery.[12] President Velasco Ibarra added to this small list in 1971 when he announced the creation of a state merchant marine fleet and a food distribution company. Nonetheless, public-sector investment in enterprises remained insignificant. The expenditures of the central government in industry and commerce amounted to only 0.14 percent of total expenditures in 1970; there was an increase in 1971 to 2.7 percent.[13] These modest stirrings in public-sector investment by Velasco Ibarra were enough to provoke the first expressions of discontent in the private sector. Early in 1971, representatives of banking, agriculture, industry, and commerce issued a public communiqué to the government expressing concern over what they characterized as the "strange statism" of government policy.[14]

The absence of a well-defined program during the first eleven months of the Rodríguez Lara regime created a brief hiatus in the private sector's pronouncements about the role of the state in the economy. The energies of the new government during the first few months were concentrated on consolidating power, not economic models. To eliminate any potential opposition, the regime pursued a "moralization" campaign that consisted of prosecuting corrupt officials of previous civilian regimes, imprisoning critics on the left and right, and selective censorship of the mass media.[15] No doubt the curtailment of public expression dampened the enthusiasm of the business community for directing comments against the regime, but this absence of criticism was short-lived. By December 1972, the *Plan integral* was made public and asserted the state's right to take a direct role in enterprise creation in key economic activities. A month later, the head of the "Brazilian" faction in the army, General Víctor Aulestia, was removed from his post as minister of defense and the most repressive phase of the regime was concluded.[16] By early 1973, the stage was set for renewed controversy over the state's role in the economy.

The organizational vehicles for the bourgeoisie's resistance to statism were already in place. While the military suspended the right of political parties to operate openly, class organizations were unaffected. The military's lack of interest in dismantling such organizations was testimony to the sheer political clout of these associations as well as an acknowledgment of their legitimacy in an environment where there was a longstanding tradition of mixing corporatism with liberal democratic arrangements.

The Cámaras de Producción (that is, the Chambers of Commerce, Agriculture, and Industry) were created by the state in the 1930s as the official vehicles for representing those sectoral interests and membership was made mandatory. The chambers were subdivided into regional associations; given the concentration of economic power in Quito and Guayaquil, the most powerful chambers became those representing the two regions (the provinces of Pichincha and Guayas). These regional producers' associations of the sierra and coast were granted functional representatives in the legislature. In addition, the chambers were permitted to designate representatives to sit on the boards of some state agencies.[17]

Thus, industrialists were grouped into two important regional peak associations, the Cámara de Industriales de Pichincha and the Cámara de Industrias de Guayaquil. Joint actions between the groups were coordinated by the Federación Nacional de Cámaras de Industrias, whose headquarters rotated yearly betweeen the Quito and Guayaquil chambers. Commercial and agricultural interests were loosely organized in similar national confederations.

While the rhetoric used by private-sector organizations was strictly laissez-faire, in practice the industrial bourgeoisie was selective in its resistance to the state intervention undertaken by the Rodríguez Lara regime. When the regime moved to make "lumpy" investments in basic industries or aid ailing industries, business associations were silent. The most important state enterprise created under the regime was the state oil company, CEPE, founded in 1972. In the same year, the state monopoly over telephone and wire services, IETEL, was created. The state also moved to bail out several large private firms on the brink of financial disaster. Both the national airline, Ecuatoriana de Aviación, and a fertilizer plant, Fertisa, S.A., were taken over when they faced bankruptcy in 1972. In 1974, the state became a majority shareholder in two troubled firms: La Cemento Nacional, the largest cement plant in the country, and Aztra, the third-largest sugar mill.

In addition to forming state enterprises, the Rodríguez Lara regime encouraged an acceleration of public investment in mixed enterprises. These new investments were channeled largely, though not exclusively, through the Corporación Financiera Nacional (CFN). Prior to 1970, the CFN functioned primarily as a provider of low-cost loans to industry. From 1970 to 1974, the CFN went from being a stockholder in five firms to twenty-eight. By 1974, the investments of the CFN extended across a number of product lines including processed food, pharmaceuticals, clocks and watches, and cement.[18] Other state entities such as the Banco Nacional de Fomento, the Ministry of Agriculture, Ministry of Health, and the Institute of Social Security, also became stockholders in a number of important firms.[19]

Industrialists generally did not oppose the state's participation in firms as a minority stockholder, particularly through the CFN whose institutional philosophy stressed the notion of eventually turning over the enterprises to private investors. The policymakers of the CFN constantly emphasized the agency's complementary, not competitive, stance vis-à-vis the private sector.[20] These three features of state intervention—the formation of public enterprises in basic industries, the takeover of ailing firms, and state minority shareholding—received the tacit approval of industrialists and the rest of the business community.

The first signs of discord between the regime and industrialists arose in relation to the creation of new state structures that appeared to preempt private-sector initiatives. The most threatening organizational innovations came from the armed forces. In August 1973, the army announced the establishment of the Dirección de Industrias de Ejército (DINE). The entity was founded for the purposes of overseeing the army's investments in basic industries, particularly metals. Together with the state development bank and a Peruvian firm, DINE founded Compañía de Industrias de Acero Cotopaxi (INDACO) to produce drill bits, taking advantage of Ecuador's sectoral assignment in the Andean Pact agreements. In addition to this mixed enterprise, DINE invested in firms producing uniforms and boots for the army. The director of DINE, Colonel Jorge Enrique Marroquín, expressed the military's perspective on the role of the state in the economy: "In place of the blind and inflexible devotion that many businessmen have to economic liberalism, we have wanted to demonstrate that instead of Adam Smith's invisible hand what is necessary is the orienting hand, the firm pulse, the unconditional support and creative persistence of the state."[21]

Not to be outdone by the ambitions of the army, the navy also announced its 1973 plan to establish its own commercial fleet. Meanwhile, the air force was already busy operating an internal commercial airline, TAME, in direct competition with two private airlines. These investments made by the armed forces deviated from most of the other public-sector investments of the same period, since the enterprises singled out by the military either had counterparts in the private sector (such as transportation industries) or represented areas of prospective interest to the private sector in light of the Andean Pact assignments (for example, the metal industry).

Just as the armed forces began to intervene in the market, industrialists were subject to what they perceived as another assault on private-sector domination of the market with the installation of price controls. In February 1973, the Superintendencia de Precios was established and given broad regulatory powers. The Superintendencia extended controls over the prices of soft drinks, edible oils, cigarettes, flour, beer, milk, meat, and medicines. Thus, the largest single branch of Ecuadorean industry, food processing, was subject to regulation. To enforce compliance with the official pricing system, two state enterprises (ENAC and ENPROVIT) were created to act as food purchasers and distributors. With the creation of these two state enterprises, the regime asserted not only its right to intervene in the market to set prices but its willingness to create a bureaucratic structure that would reduce the state's dependence on voluntary private-sector cooperation in price control.

By late 1973, the chambers began to mobilize publicly against what they interpreted as the regime's attack on market mechanisms. In April 1973, the president of the Guayaquil Chamber of Industries and chief executive officer of the Noboa group enterprises, León Febres-Cordero, was briefly jailed for tax evasion and this added to the growing sense of violation on the part of the private sector. These anxieties were particularly acute in Guayaquil where the surge in state intervention and the imprisonment of one of its leading businessmen were interpreted by the press as yet another example of the regional domination of Quito.[22] The disclosure of the formation of DINE and other military enterprises brought a reply from the private sector in the form of an August manifesto entitled "The State and Private Property." The document was signed by a group identifying itself only as the private entrepreneurs of Ecuador. The document contained a ringing condemnation of the state as entrepreneur, arguing that the enormous resources at the disposal of the state would allow it to dominate the private sector.[23]

Industrialists used the occasion of a conference sponsored by the Banco de Guayaquil in November 1973 to continue their public attacks on the state's intervention into economic enterprises. León Febres-Cordero painted a bleak picture of the mood of the industrial class toward the regime. According to Febres-Cordero, the industrial sector was undergoing a crisis of confidence. It was "fearful and suspicious of the attitude of the administrative apparatus." Speaking on behalf of the Chamber of Industries, Febres-Cordero declared that public-sector investment should only take place in areas that could be served by the private sector.[24] Another leading *guayaquileño* industrialist at the same conference, Ernesto Jouvín Cisneros, joined with Febres-Cordero in condemning the expanded role of the state. In view of Jouvín, the adoption of "paternalist state policies" functioned only to "limit the efficiency of private initiative, discourage entrepreneurial impulses, and brake the development of industry."[25]

Throughout 1974, dominant-class attacks on statism continued unabated. Speaking on behalf of the Chamber of Industry of Guayaquil, León Febres-Cordero reiterated his conception of the proper role of the state with appeals on religious and libertarian grounds, arguing that state enterprises should only act in a "subsidiary way," lending support and infrastructure to the private sector.[26] A month after these declarations, the annual meeting of the Federación Nacional de Cámaras de Industrias was held in Quito. The resolutions passed at the meeting echoed the sentiments of Febres-Cordero in his numerous public statements. The Federación admonished that state involvement in firms should be temporary and that public participation should be terminated when the private sector demonstrated an ability to take over the firms. Otherwise, the *estatización* of the economy would only damage the investment climate.[27]

The most dramatic clash over statism came in January 1975 when the government revealed that it had already signed into law the reform proposals formulated by the Superintendencia de Compañías with regard to the legal treatment of *compañías de responsibilidad limitada* (companies not engaged in public sale of their stocks).[28] These firms, primarily in commerce and industry, were generally owned by a very small number of stockholders, often members of the same family. Over two thousand such companies were operating, representing a segment of the national economy virtually untouched by government regulation. Unlike the *compañías anónimas* (companies engaged in public sale of their stocks) that were required to make disclosures to the Superintendencia concerning the identity of their stockholders and the details of their internal finances, the "limited responsibility" companies were exempt from such reporting procedures. The major thrust of the Superintendencia's reforms in Decree 1353-A was to provide some mechanisms for the state to monitor the behavior of these firms. The key features of the reform proposals included: (1) mandatory stock registration and an elimination of the anonymous "shares to the bearer" registration, (2) government control over stock transfers to foreign investors, and (3) the Superintendencia's reservation of the right to appoint an intervener to oversee any firm in the event of irregularities in its operation or of failure to provide the Superintendencia with adequate information concerning its operations.

The reforms were part of a broader program of modernization envisioned by the head of the Superintendencia, Marco Antonio Guzmán. Guzmán, a lawyer who had represented Ecuador in Andean Pact negotiations, believed that Ecuadorean capitalism could be strengthened by a "democratization" of capital. But Guzmán's conception of democratization was by no means radical. He hoped to structure a greater incorporation of the middle classes into firms as stockholders through the reforms. By subjecting *compañías de responsibilidad limitada* to the same public scrutiny as *compañías anónimas,* Guzmán believed he was creating incentives for more of these firms to go public and put shares for sale on the stock market.[29]

Industrialists, in unison with the rest of the business community, swiftly reacted to Decree 1353-A. The executive board of Guayaquil's Cámara de Industrias voted its total opposition to the law. The Cámara's most vitriolic attacks were aimed at the new discretionary powers assigned to the Superintendencia to appoint interveners to oversee firms. The industrialists saw this as a direct strike at the principle of managerial autonomy; to them, the state's assertion of its right to act in that way smacked of the notion of "social property" that was used to legitimate workers' self-management schemes and firm takeovers under Allende in Chile and the Velasco Alvarado regime in Peru.[30]

The coastal lawyers' association, the Colegio de Abogados, joined with the producers' associations in criticizing the new decree. In a round-table session attended by leaders of the coastal Chambers of Commerce and Industry, a succession of speakers denounced the measure as inquisitorial and contrary to the capitalist road of development originally described in the regime's *Plan integral*. In his speech to the session, Dr. Miguel Angel Peña of the Chamber of Commerce portrayed the ultimate effect of the law to his fellow businessmen in chilling terms:

> The reforms are "statizing" in nature. The state, with the Superintendencia de Companías, acquires the most detailed information concerning the assets of its citizens, destroying privacy, destroying private life altogether. This weapon, managed according to political criteria and under pressures of the growing statist theories which are so attractive in the bureaucratic world, will serve at some point in time to destroy private enterprise and the investor, be it through controls, be it through limitations or finally through appropriating its assets.[31]

Guzmán responded to these criticisms by maintaining that the legal precedent for the reforms was established with Ecuador's signature on Decision 24 of the Cartagena Agreement in 1971; Decree 1353-A only reiterated the obligations of firms under that Andean Pact agreement. According to Guzmán, the decree was the means to ensure compliance with the provisions of the Cartagena Agreement which were being ignored both by smaller family-run firms and *compañías anónimas*.

The ferocious public attacks by business organizations forced government policymakers to back down from the most controversial aspects of the Guzmán reforms. In late January 1975, a cabinet committee voted to maintain the reforms of Decree 1353-A. But this approval came with the proviso that the decree would be amended to clarify the parameters of the Superintendencia's right to intervene in firms and to assure the confidentiality of the data it collected. In effect, this left the reforms on the books with no machinery to insure compliance. Even after the announcement of the cabinet decision, business associations lost no time in registering their dissatisfaction with government's decision to let its verbal commitment to the law stand. A public condemnation by the Chamber of Commerce was followed by a joint communiqué from the Chambers of Industry and Commerce of Guayaquil. In yet another of their frequent allusions to the Peruvian and Chilean economic experiments, the chambers referred to the Superintendencia's attempts at change as "inspired by legislation that has caused serious upheavals in neighboring countries."[32]

The Rights of Capital: Rejecting Regulation

The industrial bourgeoisie's defense of autonomy and market principles was not narrowly focused, but extended to the property rights of other groups. In conflicts over the state's attempts to regulate their behavior, landholders and foreign investors found key allies in industrial associations.

The private sector as a whole had already expressed its dissatisfaction with attempts to regulate the direction of foreign investment even before the 1972 coup. Under the previous Velasco Ibarra regime, in 1970 Ecuador became a participant in the Andean Pact negotiations that led to the adoption of a regional code on foreign investment known as Decision 24. Joining Ecuador as original signatories of Decision 24 were Venezuela, Colombia, Peru, Bolivia, and Chile. More moderate in its final form than in its original conception, Decision 24 established a uniform legal framework in the Andean region for the purposes of regulating the flow of foreign capital and technology. The decision mandated a gradual divestment by foreign firms, created incentives for joint-venture operations, and specified preferred areas for national and foreign investment. During the negotiating process, the code was stripped of its stricter provisions concerning divestment. As one analyst of the pact noted, the code became in its final form "not a thorough-going mechanism for the reduction of dependency, but rather a mechanism for the regulation of selected internal linkages in the interests of a potential national bourgeoisie."[33]

But, from the moment of the code's enactment, Ecuadorean industrialists were hard pressed to interpret the application of Decision 24 as in their interest as a "potential national bourgeoisie." Instead, they regarded Decision 24 as a perverse instrument that would halt the flow of foreign capital and technology critical to future industrial development. Following the code's approval, industrialists once again joined with the commercial community to create a vigorous public lobby against the enforcement of the pact, particularly those provisions that restricted direct foreign investment in banking, construction, personal services, and consulting. Throughout the first six months of 1971, private-sector organizations emphatically publicized its dissatisfaction with Decision 24 in the press, while representatives of the Chambers of Industry, Agriculture, and Commerce met with members of the Velasco government in an effort to amend the decision.[34]

The lobbying effort was successful. In mid-July, the administration enacted Decree 1029 which exempted foreign investors from complying with the "hands-off" provision of Decision 24 in public services, insurance, commercial banking, finance, internal transportation, the news media, and product distribution services.[35] The reversal of Decision 24 by the government was immediately denounced by labor unions and left-wing parties as yet another example of rampant *entreguismo*.[36]

Fearful that the nationalist line taken by Rodríguez Lara in regard to the management of oil policy might be accompanied by a reversal of Velasco Ibarra's liberal interpretation of Decision 24, the business community mobilized once more around the issue after the coup. In December 1972, a coalition of business leaders delivered a position paper to Rodríguez Lara in which they unequivocally defended the rights of foreign capital and pointed to the need for such investment.[37]

Responding to the renewed defense of foreign capital by local businessmen, the administration made a series of statements reaffirming its commitment to the rights of the foreign investor. The point was reiterated in several public addresses by Rodríguez Lara and was a key topic of discussion in the regime's summit conference with business leaders in Salinas in 1974.[38] Marco Antonio Guzmán, the director of the Superintendencia de Compañías, also professed the regime's desire to attract complementary types of foreign investment.[39]

But Guzmán, while trying to soothe business anxieties, was an ardent advocate of regional integration and opposed any further weakening of the already modified Decision 24. On August 31, 1974, the Superintendencia de Compañías recommended that the government enforce the restrictions on foreign investment in commercial and service sectors that had been reversed by Decree 1029 in 1971.[40] After an October meeting on foreign investment organized by the business club, the Centro de Ejecutivos de Guayaquil, business leaders called again for a modification of the provisions of the code.[41] This clamoring by the private sector provoked a media blitz by the Superintendencia to debunk the claim that the enactment of

Decision 24 would deter new foreign investment. In news releases, the Superintendencia argued that new foreign investment in Ecuador increased by 141 percent between 1972 and 1974 and would continue to do so.[42]

On January 9, 1975, the government acted on the Superintendencia's recommendations and decided to enforce the original Decision 24 provisions that prohibited foreign investment in internal commercial, financial, and construction activities.[43] The decision to apply the regulations coincided with the enactment of Guzmán's reforms for a new legal code to regulate companies. Government appproval was required for any stock transfers to foreign investors. From the perspective of local capitalists, the assault on foreign capital was under way. Carlos Ponce Martínez, the head of Quito's Chamber of Commerce and an industrialist, joined with Febres-Cordero of the Guayaquil Chamber of Industry to denounce the government's decision.[44] The administration responded by empowering a cabinet level committee to launch investigations into foreign investment in order to insure that foreign investors were complying with the Decision 24 regulation on registration with the host government. Foreign investors were advised to comply with the registration requirement or face fines or forced liquidations.[45]

Private-sector criticism of the government's "get-tough" attitude toward foreign investors continued unabated. By the summer of 1975, discontent within the bourgeoisie was generalized across a number of policy areas, of which foreign investment was but one. The debate over Decision 24 overlapped with the development of a serious balance-of-payments crisis. As will be examined in the following chapter, the foreign exchange crisis further solidified business opposition, turning the bourgeoisie's malaise into outright demands for a return to civilian rule.

The inability of the government to pursue its unpopular Decision 24 policy in the face of business opposition became evident by mid-August 1975. The technocrat heading the Ministry of Industry, Rubio Chauvín, was forced to resign and was replaced by Danilo Carrera Drouet. An economist with strong ties to the banking industry, Carrera immediately announced that he would welcome foreign capital and seek to maximize the benefits offered in the Cartagena Agreement.[46]

Following an abortive coup attempt in September that was welcomed by the business community, the nationalist posture of the regime in regard to foreign investment in nonpetroleum areas was formally reversed. On September 30, the Ministry of Industry in its new role as the sole regulatory agency for foreign investment issued Decrees 849 and 850. The new laws permitted participation by foreign investors in banks and financial institutions. Retreating from the pro–Andean Pact position of his predecessor, Carrera declared that the Cartagena Agreement should be considered as "an instrument of integration, but not a revealed truth" and as such should not be applied when it was not in the best interests of Ecuador.[47]

The reversal by Carrera marked the demise of yet another key dimension of the reformist project. Once again, the regime had found it impossible to rally industrialists around a national capitalist developmental model for Ecuador.

Agrarian Reform and the Defense of Property

Agrarian reform was the centerpiece of the development plan put forth by the Rodríguez Lara regime. More than any other single measure, the modernization of agricultural production and the reorganization of the land tenure system were singled out as the key elements in the development proposals of the government.

In the analyses of the Junta Nacional de Planificación, the roots of injustice in Ecuador were clearly located in the countryside, specifically in the extreme concentration of landownership. High rural unemployment was the result of the monopoly over landownership coupled with capital-intensive farm production that reduced demand for agricultural labor. Massive unemployment generated an exodus of peasants from the countryside and swelled the urban marginal population. Moreover, widespread rural poverty became an obstacle in the path of industrial development by constricting the popular mass market for basic consumer goods; this insured that what industrial development took place was oriented to the demands of an extremely reduced market of middle- and high-income consumers. From the point of view of the Junta technocrats, extreme income inequality and low mass purchasing power constituted the major stumbling block to further industrial development. Agrarian reform was indispensable not only for redressing social ills in the countryside, but also as the catalyst for further industrialization in basic consumer goods.

Ecuador's agrarian structure had not been the subject of serious legislation until 1964 when pressures from modernizing landlords, peasant groups, and international organizations culminated in the enactment of the first agrarian reform law and the creation of the Institute of Agrarian Reform (IERAC).[48] The target of the first wave of reform was the tenancy arrangement known as the *huasipungo* system. Under the reform, peasants were granted titles to the subsistence plots they had cultivated as part of the traditional hacienda system.

The elimination of the *huasipungo* system had two important effects. First, it accelerated the development of modern capitalist agriculture in the sierra. Wage labor replaced tenancy and the landlords were relieved of their traditional obligations to peasants. The adoption of capital-intensive techniques further reduced landlords' labor requirements. The second effect of the reform was the proliferation of peasant smallholdings, the *minifundia*. Because granting ownership rights to these small parcels of land was not accompanied by a redistribution of the central hacienda property, a large portion of the peasantry was forced into subsistence agriculture on these plots. By 1968, more than a million people in the sierra were cultivating plots of less than one hectare.[49] Virtually no change in the overall distribution of landownership occurred as a result of the reform. While provisions within the law did place ceilings on the size of landholdings and allowed for state expropriation of holdings in excess of those limits, opposition from landowners led to a shelving of any serious attempt to break up privately owned haciendas through the application of the law. Instead, state- and church-owned haciendas were the subject of the reforms during the 1960s. In addition, the ability of IERAC to force the redistribution of privately owned hacienda land was seriously impaired by the small size of its budget.

In 1970, the Velasco Ibarra government initiated a second wave of reform aimed at eliminating the remaining forms of the sharecropping system, particularly the *precarismo* prevalent in the rice-farming zones of the coast. The results of these reforms were much the same as those eliminating the *huasipungo* in the interior. No fundamental alteration in the distribution of land took place. Rather, the reform converted peasants from tenants to owners of small parcels and forged clientelistic ties between the new tenants and the agrarian reform agency, IERAC.[50]

As feeble as these attempts at agrarian reform were, the measures stirred anxieties among many large landowners and generated capital flight from agriculture. Fearing a radicalization of the agrarian reform process, land-holders divested and moved their capital into urban construction and real estate. The large landholders who remained began to shift production from labor-intensive crops such as potatoes and corn to more capital-intensive activities such as dairy farming and ranching. This combination of capital flight and product shifts together with the proliferation of the *minifundia* aggravated the problems of agricultural production. The production crisis was particularly acute in such popular staples as potatoes, beans, and wheat. Per capita food production plummeted.[51]

The depression in agriculture had important repercussions for the industrial sector. First, the decline in food production, coupled with the rapid growth of government expenditures, aggravated the inflationary spiral. The consumer price index rose by sixty-three points from 1970 to 1974.[52] Food prices increased by 10 percent in 1972, by 17 percent in 1973, and by 31 percent in 1974.[53] Inflation took its toll on the wages of industrial workers. Real wages stagnated from 1970 to 1974. The agrarian sector's failure to produce enough food to meet urban demand meant an increase in the cost of reproducing the industrial labor force. Moreover, the state's use of oil revenues to finance food imports created pressures on the balance of payments. Imports of agricultural products increased from $56 million in 1972 to $147.5 million in 1976.[54] Industrialists feared that continued food imports would create a foreign reserve crisis, provoking devaluation and diminishing the capacity of the industrial sector to import capital goods. The Chamber of Industry of Pichincha expressed its concern about food imports in its 1971–1972 annual report, arguing that such imports were a "waste of resources" that would "condemn agricultural and industrial production to death."[55]

Against the backdrop of the growing crisis in agricultural production, Rodríguez Lara committed his regime to restructuring the land tenure system that he characterized as unjust and degrading. But, other than assurances of the continued elimination of *precarismo*, the *Plan integral* was vague regarding the specific measures to be taken. For the first year and a half after the coup, the government held discussions with landlord and peasant organizations in an attempt to fashion a compromise acceptable to both. During the negotiations, the Chambers of Agriculture of Guayaquil joined with the Chambers of Industry and Commerce and issued a joint statement spelling out their opposition to any prospective reform. The document left no doubt that the private sector considered any encroachment on private property unacceptable and called for a halt on land invasions and plans for state-sponsored expropriations.[56]

When the agrarian reform law was finally issued in October 1973, the effectiveness of the dominant-class lobby was evident. The new law differed only moderately from the original agrarian reform law of 1964. According to the revised law, the government reserved the right to expropriate large private estates that were not fulfilling their social function by producing food. Estates with less than 80 percent of their area under cultivation could be subject to expropriation by the state. Yet the definition of the social function of property in terms of productivity created a number of legal loopholes through which landholders could escape the expropriations. In addition, landowners were given two years to comply with the new productivity requirements.

Despite the conservative character of the agrarian reform, the landowners' associations refused to accept any intimation by the regime that property rights could be subject to state intervention. The controversy heightened in March 1974 when the minister of agriculture, Guillermo Maldonado Lince, stated that under exceptional circumstances estates could be expropriated with compensation if such actions were deemed to be a social necessity. The Chambers of Agriculture responded immediately to Maldonado's pronouncements by declaring him persona non grata and branding him a traitor to the nationalist revolution. The caustic attacks forced Maldonado's resignation immediately thereafter.[57]

Despite the regime's portrayal of agrarian reform as a vehicle for expanding the internal market and accelerating industrial accumulation, the industrial class dissociated itself from the agrarian program and stood by as the program was relentlessly attacked by the chambers of agriculture. The industrial chambers made no effort to come to the program's defense. Just as industrialists refused to accept the logic of the statist and regulatory component of the reformist project, the industrial class was uninterested in the regime's equation of agrarian reform with internal market expansion. Industrialists remained far more preoccupied with the need to expand agricultural production rapidly than with anything that smacked of altering property rights. According to Guayaquil's leading industrial spokesman, León Febres-Cordero, the government's agricultural policymakers had "lost sight of the real problem of productivity."[58]

Disembodied Reformism

In reflecting on these policy battles, what one finds most impressive is the rapidity with which the reformist project fizzled and fell flat. Dominant-class lobbying efforts were comprehensive and effective, defusing the project at the implementation level (evident in the cases of capital democratization and Decision 24) and sometimes even as policy was being formulated (demonstrated in the tepid character of the agrarian reform proposal). Emerging from the fray over reformism was a distinctive style in the policy process. When consultations between government and business representatives did occur, the meetings were haphazard, inconclusive, and produced no consensus on policy. Decrees were enacted that had no support in the business community, provoking endless streams of criticism from dominant-class organizations in the media and public forums. In the face of such concerted resistance from the privileged and powerful, the regime could do nothing but retreat—making itself and its aspirations for change more vulnerable with every step backward.

Why were the reformers inside the state unable to carry out at least some portions of their project? Why was the state unable to force the industrial bourgeoisie into "reactive participation" in a reform process? To return to our previous argument, the prospects for relative autonomy and reactive participation in reformism are heightened when (1) dominant-class cohesion is weakened either through external forces (such as international economic crises) or internal problems (such as serious sectoral clashes within the bourgeoisie), (2) the state is able to create a base of alternative support among subordinate classes, and (3) there is unity on policy decisions inside the state apparatus. None of these conditions was fully developed in Ecuador to allow for the formation of an alliance capable of inducing reform.

Certainly, the social changes and differentiations that took place in Ecuador during the 1950s and 1960s had complicated the social order and eroded the unilateral control that dominant classes had grown accustomed to. The banana boom, import-substitution industrialization, and the growth of the state expanded the ranks of the middle class. The middle-class presence was expressed in the development of new technocratic bodies within the state such as the Junta Nacional de Planificación. The growth of the state bureaucracy under middle-class technocrats weakened the ability of traditional dominant-class organizations such as the chambers to exclusively shape the political agenda. The technocrats embraced both ECLA doctrines and dependency theory, creating the intellectual base for Rodríguez Lara's *Plan integral*. But while the ironclad grip over political discourse was loosened by the new middle-class presence in the state, the middle classes were unable to force dominant-class fractions to accept their development formulas because of a lack of organization, mobilization capacity, and political will. Middle-class political organizations were still embryonic. The Social Democratic party, Izquierda Democrática, was formed in 1970 as the result of a schism within the traditional Liberal party; it had no ties to auxiliary popular organizations such as trade unions. Founded in 1964, the Christian Democratic party remained small, although it could boast of ties with the CEDOC trade union confederation. The organizational underdevelopment of the middle sectors reflected not only their own internal structural heterogeneity, but also their social identification with upper-class interests. Oligarchic parties lasted so long and alternative political vehicles evolved so slowly because portions of the middle class remained encapsulated within elite-dominated parties.

The economic interests of the dominant classes began to change as individuals moved their capital from agriculture and commerce to industry. But portfolio diversification and the appearance of industrial groups did not weaken political or ideological solidarity across the propertied classes. Given the windfall oil revenues, clashes between elite fractions were minimized by the availability of resources. From their perspective, Ecuador of the 1970s was indeed a multiple-sum game in which every fraction of capital could be satisfied without imposing costs on the rest. And given their constellation of structural interests, their perspective was accurate. With the growth in urban purchasing power, export opportunities, and symbiotic relations with foreign capital, Ecuador's industrial investors had little reason to be concerned with state schemes to alter the pattern of development already under way. The reforms were not just irrelevant, but ideologically distasteful. Industrialists balked at the state's assertion of its right to intervene in the economy in a systematic way to restructure accumulation. Rather, they preferred that the state continue to act as a sporadic redeemer of capital (as in the case of buyouts of bankrupt firms).

In the absence of significant divisions in the dominant strata, the military's unwillingness to undertake serious efforts to mobilize the lower classes behind the reforms undermined any prospects that the dominant classes would be forced to move away from their conservatism and pragmatically accept reforms. What clearly distinguished the Rodríguez Lara regime from its Peruvian counterpart under Velasco Alvarado was its remarkable lack of interest in creating a popular base of support for the reforms. In contrast, the Peruvian reformers at least attempted to construct some popular counterweight to elite resistance through the state-created mobilization network, SINAMOS.[59] Apart from a brief allusion to the need for popular participation in the *Plan integral,* no proposal for creating mass-based organization was seriously entertained by the Ecuadorean regime. A number of factors undermined the prospects for political development along these lines. Partly to blame were internal divisions within the military over the character of the regime and the direction of policy. Conservative factions in the armed forces were never completely neutralized by the reformist officers. Second, the military reformers could not afford to alienate their only major source of civilian organizational support, the Communist party, by creating an alternative popular organization outside of their control. But at the same time, the party itself was small, possessing only a limited mobilization capacity through their trade union organization, the Confederación de Trabajadores del Ecuador (CTE). Total CTE membership was estimated at only 40,000 in 1973.[60] As such, it could not alone provide a broad popular base to sustain the regime.

To a great extent, the inability of the reformist coalition of military and civilian technocrats to see the need to create popular sources of support for the reforms was connected to their initial belief that a "modernizing" segment of the bourgeoisie would appear to support the reforms. Moreover, the failure to focus on mass bases of support for the regime's policies reflected the extreme disorganization within society as a whole. The longstanding restrictions on the franchise retarded the development of mass-based political parties. As the recent work of Amparo Menéndez-Carrión demonstrates, populist parties such as the CFP and old Velasquista parties were fluid and fragile networks that constantly dissolved and reassembled on the basis of clientelism.[61] Other organizations such as trade unions and peasant associations represented only a small portion of the labor force. The average level of unionization in the work force hovered around 16 percent during the 1970s. Within this reduced group of the unionized, over half were members of independent unions not affiliated with any of the national trade union confederations. Many of these independent unions were company-organized entities. Moreover, political rivalries inside trade union ranks further divided the movement and weakened its mobilizational capacity. In addition to the Communist CTE, two other confederations vied for power: the Confederación Ecuatoriana de Organizaciones Clasistas (CEDOC) and the Confederación Ecuatoriana de Organizaciones Sindicales Libres (CEOSL).[62]

The absence of well-developed and militant lower-class organizations translated into relatively low class conflict. A comparison with Peru clearly illustrates the relatively passive character of Ecuadorean society and the minimal threat posed by popular organizations. Strikes and civil violence were significantly less common in Ecuador than in Peru prior to the installation of reformist regimes.[63] The low levels of threat and popular mobilization in Ecuador had an important effect on the behavior of dominant-class and state leaders. For government reformers, it meant they had no obvious allies to turn to for assistance when the "progressive" bourgeoisie did not appear. At the same time, Ecuador's reformers felt no compulsion to create popular pressures as occurred in Peru. For the dominant classes, no fear of a mass threat, coupled with a reformist coalition clearly incapable of manufacturing such a threat, placed them in a superior strategic position and strengthened their ability to resist even the most feeble attempts at change. Ideologically resistant and structurally indifferent, the industrial bourgeoisie closed ranks with the rest of the private sector to jettison the regime's proposals that in retrospect appear so disembodied—thoroughly disconnected from the real balance of class power at the time.

Disillusioned and estranged from the regime, business organizations joined with political parties clamoring for change. The exhaustion of the military-led reformism was to become the catalyst for the process of regime transformation and the eventual return to electoral politics. At the heart of the democratization process was the bourgeoisie's quest to restructure domination and create new avenues of access for their control over the policy process. The bourgeoisie's veto of the reformist project was not only an objection to a set of substantive policies, but also a rejection of a set of procedures and style that distanced them from state power.

5

The Crisis
of Representation
and the End
of Reform,
1976–1979

On the afternoon of Sunday, August 31, 1975, Ecuadorean television and radio broadcasts were interrupted by the reading of a proclamation signed by the armed forces chief of staff, General Raúl González Alvear. The statement, delivered to the stations by representatives of Ecuador's major political parties, appealed to the public to support the overthrow of the "demagogic kitchen cabinet" responsible for the absence of "social transformations." By late Sunday evening, heavy fighting between the presidential guard and rebel troops under the direction of González and his brother-in-law, General Alejandro Solís, was under way in the area around the presidential palace. During the fighting, General Rodríguez Lara was able to escape and headed south to organize the resistance.

González was successful in the siege of the palace, but failed in his bid for support among the rest of the armed forces. By Monday morning, the commanders of the navy and air force declared their loyalty to the existing regime. The air force began attacks on the rebel tanks. At 5:30 P.M. on Monday, Rodríguez Lara and his cabinet were able to reenter the presidential palace. Thirteen soldiers and six civilians lay dead as a result of the conflict. González Alvear fled to the Chilean embassy and asked for political asylum. The embassies of several other Latin American countries received similar requests from the leaders of the political parties who had publicly supported the coup attempt.[1]

The violence was the culmination of stormy policy conflicts between dominant-class organizations and the government during the summer of 1975. These conflicts were rooted in the increasing pressures of traditional bourgeois political parties for redemocratization and the opposition of the chambers of production to the government's policy of selective importation enacted in the wake of a renewed balance-of-payments crisis. Within this context, the coup attempt took place.

Yet, even as Rodríguez Lara was winning the military battle against the small group of insurgents, it was already evident that he had lost the broader political struggle to construct a reformist alliance with modernizing elements within the bourgeoisie. Although the coup attempt failed to remove Rodríguez Lara as head of state, the political message of the event was unmistakable. In the weeks following, changes in the cabinet were accompanied by important reversals in economic policy. The calls for a transition to democracy by centrist and right-wing political parties continued unabated. Popular disillusionment with the failure of reform was expressed in a one-day nationwide general strike. In early January 1976, Rodríguez Lara finally announced his resignation. Upon assuming power, the new military triumvirate, headed by Admiral Alfredo Poveda Burbano, immediately announced its plan for a *retorno constitucional*.

This chapter examines the final conflict between business associations and the regime that brought about the termination of the Rodríguez Lara administration. The clashes over the questions of political participation and economic policy served as rallying points and turned dominant-class malaise into a consolidated opposition. The unfolding of events during the summer and fall of 1975 attested to the the absence of a progressive industrial bourgeoisie. Rather than disorganizing and weakening economic elites, the regime had only succeeded in clarifying the overlapping character of their material interests and intensifying their ideological cohesion and opposition to change.

The Crisis of Bourgeois Representation

Whether or not capitalists directly benefit from a particular military regime's policies, the leadership of the state by military personnel creates enormous political problems for the bourgeoisie. Namely, the dissolution of parliamentary institutions and the suspension of civil liberties that usually accompany military rule mean a cessation of "regulated and orderly class representation."² Under these circumstances, the access of capitalist classes to key policymaking bodies within the state can become extremely haphazard and personalized. The dismantling of the institutional mechanisms of representation introduces uncertainty and instability into the bourgeoisie's involvement in the capitalist state. Nicos Poulantzas pinpoints this crisis in bourgeois political participation as key to the emergence of bourgeois opposition to the dictatorships in Spain, Portugal, and Greece.³ Guillermo O'Donnell portrays the problem of regularizing bourgeois access to influence as an important source of tension within the bureaucratic-authoritarian regimes of the Southern Cone and Brazil.⁴

Underlying and aggravating the substantive policy disputes between industrialists and the Rodríguez Lara administration was the procedural issue of institutionalizing private-sector access to the regime's military and civilian policymakers. The absence of regularized consultation with business became part of the industrial bourgeoisie's opposition to the entire Rodríguez Lara reform package.

The dissolution of Congress and the banning of political activity following the coup eliminated the party system as one of the vehicles of dominant-class influence. Yet the coup did not completely close off all channels. Representatives of the business chambers continued to sit on the boards of important economic entities such as the Junta Monetaria and the Corporación Financiera Nacional. At the same time, civilians remained as the directors of the Ministries of Finance and Industry and the Central Bank. The peak associations, the Chambers of Industry, Commerce, and Agriculture, functioned without interruption. In the absence of political parties, the chambers became the primary institutional vehicles for articulating dominant-class interests.⁵

Nonetheless, these remaining channels of representation seemed inadequate. While the private sector was still represented within the Junta Monetaria and the Corporación Financiera Nacional, these representatives were only assigned the status of *vocales* (that is, they could participate in board meetings but had no voting rights on board decisions).⁶ In one of his numerous verbal assaults on the regime, León Febres-Cordero, director of the Guayaquil Chamber of Industry, linked the erosion of entrepreneurial confidence in the government to the absence of formal channels of representation for the private sector, "Is it possible by chance that one could demand a genuine participation by private enterprise for the accomplishment of developmental goals while pretending that we should not have a role in the organs of planning, credit, or monetary policy? . . . We cannot accept the assignment of great responsibilities without participation."[7]

In addition, while the regime did maintain civilians in the top economic posts, a number of the key members of the regime's "economic team" were technocrats, not businessmen. Pedro Aguayo, an economist from the University of Guayaquil, headed the Junta Nacional de Planificación. After the brief tenures of a *quiteño* lawyer and a *costeño* insurance executive, the Ministry of Finance was directed by Jaime Moncayo, a career civil servant. The minister of industry, Rubío Chauvin, was also a career civil servant. Thus, key positions in the economic policy apparatus were controlled by outsiders, individuals without direct economic and social links to dominant class fractions. In addition, the social rift between military officers and the economic elite was particularly acute. The officer corps were largely middle- and lower-class. Few officers were members of the elite social clubs frequented by businessmen.[8]

Given the elimination of some of the normal channels of bourgeois representation (parties, Congress) and the limited character of those that remained (consultant status, civilian presence within ministeries), industrialists relied heavily on pressure tactics ranging from intense lobbying of bureaucratic agencies to using the press as a forum for expressing class grievances. The bourgeoisie's attempt to construct a patchwork of influence, combined with the regime's constant vacillations, produced policy confrontations that were resolved by "sudden blows, jerkily, and behind the scenes."[9] The conflicts described in chapter 4 over the democratization of capital, foreign investment, and agrarian reform, were typical of the style of interaction between the state and the private sector during this period. Major policy initiatives by the regime were met by unbending opposition from the private sector expressed in the press and other public forums. These public confrontations were similar to those in neighboring Peru between business and the Velasco Alvarado regime. But in contrast to the Peruvian case, private-sector opposition to reformism in Ecuador was generally effective, often resulting in embarrassing policy reversals by the regime (for example, regulation of foreign investment) or a quiet abandonment of policy implementation (such as democratization of capital, agrarian reform). Although industrialists, landowners, and merchants were relatively successful in their attacks on government policy, the absence of formal institutional channels for voicing their grievances, plus the lack of clarity in the rules of the game for the opposition, imparted an ad hoc quality to the policy process and aggravated the uncertainty of the investment climate.

No single event more clearly attested to the extent of dominant-class concern and the inconclusiveness of the regime regarding representation than the summit conference between the administration and the private sector in January 1974.[10] In an attempt to assuage business leaders' criticism, General Rodríguez Lara assembled his full cabinet in the resort city of Salinas to confer with members of the coastal business community. The first wave of conferees came from the industrial sector. Those invited to attend the secret five-hour session with the cabinet included León Febres-Cordero, the government's most unrelenting critic and head of the Noboa group enterprises. Along with Febres-Cordero, Guayaquil's industrial elite was represented by Jacinto Jouvín Cisneros, owner of the country's largest paper plant and former cabinet minister, and Juan Vilaseca, an important industrial investor. The leading Quito newspaper, *El Comercio*, reported that as a result of the meeting the government had agreed to restore direct representation to the private sector in "matters of their own concern." The meetings also produced a government agreement to reconsider policies regarding the application of Decision 24 and to review labor legislation. Similar consultations were held with representatives of coastal agriculture and finance.

The rapprochement between business and the Rodríguez Lara regime was short-lived. While the regime did accede to a substantive demand for a revision in labor policy, it made no systematic attempt to establish new mechanisms for private-sector participation in policymaking. A scheme to restructure the peak associations by creating an agro-industrial chamber combining firms already represented by the Chambers of Agriculture and Industry was characterized as absurd by the Guayaquil Chamber of Industry. The chamber regarded the projected reorganization as an attempt to weaken it by dividing its membership.[11] Typically, the government reacted to the criticism by dropping the proposal.

The crisis deepened during 1975 as the leadership of the traditional political parties pressed for a return to civilian rule. The parties, which had been banned from engaging in public activities but not dismantled, became progressively more audacious. In violation of the ban on political gatherings, the Conservative party held an assembly in early May 1975. The regime responded by imprisoning the head of the party and vice-rector of the Universidad Católica of Quito, Julio César Trujillo Vásquez.[12] This move only heightened party opposition. Right-wing and centrist parties (Frente Radical Alfarista, Frente Poncista, Velaquismo, Partido Democrata Cristiana, Partido Nacionalista Revolucionario, and Izquierda Democrática) unanimously denounced Trujillo's incarceration. Joining in their demands for his release were the faculty of jurisprudence, the student federation, and the employees' union of the Universidad Católica.

The conflict between the government and the civilian politicians continued through June and July. The parties pressed their demands for a restoration of civilian rule and offered their visions of how the *retorno* should take place. The Frente Alfarista proposed the selection of an interim civilian president who would preside over new elections. The Radical Liberal party offered a similar suggestion, except that it would have banned any former president from the interim slot. The Izquierda Democrática recommended the immediate announcement of a target date for the military's withdrawal. The CFP (Concentración de Fuerzas Populares) called for a national plebiscite to decide on the mechanisms for the return. The Conservative party proposed the creation of a constituent assembly to oversee the process.[13]

The government responded with a full-fledged rejection of the idea of returning the political system to civilian politicians. Government spokesmen characterized the parties as the groups directly responsible for the country's previous "false democracy" along with the "paralysis and permanent marginalization" of the lower classes. The minister of government, General Durán Arcentales, declared that the regime's references to the need for a political "institutionalization" did not include any projected return to civilian rule. In a press conference in late June, Durán pointedly remarked that as far as the government was concerned, "No one has spoken of a return." In July, Durán continued with his attack on the parties, accusing them of complicity in a plot to overthrow the government.[14]

This running conflict over representation might have continued without resolution had it not coincided with yet another wave of bourgeois opposition to a substantive point of economic policy. The emergency measures adopted by the regime in the summer of 1975 as a response to the renewed balance-of-payments problem provoked fierce resistance from merchants and industrialists. The battle over the policy of selective importation provoked the final mobilization of dominant-class groups against the regime.

The Turning Point: Fiscal Crisis and Selective Importation

Ecuador's shift from a reliance on agricultural exports to petroleum did little to alter the dependent character of the economy. The balance-of-payments crisis of 1975 underscored the enduring vulnerability of the economy to price fluctuations in the international market. Politics during the course of the oil boom was still wedded to uncertainties in the international market, much as it had been during the reign of banana and cacao.

The catalyst triggering Ecuador's renewed balance-of-payments difficulties was the abrupt change in the world price of oil. Surplus, not scarcity, characterized the market by mid-1974. This was a sharp contrast to the two previous years in which the Organization of Petroleum Exporting Countries (OPEC) had successfully maintained a scarcity that resulted in an unprecedented surge in the international price of petroleum. Consistent with the nationalist stance of the military government, Ecuador had joined OPEC in 1973 under the direction of the outspoken minister of natural resources, Admiral Gustavo Jarrín Ampudia. The price for Ecuadorean crude increased from $2.53 to $13.90 per barrel in the period 1972–1975.[15] As oil prices climbed, government revenues and international monetary reserves expanded even beyond the optimistic expectations of government technocrats and planners, straining their capacity in many instances to utilize the revenues efficiently.

In political terms, this financial bonanza gave the military regime a clear margin of maneuverability vis-à-vis all social classes. The newfound solvency allowed the government to pursue policies that subsidized simultaneously popular consumption and private-sector accumulation. Given the regime's tenuous political base, it is no wonder that it attempted to buy support from different social sectors by underwriting a wave of consumption.

In order to check inflation and promote popular consumption, the regime held down prices on a number of food items through direct subsidies to certain industries. This included payments to the producers of flour, sugar, and vegetable oil. Flour and vegetable oil firms were allowed to maintain profits and abide by government price controls even though raw materials in the international market were rising in cost. In the sugar industry, government subsidies were accompanied by strict limitations on sugar exports. Added to these subsidies for basic food items was the maintenance of extremely low gasoline prices: gasoline was still $.20 per gallon in 1975.[16]

Direct subsidies to industries accomplished the dual purpose of expanding popular consumption while underwriting private accumulation. The regime transferred a significant portion of the new oil revenues to the private sector through a number of other mechanisms as well. The expansion of the credit system was one of the vehicles of the transfer. In 1972–1975, the Central Bank expanded credit to both state entities and private banks which in turn made loans available to the private sector at low interest rates. Credit to government entities (which included such agencies as the Corporación Financiera Nacional) rose from S/.573 million to S/.2,577 million during this period. The Banco de Fomento credit increased from S/.502 million to S/.3,504 million. Credit to private banks increased from S/.66 million to S/.766 million.[17]

The expansion of the credit system, coupled with the generous incentives provided by the industrial development laws, accelerated imports of raw materials and intermediate and capital goods. The import of capital goods and transportation equipment tripled from 1973 to 1975, increasing from $148 million to $448 million. Raw materials and intermediate goods doubled in the same period from $174 million to $375 million. While consumer goods as a proportion of the total import bill decreased, expenditures for these items continued to increase in absolute terms. In the space of one year (1973–1974), consumer goods imports increased from $10 million to $64 million.[18] This increase was in part a response to relaxed tariffs on such items as color televisions, economy cars, and luxury foods. This liberalization in import policy was enacted in March 1974 as the country's international monetary reserves reached new highs.[19]

By June 1975, the limits on these policies of unrestrained consumption had been reached. For the first time since petroleum export began, imports outpaced export revenues. Petroleum exports, suffering under the weight of a drop in world market prices and a continuing conflict between the multinationals and the state over oil policy, dropped off drastically between March and June. This was accompanied by a sharp decrease in Ecuador's international monetary reserves. Under these deteriorating economic conditions, the regime lost its margin of maneuverability. The state had to impose the costs of curbing consumption on dominant-class fractions openly hostile to it, fractions whose antagonism had already been made clear in the clashes over political representation, the regulation of foreign capital, the democratization of capital, agrarian reform, and state intervention in the economy.

The first measure restraining imports was enacted in June 1975. Regulation 734 temporarily suspended auto imports. At the same time, Decree 773 placed a ceiling on the amount that banks were permitted to loan business enterprises. Not surprisingly, these decrees were greeted with strident denunciations from auto importers and their representative organizations, the Chambers of Commerce.[20]

But the June measures represented only the first wave in the government's attempt to establish import austerity. On August 22, the Monetary Board issued a series of new, more stringent restrictions. Under Decree 738, import duties on goods classified as List 2 (nonessential) were raised by 60 percent until January 1976. In addition, the decree raised import taxes on List 1 (capital goods) items from 5 to 25 percent depending upon the payment arrangements for such goods. Along with the tariff hikes, a number of goods lost their privileged List 1 classification and the import of seventy-five other items was banned completely. The suspension of car imports was extended until the end of the year.[21] Within the space of three months, the regime found itself forced to freeze abruptly the consumption expansion that it had nurtured during its first three years of existence.

Dominant-class reaction to the proposals was swift. Among those most seriously affected was the commercial fraction of the bourgeoisie—the major importers of Quito and Guayaquil. The reverberations of these measures, however, were felt outside of the importing sector as well. Given the enormous overlap of interests between the commercial and industrial classes, industrialists were drawn into the conflict over selective importation. As was detailed in chapter 2, a significant portion of the industrial class maintained interests in commercial firms. But even apart from the direct interests of certain industrialists in the import trade, the class as a whole stood to suffer under these measures since they tightened regulations governing the importation of capital goods and increased tariffs on luxury items. If, as a number of Ecuadorean analysts argue, the tariff measures represented a last-ditch effort by the regime to divide dominant-class opposition by rallying industrialists around protectionism, it was a poor strategy, considering the structural position of the industrial bourgeoisie.[22] Rather than regarding the new tariff barriers as a possible opportunity to be exploited by local industry, industrialists regarded selective importation as further restraint on their economic activities. The prospect of an increase in economic regulation only solidified dominant-class opposition.

On August 26, the Chamber of Commerce of Pichincha published a critique of the new measures. This was followed by a communiqué issued by Jaime Robalino, director of the Chamber of Industrialists of Pichincha agreeing with the position taken by the Chamber of Commerce. He emphasized that higher import prices create inflationary pressures and stressed the need for measures to stimulate production. The chamber called for a rationalization of petroleum policy and curbs on government spending. Robalino argued that the roots of the fiscal crisis lay in an overly nationalist oil policy that generated conflicts with multinationals and slowed down production, along with increased nonproductive consumption expenditures by the government.[23]

On the same day, the director of the Guayaquil Chamber of Industry, León Febres-Cordero, issued a statement in which he interpreted the new economic measures as an indicator of the total failure of the government's economic policies. He stated: "The desperate and unadvisable economic measures recently enacted make the following realities public: (A) The official acceptance of the grave fiscal and monetary crisis (B) That this crisis is the result of a lack of opportune and suitable measures to ward it off (C) That those responsible are the directors of this country's economic policy."[24] Like the other representatives of business organizations, Febres-Cordero concluded his statement by calling for a revision of oil policy and the application of austerity in public spending.

The traditional political parties, already at odds with the regime over representation, joined with the Industrial and Commercial Chambers in attacking the measures. The solidarity expressed among the business chambers was paralleled by an alliance formed among opposition political parties. On August 29, leaders of the Conservative, Socialist, Velasquista, Institutionalist Democratic Coalition, and National Revolutionary parties met to declare the formation of the Junta Cívica, an umbrella organization of parties dedicated to the "reestablishment of the constitutional order." The first statement of the junta presented an analysis of the fiscal crisis similar to those formulated by the Chambers. The junta blamed the fiscal crisis on excessive government spending and the mismanagement of oil policy. The junta went on to condemn the regime for its demagogic agrarian reform, its collaboration with the Communist party, and its "aggression against the private sector."[25] With the traditional parties and business peak associations clearly united in opposition to the regime, the stage was set for the abortive coup attempt undertaken by González Alvear on August 31. Openly cooperating with the insurgents, members of the Junta Cívica read González Alvear's proclamation on national television. In the statement, the rebels pledged the restoration of civilian rule and the military's "return to the barracks."

The Final Months

Although the military action taken by González Alvear failed to provoke the immediate removal of Rodríguez Lara as head of state, the attempt did produce ministerial changes and policy reversals aimed at quelling private-sector opposition.

Jaime Moncayo, the minister of finance who had presided over the selective importation policy, was the major casualty of the González Alvear affair. He was replaced by Jaime Morillo Batle, who immediately declared that the government should not provoke confrontations with the diverse sectors of the country. Within the first two weeks after the coup attempt, significant alterations were made in import policy. Most notably, the 60 percent tariff hike on List 2 items was reduced to 30 percent. The increase of the tariff rate on List 1 items was dropped completely. Concurrent with this reversal on import policy, the government enacted measures to centralize the regulation of foreign investment in the Ministry of Industry. This restructuring of economic policy was announced shortly after a meeting between the ministers of finance, industry, and the Central Bank with representatives of the private sector.[26] By mid-September pressures from the private pressures had proved effective not only in forcing a government retreat on selective importation, but also in establishing a clear institutional locus for decisions relating to foreign investment.

Notwithstanding the regime's renewed promise to engage in a dialogue with the private sector after the coup attempt, the hasty policy reversals of

September left unresolved the issue of rationalizing bourgeois representation in the policymaking process. The substantial concessions made on economic policy contained no provisions for expanding dominant class participation in the procedures. With the question of access for the bourgeoisie still unresolved, political parties continued to press their demands for a restoration of civilian rule.

The leadership of the exiled Junta Cívica regrouped in Bogotá. In November, the junta announced its plan to return clandestinely to Ecuador to participate in a "final action" against the government.[27] At the same time, the political parties not directly linked to the junta continued with their criticisms of the regime and calls for elections. The government responded to the criticisms from this core of civilian politicians with sporadic and haphazard attempts at repression. In early November, Julio César Trujillo, the head of the Conservative party, and Carlos Julio Arosemena, the ex-president of the republic and legal counsel for members of the exiled Junta, were arrested and deported to Bolivia on conspiracy charges. But, the singling out of high-profile members of the opposition for punishment turned out to be counterproductive. The Arosemena and Trujillo deportations only provoked further protests from opposition groups. The Universidad Católica of Quito, a number of political parties, and the National Federation of Lawyers, all registered complaints about these actions. Even the church joined in the criticism, calling for a "constitutional and juridical reordering of political authority."

The continuing pressures mounted by the political parties and pressure groups coincided with an erosion of the passive, popular support for Rodríguez Lara that had been led by the Communist party of Ecuador. Since the coup in 1972, the party had adopted a policy of guarded support for the regime and constituted its only major ally among civilian organizations.[28] By 1975, however, the Communist party and its trade union CTE along with CEDOC and CEOSL had grown steadily weary of the constant frustrations of the regime's reform attempts. In August 1975, the trade union organizations announced their plan for a one-day national strike to demand the regime's compliance with its original "philosophy and plan of action." In addition, the strike was posed as a response to those sectors pressuring for the installation of a "repressive government, one docile to imperialism."[29] The strike was intended to question the motives of traditional parties in their campaign for *retorno* as well as demonstrating union dissatisfaction with the halt of the reform process. Redemocratization was conspicuously absent from the strikers' agenda.

The call for a general strike was successful and the event took place peacefully on November 5. The nine-point manifesto issued by the trade unions on the day of the strike called for a derogation of the legal constraints on strike and union activities, a 50 percent increase in the minimum wage, a freeze on prices, the enforcement of agrarian reform laws, and the nationalization of petroleum, electricity, foreign trade, and food distribution.[30] The response of the Chamber of Industry of Pichincha to the strike was predictable. The body condemned the strike for generating losses in production detrimental to national development.[31]

Sharp exchanges in later November between the Chambers of Production and the new finance minister over the issue of government spending underscored the ongoing displeasure of the private sector with the regime even in the light of the September adjustments in economic policy. In a joint statement issued by the Chambers of Industry and Commerce, government spending was portrayed as the major source of the drain on oil revenues. The chambers recommended the elimination of government purchases of real estate, luxury furnishings, and bureaucratic expenditures as the way to remedy the budget deficit. Finance Minister Morillo depicted the chambers' recommendations as "demagogic," arguing that a reduction in public expenditures would mean "paralyzing infrastructure projects, unemployment and a recession."[32]

The erosion of popular acquiescence vis-à-vis the regime that was evident in the general strike coupled with the unabated hostility voiced by bourgeois organizations regarding problems of representation and the management of the economy finally forged a consensus within the armed forces on the removal of Rodríguez Lara from office. With a consensus clearly established within the ranks of both the military and civilian establishments, no coup was even necessary. Under pressure from his cohorts, Rodríguez Lara resigned his office on January 11, 1976. A new military triumvirate under the direction of Admiral Alfredo Poveda Burbano was installed and vowed to preside over the return to civilian rule.[33]

With the political defeat of Rodríguez Lara and the reformist project, a continuation of industrialization in the style in which it had proceeded since the early 1960s was assured. Industrialization would continue to be largely shaped by the local bourgeoisie in cooperation with foreign capital and adjusted to the peculiarities of an internal market characterized by extreme income inequalities. Under the new military government, local industrialists turned their energies to consolidating this model by extending their alliance with foreign capital and supplanting the reformist focus on the limited internal market with a vision of limitless opportunities in external markets.

Conclusion: Industrialists Under the Triumvirate

The period from January 1976 to August 1979 was marked by a readjustment in the relationship between the industrial class and the state. The termination of the reformist project produced a greater correspondence between the demands of the industrial class and the public policies enacted by the military junta. The new junta (officially referred to as the Consejo Supremo de Gobierno) clearly distanced itself from the reformist interregnum by adopting a militant stance toward labor and actively courting foreign investors. At the same time, industrialists sought to create a consensus within the dominant classes and the state bureaucracy on the direction of future industrial development—a development directed away from the problematic internal market and toward exports.

The first sign of the industrial bourgeoisie's developing interest in an export strategy came in 1976 with the creation of FEDEXPOR, an organization representing industrial firms specializing in nontraditional exports. Drawn together by the prospects of increased business with Andean Pact countries, the original founders of FEDEXPOR included some of the largest producers of consumer goods in Ecuadorean industry.[34] Pharmaceuticals were represented by the Dow affiliate, Laboratorios Life, and textiles by La Internacional, S.A. One of the top financial contributors to the organization was Ecasa, S.A., Ecuador's first producer of household appliances.

The analysis formulated in the initial documents issued by FEDEXPOR stressed the inherent instability introduced into the economy by Ecuador's traditional reliance on the export of agricultural commodities. From the perspective of FEDEXPOR, the remedy to the cyclical crises of agricultural export lay in a diversification of the export structure to include industrial products. According to their analysis, diversification constituted the "best and only" development strategy available. In contrast to external markets, the internal market offered no prospects for growth. With at least 40 percent of the population unavailable as consumers, FEDEXPOR concluded that exports would continue to be the "base of internal development."[35]

Similar sentiments were expressed by members of other industrial organizations. In a business round table in May 1977, the president of the Pichincha Chamber of Industry, Gonzalo Vorbeck, argued that the future of Ecuador's industries would depend on external markets given the limitations in the internal market and the skewed distribution of income.[36] The annual reports of the Chambers of Industry from 1976 to 1979 reflected the stand taken by Vorbeck and emphasized the need for improved tax incentives for the export industry.

By early 1978, it was evident that these efforts by elements within the industrial bourgeoisie to recast the framework of industrial policy from import substitution to outward-oriented growth were producing results. New subsidies for exports were incorporated into the revised Industrial Development Law of 1976.[37] Moreover, a further shift in policy emphasis was signaled in remarks by Rodrigo Espinoza Borja, director of the Central Bank, in January 1978. Espinoza observed that the "traditional scheme of industrial development must be given a gradual but firm twist which would lead to the adoption of an outward oriented growth model."[38] This pronouncement was followed by a similar statement from the head of the Corporación Financiera Nacional, Alberto Quevedo Toro, who declared that the process of import substitution had reached its limits.[39] JUNAPLA joined in the new official calls for export-oriented strategies and underscored the need "to draw a new industrial incentives policy so that industrial development on the basis of import-substitution can be oriented toward the capture of foreign markets, toward exports."[40]

This shift in market priority from internal to external markets was accompanied by an aggressive search for new foreign investment. The search was spearheaded by the new minister of industry, Galo Montaño. Along with representatives of other government agencies, Montaño toured the United States in 1977 speaking to groups of potential investors on the virtues of Ecuador's industrial developmental laws, particularly the List of Directed Investments (LID) enacted in 1976. The LID provided a range of generous tax breaks to firms willing to invest in targeted industries. To complement this new public relations offensive, government entities ranging from CENDES to the Central Bank issued slick new promotional pamphlets outlining the incentives provided in the industrial development laws.[41] The pursuit of new foreign capital was facilitated by the generalized retreat of all Andean Pact countries from applying the more stringent regulations governing the behavior of foreign capital under Decision 24. By 1976, the Andean Pact signatories had agreed to raise the ceiling on the repatriation of profits from 14 to 20 percent.[42] Meanwhile, as the legal framework of the pact was progressively weakened through liberalizations, business associations in Ecuador continued to call for a broad interpretation of the foreign investment code by the central government.

The new rapprochement between industrialists and the Consejo Supremo was also expressed in the regime's adoption of a hard-line position vis-à-vis the labor movement.[43] To create an attractive investment climate for both local capitalists and multinationals, the regime turned to repression to restore labor discipline and contain strike activity. The army's well-known hard-liner, Durán Arcentales, took over as minister of labor. As minister, Durán presided over government intervention in a number of strikes which ended in police actions against strikers. Such incidents occurred in the strikes at Texaco (November 1976), the Anglo refinery (September 1977), Enkador (December 1976), and the Vernaza hospital in Guayaquil (January 1977). The most notorious incident occurred in October 1977, when workers struck the government-owned sugar mill, AZTRA. At least twenty-three, but perhaps as many as one hundred strikers, died during an eviction of the plant premises by the police.

Notwithstanding the alliance between the state bureaucracy under the triumvirate and the industrial bourgeoisie (particularly with regard to labor policy), the relationship between the two actors was not completely devoid of tension. While a consensus was reached on the need for a greater emphasis on exports in developmental policies, the question of precisely what types of industrial exports would be promoted proved to be one of enduring controversy. The policies of Galo Montaño at the Ministry of Industry sought to commit Ecuador firmly to carrying out the sectoral programming assignments mandated by the Andean Pact in the automotive and petrochemical fields. In Montaño's perspective, export-led growth was to be derived from the development of such basic industries, with the Andean Pact countries acting as the prime market for these products.[44] Montaño was supported by a coterie of *quiteño* industrialists who stood to benefit from the location of the new plants in the sierra. Guayaquil's industrialists, however, were much less enthusiastic about the sectoral assignments and favored the abandonment of such an approach in favor of the development of agro-industries. This was also the position taken by the leaders of the Chambers of Agriculture and Commerce who launched vigorous attacks on Montaño's policies, labeling the projects as "false industries."

The Industrial Chambers were somewhat successful in pressing their demands for improved representation in the key economic policy-making agencies. Voting rights of the Chamber representatives in such governmental bodies as the Monetary Board were restored by the regime in November 1976.[45] CENDES, the agency charged with the promotion of industrial projects, did act to integrate industrialists directly into the agency by designating Gonzalo Vorbeck (president of the Pichincha Chamber of Industry) as vice-president of the organization in 1977.[46]

Even more serious than the industrial bourgeoisie's irritation over the incomplete integration of its representatives into the economic policymaking apparatus was its open opposition to the methods and schedule for democratization proposed in the military's "Plan for the Juridical Restructuring of the State" which had been formulated in consultation with the political parties.[47] Both the Guayaquil and Quito Chambers of Industry publicly opposed the plan. The initial attacks centered around what they considered to be unrepresentative composition of the boards revising the two constitutions. The constitutions were to be subject to a popular referendum in January 1978. Moreover, one of the new constitutions developed by the board provided for the enfranchisement of illiterates, the elimination of the traditional functional representatives of the chambers in Congress, and the establishment of communal property as one of the four types of property within the Ecuadorean economy. León Febres-Cordero, head of the Guayaquil Chamber of Industry, led the campaign protesting the provisions and urged individuals to cast null ballots to demonstrate dissatisfaction. In opposition to the Febres-Cordero campaign stood the three national labor federations and the majority of the political parties whose primary interest was in the reestablishment of the political game. The industrialists lost the struggle of the ballot box. The new constitution was adopted with 43 percent of the vote. The null ballot option promoted by the private sector accounted for just 23.3 percent of the vote. Despite the loss in the referendum, the chambers continued their attack on the constitution, particularly in regard to the provision concerning the development of a "communal property" sector of the economy.

> Even greater is the confusion if we consider the questions provoked by certain ideological postures prone to introduce into the country the social and economic experiments similar to those which provoked the misfortunes that Chile and Peru suffer from today. One observes with particular pessimism the insistence on promoting utopian theories of "communitarianism" which lead to the surrender of the means of production to workers so that through self-management they generate benefits that will be shared by the collectivity in general. The afore-mentioned absence of positive norms which will regulate this delicate subject will increase uncertainty, above all if we consider that expectations will serve to promote a commotion within known groups of agitators and suspicion among businessmen.[48]

Although the chambers lost the initial constitutional skirmish over the principle of communal property, they won the battle in the long run. The election of the populist candidate, Jaime Roldós, to the presidency in 1979 brought with it no serious attempt to install a communal property sector. The notion remained enshrined in the constitution, but ignored by the new civilian government which had been forewarned of virulent private-sector opposition.[49]

The peace established between the Consejo Supremo and the industrial class in the period 1976–1979 was incomplete. The issues of bourgeois representation, the mechanics of the *retorno,* and the priorities in export policy generated points of contention between the military triumvirate and industrialists. Nonetheless, the industrial class was to fare better under this second wave of military rulers than they had under Rodríguez Lara. The terms of the debate over development policies had shifted along lines more acceptable to the industrial class. The rhetoric of redistribution and nationalism was replaced by a productivist ideology compatible with the style of industrialization in progress.

6

Restructuring
Domination Through
Democratization,
1979–1984

More than a decade after General Rodríguez Lara proclaimed the "nationalist revolution," dominant-class efforts to rebuild modes of direct control over the policymaking within the framework of democracy climaxed in the inauguration of León Febres-Cordero as Ecuador's chief executive. Accepting the presidential sash in a ceremony on the tenth of August, 1984, Febres-Cordero pledged an end to state interventionism, welcomed foreign capital to Ecuador, and promised to fight inflation and increase income "through the road of production."[1]

From the perspective of the bourgeoisie, Febres-Cordero was truly one of their own. Indeed, his public and private life neatly paralleled the economic interests and the political trajectory of the emergent industrial bourgeoisie as a whole. From an old-line family of Guayaquil, Febres-Cordero was trained as an engineer at Stevens Institute in Hoboken, New Jersey. By the mid-1960s, he was the general manager of the Noboa group enterprises as well as heading his family-owned companies. He turned to public life through the Chamber of Industry of Guayaquil. From his position as president of that organization, he became a leading critic of the Rodríguez Lara government. With reform defeated and democratization under way, Febres-Cordero moved into party politics and affiliated with the rightist Social Christian party just prior to the congressional elections of 1979. Well known from his high-profile tenure at the Chamber of

Industry, Febres-Cordero won a legislative seat. As a congressman, he attracted media attention with his unrelenting attacks, especially those aimed at the government of the young Christian Democrat, Osvaldo Hurtado.[2] After establishing a public image as a macho no-nonsense personality, Febres-Cordero became the candidate of a united front of rightist parties in the presidential elections of 1984. Defying the predictions that the right was exhausted as an electoral force, Febres-Cordero won a narrow victory over his social democratic rival, Rodrigo Borja, in the May runoff election.

León Febres-Cordero was a central figure in the movement by industrialists and other economic leaders to fashion new means to control the state so that reformist projects could not resurface out of the shuffle of democratic politics. Parties representing private-sector interests and organizations of that sector played a dual game during the transition to democratic rule and thereafter. On one hand, they were advocates of and participants in the democratization process, seeking to structure at every turn a political environment they could dominate. But at the same time, organizations on the right kept open extraconstitutional options by questioning the legitimacy of the process and the integrity of their rivals to the center and left.

As dominant-class representatives mobilized to create political defenses against reformism, a new set of circumstances in the international arena were creating new economic restraints on the pursuit of reform. With declines in the world market prices for oil and fiscal pressure mounting for the repayment of the international debt, the state in Ecuador was progressively losing its margins to manipulate resources. Policymakers, regardless of their ideological inclinations, were increasingly forced to deal with the issue of how to distribute austerity in the economy rather than promote reform.

This chapter does not attempt an exhaustive description of all the events surrounding the transition to democracy in Ecuador.[3] These final reflections will delineate how industrialists and their colleagues in the business community moved to reestablish control over the state during the process using traditional corporate lobbying organizations and rightist political parties. The political revitalization of the forces on the right intersected with the constraints posed by economic crises to dramatically restrict the prospects for a resurgence of reformism.

Resuscitating the Political Right

As discussed in the preceding chapter, the schism that opened between dominant-class organizations and the military was not completely closed by the defeat of the Rodríguez Lara program. The divergence between the two actors was most pronounced with regard to the mechanics of the transition to restore civilian rule. Nonetheless, the military government under the triumvirate was able to retain important margins of control over the process, even in the face of dominant-class complaints about the structure and pace of the transition. In comparative perspective, it is an example of a controlled transition, that is, one in which the armed forces retained the lead in dictating the terms of the process.[4] In this way, democratization in Ecuador diverges sharply from other recent cases such as that of Argentina where the military lost its negotiating powers vis-à-vis civil society and retreated from power in a hasty and disorganized way.

The ability of the Ecuadorean military to veto elite proposals on the structure of the transition originated, in part, in the lack of consensus among dominant-class groups themselves over exactly how civilian rule should be restored. As described in the previous chapter, the split across the forces on the right became evident in the different positions taken by corporate organizations and parties regarding the constitutional plebiscite of 1978. For future electoral purposes, the traditional parties of the right had little to gain by appearing overly obstructionist and took positions supporting one of the two constitutional options on the ballot. Meanwhile, business interest organizations urged voters to protest the plebiscite by casting invalid ballots. Divisions continued as the electoral process got under way in 1978 when right-wing parties fielded two candidates in the first round of the presidential elections in July. The Liberal party chose its longstanding leader, Raúl Clemente Huerta, as its candidate; the Conservative and Social Christian parties backed Sixto Durán Ballén, the former mayor of Quito.[5]

For forces on the center and the left, the disarray on the right created an important opportunity for these new political groups to play a critical role in defining the shape of the transition. The economic boom of the 1970s expanded middle- and lower-class constituencies; these new social differentiations were reflected in the range of groups that the military consulted in the the public "dialogues" on the transition. Moreover, emerging out of the political parties that aspired to represent these new social forces was a whole new generation of political leaders. The leadership skills and dynamism of this new political cohort allowed them to occupy center stage in the transition. Jaime Roldós of the Concentración de Fuerzas Populares and Osvaldo Hurtado of the Democracia Popular directed two of the commissions created by the military to work out the legal structure of the transition. In contrast to these young luminaries in the party system (which included Rodrigo Borja of the Izquierda Democrática and Francisco Huerta of the Partido Democrata, along with Roldós and Hurtado), the traditional parties were plagued by old and uninspired leadership.

While the military did not allow a unilateral takeover of the transition by any group, two key decisions were made that enhanced the electoral prospects of the right. First, the military proscribed the presidential candidacy of Assad Bucaram, leader of the populist CFP and the obvious front runner. The proscription of the Bucaram candidacy had long term repercussions on the development of the CFP. Forced to pick another presidential candidate, the party settled on Jaime Roldós, a young *guayaquileño* lawyer linked to the Bucaram family through marriage. With Roldós's victory in the presidential election in 1979, rivalries between him and Bucaram over the leadership of the party broke apart the progovernment majority in Congress. This proved to be a costly rupture that allowed the right in Congress to ally with disgruntled Bucaramistas and create a powerful congressional bloc.

The second key decision favoring the right involved the extensive recount of the results of the first round of presidential elections held in July 1978. The recount resulted in a massive disqualification of votes for the CFP-DP ticket of Jaime Roldós and Osvaldo Hurtado that drastically narrowed the margin between their ticket and that of rightist candidate Sixto Durán Ballén.[6] In addition to creating the image that Durán Ballén could win in the second round, the recount delayed the scheduling of the the runoff until April 1979 and allowed the divided right more time to regroup around the Durán candidacy.

But the presidential campaign revealed how ill-prepared the old parties of the right were to compete and assume creative roles in the newly structured political system. Under their forced hiatus from political life under military rule, the traditional parties ossified while corporate entities such as the Chambers of Industry and Commerce became the key institutional voices for the right in the policy process. Their programmatic underdevelopment was matched by their institutional underdevelopment. Prior to the presidential elections of 1979, no more than 18 percent of the population had ever participated in an election. Restrictions on the suffrage ranging from literacy to registration requirements had effectively disenfranchised the mass of the citizenry. The traditional Liberal and Conservative parties had always operated as electoral vehicles at the service of the country's elite within the context of the extremely restricted electoral system. As such, they were never mass-based parties. With the expansion of the franchise to include illiterates (mandated by the adoption of the new constitution in the 1978 plebiscite), a whole new body of voters was integrated into the electorate that had no past ties or loyalties to the traditional parties. The right's limited electoral appeal to this new electorate was further undermined by the lackluster style and organization of the Durán Ballén campaign.

Certainly, the parties of the center and the left were also debilitated by the atrophy of the electoral system for seven years under the military. Parties that were created in the years just prior to the coup such as the ID and the DP had not had the chance to develop well-established constituencies in the electorate. Moreover, their marginalization from policymaking and state power under the military meant that one of the traditional routes of party building—through clientelism—was not available. For the older populist CFP, the linkage problem was not so acute because they could rely on previously established clientelistic networks to mobilize coastal voters. What the Roldós-Hurtado ticket did effectively was to combine the mobilization capacity of the old CFP with attractive young candidates who could appeal to the new masses of middle- and lower-class voters. The result was an overwhelming victory for Roldós-Hurtado in the second-round runoff held in April 1979. Roldós took over 60 percent of the vote nationally, receiving a majority in all but one province.

The Roldós victory was a clear setback for dominant-class organizations and rightist parties in their quest to reestablish unambiguous control over the state apparatus. Nevertheless, the eclipse of these groups was not total. On the ideological level, the incessant accusations of communism hurled at Roldós and Hurtado (most notably by León Febres-Cordero) forced the candidates into a position of studied moderation. Their "twenty-one-point" platform was mild, vague, and decidedly on the side of a market model of the economy.[7] Indeed, political commentators during the campaign often pointed to the similarities in the platforms of Durán Ballen and Roldós. Once elected, Roldós bolstered private-sector confidence by appointing well-known businessmen to his economic team.[8] From the perspective of the private sector, the new democratic state under Roldós was highly permeable, both at the institutional and ideological level.

But despite this permeability, a great deal of uncertainty reigned in business circles during the first year of the Roldós administration regarding the precise policy course that would be followed. During the campaign, Roldós proclaimed the ticket as the *fuerza del cambio*—and for a bourgeoisie already rattled by aspirations for reform, there was no telling exactly where Roldós's broad popular mandate and populist roots would lead him. Given the prospective uncertainties in the conduct of the executive branch, Congress stood as the key institutional site that could give the private sector access to the policy process and a channel for vetoing any reformulation of the reformist project. The problem, of course, was that the right fared poorly in the congressional elections and occupied just twenty-two of the sixty-nine seats in the unicameral Chamber of Representatives. But the lack of intraparty cohesion and the debility of party alliances across parties of the center and left allowed right-wing party leaders to assume a highly visible and important role in the legislature, despite their minority status.

The opening for rightist parties in Congress came immediately after Roldós's inauguration in August 1979 and was the product of the fissure within the majority party, the CFP. Assad Bucaram, the longtime leader of the the CFP who was barred from the presidential campaign by the military, was elected president of the Congress. Even though Jaime Roldós had been elected president, Bucaram made it clear that he considered himself to be the head of the party. In effect, Bucaram believed the slogan that had circulated among stalwart CFP supporters during the campaign, "Roldós a la presidencia, Bucaram al poder" (Roldós to the presidency, Bucaram to power) would be put into practice. Roldós, however, moved to distance himself from Bucaram during the campaign and immediately thereafter. The struggle for party leadership broke out during the deliberations on cabinet appointments with Roldós defying Bucaram's desire to see only loyal party veterans in the posts. The struggle over party leadership broke the CFP congressional delegation into Roldocista and Bucaramista factions of approximately equal size. In order to maintain his control over Congress, Bucaram engineered an alliance that combined his faction with deputies from the Conservative, Liberal, and PNR parties. With this antigovernment alliance in place, a continual clash between the executive and legislative branches (dubbed the *pugna de poderes*) resulted in a near-complete policy paralysis in both branches.

The disintegration of the CFP congressional bloc would have not proved so favorable to the right had forces on the center and left regrouped to form a stable progovernment coalition. Taken together, the deputies from the Izquierda Democrática, Democracia Popular, the Partido Democrata, and the Roldocista CFP did constitute a majority in the chamber. But the vacillating position struck by the Izquierda Democrática, under the leadership of Rodrigo Borja, made the creation of a durable congressional bloc impossible. Believing that any association with the government (that was contending with a deteriorating economic situation) would damage the electoral prospects for ID in the 1984 elections, Borja steered the social democratic party away from any consistent support for the government. In moments of "crisis" when the survival of democratic arrangements appeared to be at stake, the ID did cooperate with progovernment forces in the Congress. The experience of the Convergencia Democrática agreement in 1983 illustrates the ID's approach to congressional alliance politics during the period. The government of Osvaldo Hurtado, who succeeded to the presidency after the death of Jaime Roldós in a plane crash in May 1981, became the subject of increasingly vicious attacks by business associations who were seeking intervention by the military. In the context of this heightened threat to the democratic system, the ID joined together with the Democracia Popular and Roldocista faction in congress in the Convergencia to defend democratic arrangements.[9] Once the prospects of a coup receded, however, the ID drifted away from its congressional alliance. Just weeks after the Convergencia agreement, the ID joined together with the right-wing bloc, now visibly led by Febres-Cordero, to censure Hurtado's minister of government, Carlos Feraud Blum.

The mobilization of the right against the Roldós-Hurtado governments involved attacks both from the political right (through parties) inside Congress and the economic right (through the chambers). The level of attacks accelerated after Hurtado's succession to the presidency and coincided with the deepening of the economic crisis.[10] Business leaders openly questioned Hurtado's competency and called for military intervention.

The attacks on the Hurtado government are an especially fascinating phenomenon of the period because they clearly demonstrate the bourgeoisie's fixation on the issue of access to influence and policymaking style and how important their perceptions are in structuring their behavior toward a regime. Despite the radical rhetoric of his past, Hurtado presided over a government that carried out policies highly favorable toward the private sector. Nevertheless, his government was constantly subject to verbal assaults by business groups that were reminiscent of the attacks on Rodríguez Lara. Political style rather than the substance of economic policy was the source of the rocky relationship between Hurtado and the business organizations.[11] Hurtado consciously sought to insulate economic policymaking from the direct pressures of producers' associations. As Hurtado himself later acknowledged, the attacks on his government by business groups were caused by the fact that "they knew they couldn't pick up the phone and give me orders in a country where the government traditionally ruled in consultation with the Chambers."[12]

Spokesmen on the right invoked extraconstitutional options at various points during the period. During the popular unrest in October 1983 that occurred in response to Hurtado's economic austerity plan, León Febres-Cordero suggested that Hurtado resign and that Congress name his successor, an act that clearly contradicted the succession procedure laid out in the constitution.[13] The rumors and threat of a coup were chronic during the Hurtado administration. Hurtado later remarked that "there wasn't a cocktail party or a social get-together" where members of the armed forces were not approached by civilian leaders on the subject of a coup.[14] But a number of factors were at work that reduced the likelihood of an interruption of the democratic game. Having lost prestige and popularity in their previous attempt at government and because of their poor performance during the brief Paquisha border war with Peru in 1981, the military itself had little institutional interest in intervention, particularly within an atmosphere of economic crisis. Added to this were the pressures from the U.S. embassy against intervention and its unequivocal support for the Hurtado administration. Moreover, there was no overriding consensus across the multiple groups on the right on the desirability of interrupting the democratic process. Party leaders on the right distanced themselves from the more provocative stances of the Guayaquil chambers, claiming their loyalty to democracy.[15] Time eventually solved the question of how the right would proceed. As the 1984 presidential and congressional elections approached, the talk of a *golpe* receded as the prospects for an electoral victory by the right became palpable.

While the idea that the right could recapture the state through the ballot box appeared preposterous after the rout by Roldós in 1979, by 1984 it was much less so. Popular disappointment with the Roldós-Hurtado governments and internal developments within the political forces on the right favored an electoral recuperation. Despite their election as the *fuerza del cambio*, Roldós and Hurtado were forced to preside over governments associated with a deteriorating economy. The four years of democratic government had produced nothing dramatic or new in terms of policies. The instability in congressional alliances and the constant attacks on the government turned the maintenance of democratic arrangements themselves into the number one priority of these administrations. Given that the other parties of the center and left had collaborated at various points with the Roldós-Hurtado governments, the parties of the right were able to claim the space as the opposition and to play on popular frustrations over the economy. Right-wing strategists believed that their electoral prospects were going to be greatly enhanced by such "retrospective" voting on the economy.[16]

The problems posed by the fractionalization of the right across six parties (Conservative, Liberal, Social Christian, Nationalist Revolutionary, Velasquista, and the Institutionalist Democratic Coalition) were "solved" by the formation of a united electoral front, the Frente de Reconstrucción Nacional (FRN). One of the intellectual architects of the FRN was Sixto Durán Ballén whose own presidential candidacy had suffered as a result of the lack of unity on the right. Almost immediately after his defeat in 1979, Durán Ballén began to lobby other party leaders to create a single electoral vehicle for the right.[17] The poor showings of these parties in 1979 and the municipal elections of 1980 only underscored the need for an innovative electoral strategy. To win, the right needed the charisma and notoriety that someone like León Febres-Cordero could provide. The rise of Febres-Cordero as a well-known political personality provided the practical incentive for the coalescence of the FRN. In a surprising show of unity, these parties of the right joined together to support a single candidate for the first round of a presidential election. In contrast, the parties of the center and left fielded seven different presidential candidates. With the center and left vote dispersed across so many candidates, the FRN ticket was able to attract 22 percent of the first-round vote. This gave Febres-Cordero a spot in the second-round runoff against the top vote-getter, Rodrigo Borja of the Izquierda Democrática, who took 23 percent of the first-round vote.

The electoral strategy of the right underwent some important shifts over the course of the two-round campaign that ran from summer 1983 through May 1984. The vague slogans of the first round ("León: Decisión Nacional" and "Ecuador es mi partido") were replaced by populist promises of bread, work, and housing ("Pan, Techo y Empleo"). The large stadium rallies and high-profile media events of the first round were dropped in favor of a grassroots campaign organized around door-to-door appeals in lower-class neighborhoods.[18]

The adaptability and flexibility demonstrated by the Febres-Cordero organization was never matched by the Borja campaign. The errors of the Borja campaign were both stylistic and tactical, deeply rooted in Borja's personal convictions about his own mission and the transcendent character of his party. To Borja, the ID represented an attempt to create a modern political party—one that was ideologically coherent, disciplined, and unbound by the personalist and patronage considerations that marked the behavior of other parties.[19] In the image battle between the two candidates, Borja's studious and cultured style appeared timid in comparison with Febres-Cordero's conscious cultivation of machismo. Borja's aloofness was not strictly stylistic; it carried over into the relationships between ID and other parties in the second round. With his refusal to make concrete deals on the distribution of power and patronage, Borja alienated two key regional parties from his ticket, the CFP and the FRA. As a result, the leaders of these parties struck an informal understanding with the FRN and openly campaigned for Febres-Cordero in the coastal provinces. Thus, Febres-Cordero's appeal to coastal voters as a *guayaquileño* was combined with a mobilization by the clientelistic FRA and CFP organizations in a region where ID was already weak. Two parties of the left, the Movimiento Popular Democrático (MPD) and the Partido Socialista also abstained from a Borja endorsement. Believing that the previous regime was highly unpopular, Borja did not call on Osvaldo Hurtado's Democracia Popular or Francisco Huerta's Partido Democrata for help. With the exception of the active support of the Communist-led FADI coalition, the ID's isolation in the party system was near complete.

But even as the electoral tide was turning in favor of Febres-Cordero, the right maintained its dual strategy of participating in democratic politics while setting the stage for a possible repudiation of the outcome. The Tribunal Supremo Electoral's switch to a computerized registration system and ensuing technical foulups led to charges by FRN leaders of an attempt to rig the elections for Borja. They called for an impeachment of TSE members and questioned the legitimacy of the first-round results.[20] The controversy over the returns evaporated after Febres-Cordero's second-round victory.

Still the Febres-Cordero presidency did not signify a complete takeover of the state by the right. Parties of the center and left dominated the congressional contests that coincided with the first round of the presidential race and constituted a clear majority in the new legislature, winning forty-two of seventy-one seats. The unexpected shock of the the Febres-Cordero election brought these parties together into the Frente Progresista (FP) legislative bloc that included the Izquierda Democrática, Partido Democrata, Democracia Popular, Partido Roldocista Ecuatoriano, Movimiento Popular Democrático, Partido Socialista, and the Frente Amplio de Izquierda which included the Communist party. The FP pledged to undertake a concerted opposition to the regime's proposed neoliberal economic project. So while democratic politics did produce an opening of the state to the private sector (through the executive), it was certainly not a total one. Nor was the victory without its own internal contradictions as groups within the economic and political right began jockeying for power within the Febres-Cordero administration. The demands of the professional political right (that is, the leadership of the FRN parties along with the allied CFP) for patronage collided as fractions of industrial and financial capital maneuvered to control the key economic policy-making posts.[21]

The Febres-Cordero administration moved forcefully in its first year to neutralize the sources of opposition inside state institutions. A two-pronged approach was used for these purposes; pressures on individual congressmen within the Frente Progresista legislative bloc to desert it were combined with a systematic undermining of the powers of Congress as well as that of autonomous entities such as the Supreme Court. Opposition congressmen reported offers of cash and control over provincial patronage to induce defections from the Frente Progresista.[22] Internal conflicts from within the parties constituting the FP added to these disintegrative pressures. By August 1985, defections from the FP parties and alliances between the FRN, CFP, and FRA parties allowed for a recomposition of forces in Congress that gave the Febres-Cordero government a legislative majority.

As the executive worked to undermine the unity of the FP, Febres-Cordero set out to build an imperial presidency. At various points in his multiple conflicts with Congress during the first year, Febres-Cordero asserted his right to act as the final arbiter of constitutional issues and control the legislative agenda. The tone of the Febres-Cordero presidency was set immediately after his inauguration in August 1984 when he clashed with the FP coalition in Congress over new appointments to the Supreme Court. The controversy paralyzed congressional business from August through December. The FRN parties disrupted debates on the floor of the Congress with tear gas bombs, fist fights, and by packing the galleries with hostile FRN supporters. During the course of the clash over the legality of the appointments, President Febres-Cordero sent the police to physically bar the new justices from entering their offices. Long and tortuous negotiations between Febres-Cordero and Raúl Baca Carbo (president of Congress and leader of the FP bloc) brought an end to the confrontation. The terms of the resolution revolved around *la troncha*—a distribution of Supreme Court appointments among parties that included the FRN and the CFP.[23] In short, the FP acceded to the FRN's demands for stable access to the institutions outside of direct executive control. As FP leaders admitted at the conclusion of the conflict, their decision to give in was based on the fear that continuation of the conflict might have provoked extraconstitutional actions by Febres-Cordero such as a closing of Congress.[24]

The 1979–1984 track record of democracy in Ecuador was marked by a partial repenetration of the state by dominant-class representatives. Without question, this repenetration took place a context much changed from the old days of oligarchic politics. For the first time, the right had to compete for the support of a broad-based electorate and share space in democratic institutions with representatives from Social Democratic, Christian Democratic, and far-left parties. But while many of the key actors and relationships within the political system were altered by the social change and modernization of the 1970s, there is still little evidence at this point which indicates that the political right (parties) and the economic right (the *cámaras*) have coalesced into a sturdy democratic right—that is, one committed to maintaining democratic procedures and norms under difficult circumstances. Rather, the right took shifting and ambiguous positions vis-à-vis democratic arrangements during the period. These shifts were related to their attempts to maximize their access to the state apparatus and remove reformism from political discourse.

The New Economic Limits

Removing reform from the political agenda during democratization in Ecuador was the product of a dual movement. The regrouping of the political forces on the right coincided with changing circumstances in the international and domestic economy that created limits on state autonomy and restricted the fiscal capacity of state managers to promote reform measures.

By the end of the 1970s, the petroleum-induced economic expansion in the Ecuadorean economy was coming to a close. The revitalization of democratic institutions after 1979 was to take place within an atmosphere of recession, rather than the boom of the previous decade. At the core of the economic crisis of the 1980s were two factors: (1) the deteriorating performance of the export sector, and (2) the increasing fiscal burdens imposed on the state by the servicing and the repayment of the international debt.

The dynamism of the petroleum sector during the 1970s owed much to the buoyancy of prices on the international market. The volume of Ecuador's production actually stagnated after 1973. Moreover, the volume of oil exports fell as domestic demand increased dramatically under the protection of government price controls. The prices of petroleum derivatives were frozen in 1972 and remained so until 1981. With prices well below those prevailing on the international market and with increases in purchasing power, domestic demand increased at an annual rate of 14 percent from 1972 to 1981, reducing the amount available for export. Falling prices for petroleum on the international market starting in 1982 only aggravated the growing crisis in the sector.[25] The performance of nonpetroleum exports (bananas, coffee, cocoa, fish/shrimp) was unimpressive during the 1970s and grew worse in the 1980s. In short, there was no alternative engine of growth in the Ecuadorean economy that could replace or significantly compensate for loss of petroleum revenues.

As with other countries in the region during the 1970s, both the public and the private sector in Ecuador increased their borrowing from international creditors. The availability of petrodollars in the international money market and the business confidence created by Ecuador's status as a petroleum exporter allowed the two military governments to engage in a policy of "aggressive indebtedness." Between 1970 and 1976, the debt increased from $241 million to $693.1 million. The pace of indebtedness increased in the last half of the decade, bringing Ecuador's foreign debt to over $5 billion by 1981. While in 1973, Ecaudor's payments to service the debt amounted to only 8.8 percent of the country's exports, by 1981 they accounted for 84 percent of export revenues.[26] Given the deterioration in export revenues and the impossibility of continuing payments, President Osvaldo Hurtado undertook negotiations with private international creditors and the International Monetary Fund to refinance the Ecuadorean debt.

As in other Latin American cases, the sine qua non of debt renegotiation was austerity. In October 1982, President Hurtado and his economic team announced the enactment of a stabilization program that included new taxes on consumption, the elimination of subsidies on wheat and gasoline, and an increase in transportation fares. Currency devaluation became a permanent part of the program through a system of regular "minidevaluations" that went into practice in March 1983. Hurtado moved to curb government spending and was able to reduce the deficit by 1983. In short, the severity of the economic crisis and the necessity of debt renegotiation seriously constricted the range of policy choices open to the Hurtado government and turned the idea of undertaking structural reforms into an impossibility. In a system wracked by economic stress and popular unrest, the maintenance of democratic arrangements rather than policy innovations aimed at structural change became the key policy concern of the government.

By the 1980s, long-term structural conditions and short-term conjunctural factors had come together to produce a powerful antireform coalition in Ecuador. Held together by overlapping interests and offended by the military's visions of change, dominant-class fractions mobilized first through business associations for their defense. Seeking to regain direct access over the instruments of the state, they later turned to democratic politics and the party system. Their footholds inside the newly created democratic institutions (through their representation within the legislature from 1979 to 1984 and the executive branch after 1984) created opportunities to defuse and discredit the idea of reform and its advocates. In the battle to shift the tone of the political debate in Ecuador from reformism to economic orthodoxy, this antireform coalition could look to powerful allies in international banking and financial circles. With a politically rejuvenated bourgeoisie in place and an array of international creditors in the wings, a refurbished conservatism took center stage in Ecuador of the 1980s.

7

From Military
Reformism
to Democratic
Authoritarianism

The installation of bureaucratic-authoritarian regimes in Brazil, Chile, Argentina, and Uruguay in 1960s and 1970s continues to haunt the study of Latin American politics. While nondemocratic politics is no stranger to Latin America, the particular ferocity and repressive capabilities of these regimes provoked a wave of inquiry into the origins of this "new authoritarianism."[1] A compelling question left in the wake of this discussion is what extent these experiences portend for the political future of the smaller and poorer countries of the region. To what extent will the tragic experiences of the more advanced nations be repeated? Are grim forecasts of the future to be found in the analyses of Fernando Henrique Cardoso and Guillermo O'Donnell, who linked the origins of these bureaucratic-authoritarian regimes to crises brought by dependent industrialization? Julio Cotler suggests a possible convergence of political forms in the region toward the authoritarian end of the spectrum.[2] Similarly, Marcelo Cavarozzi points to a narrowing in the range of political options as industrialization proceeds.[3] The noted Brazilian sociologist, Florestan Fernandes writes, "It appears that capitalist development points to the [autocratic] route as normal. . . . The significance of present day Brazil is that it contains the future of other countries which belong to the periphery of the capitalist world and cannot put themselves directly on the road to socialism."[4]

But if the contemporary histories of Brazil, Argentina, Chile, and Uruguay do tell us something about the fate of other countries, it is a revelation that is partial and uneven. While industrialization in nations on the periphery does structure the political choices and alliances available to social classes, this structuring takes place within already crystallized class and state structures and is subject to variations by changes in the character of the industrialization process itself. As Alexander Gerschenkron has shown, industrialization never repeats itself in quite the same way. Rather, as industrialization is played out from country to country, the technological advances and organizational arrangements of earlier industrializing countries are mimicked and combined to produce new hybrids in the processes. The social and political consequences of industrialization are constantly transformed as the process is itself altered through time and inserted into distinctive social formations.

The first wave of horizontal import substitution in the more advanced countries in Latin America gave rise to the classic populist reform projects of the 1940s. At the same time, the problems directly generated by horizontal import substitution (for example, its import intensity and its draining effect on foreign exchange) combined with the accumulation and consumption demands placed on the populist state by capital and labor to erode the economic margins that made reform possible and paved the way for the installation of bureaucratic-authoritarian regimes. But the second wave of horizontal import substitution that began in many of the less-developed countries during the 1950s did not generate the same sets of social forces or political formulas. The extremely late-starting industrialization in Central American and central Andean countries did not produce a "reactive participation" of the emergent industrial bourgeoisie in reformist projects, but nor did it bring bureaucratic authoritarianism. Instead, industrialization has been accompanied by dominant-class resistance to military-led reformism, followed by an ironic reversion to competitive politics and the emergence of what many analysts are now calling "democratic-authoritarian" regimes, that is, regimes marked by an extreme concentration of power in the executive branch, feeble legislatures, and debilitated party systems.[5]

Industrialists in Comparative Perspective

The industrial bourgeoisie that emerged in the late-starting process of industrialization in Ecuador bears little resemblance as a class to its Southern Cone counterparts of forty years ago. It was not forced into learning political flexibility as the Chilean industrialists of the 1930s had to do. Unlike Argentine and Uruguayan industrialists of the 1940s, the ability of Ecuadorean industrialists to engage in political compromise is undermined by peculiar and often distant ties to the internal market.

Important differences in their relationship to markets and labor separate the early industrial classes formed during the first wave of import substitution from the recently formed industrial class in Ecuador. In the Southern Cone cases in the 1940s, the industrial class largely specialized in producing basic consumer goods for an urban mass market. In Argentina, an urban proletariat formed in the meat-packing and subsidiary industries around Buenos Aires. In Chile and Uruguay, early urbanization produced a rapid growth in the service sector and the industrial labor force by the 1930s and new industries were created to serve this heterogeneous group of consumers.

In contrast, the export trade in cacao and bananas in Ecuador generated only a minimal expansion in white-collar and industrial employment. Moreover, the export economy of the coast left traditional agricultural life in the sierra undisturbed. As a result, when import substitution began during the 1950s, over half of the population still remained trapped within the antiquated agrarian structures of the sierra and were lost as potential consumers of industrial goods. Given the peculiarities of this internal market, the production of consumer nondurables as well as durables became extraordinarily dependent upon a reduced group of middle- and upper-class consumers. Industrialization was nurtured by incentives created by the state and high tariffs.

With the oil boom of the 1970s, the ranks of the the middle classes grew and their purchasing power expanded. This triggered a process of product diversification in existing industries and provoked new interest from multinational corporations in the Ecuadorean market. At the same time, the takeoff of export-oriented industries such as cacao semielaborates and fish transformed segments of the old commercial elite of the coast into a new export wing of the industrial bourgeoisie. Andean Pact assignments encouraged further investment in export industries and expanded the industrial bourgeoisie's vision of its potential market. All these economic changes converged to produce an industrial class whose expansion was built on the external market, a limited internal market, and a continued subsidization by the state.

The political impact of this structural constellation was that it reduced the industrial bourgeoisie's capacity to tolerate reform projects, even the relatively mild national-capitalist developmental model proposed by Rodríguez Lara. Industrialists looked at economic concessions to the popular classes as sources of increased costs to them, not as a necessary vehicle for internal market expansion. Moreover, they were uncomfortable with the ideological costs of increased state intervention into the economy and resisted the state's attempts to regulate managerial behavior. With regard to agrarian reform, the style of Ecuadorean industrialization rendered the rural masses irrelevant to continued economic growth. The commitment of the industrial class to the defense of private property was strengthened by its social links to agricultural capital. Nationalist appeals struck no responsive chord because of the close association between the local private sector and multinational corporations.

From the perspective of the industrial class, there was nothing to gain and potentially much to lose with the Rodríguez Lara program. The industrial bourgeoisie correctly perceived that there would be no penalties for noncooperation in the project. The state's willingness to subsidize private-sector expansion with new oil revenues was never in doubt. Argentine industrialists in the 1940s, however, had somewhat different structural interests in relation to the reform project of Perón. Given the separation between agricultural and industrial capital in Argentina, the industrial class had a vested interest in the partial assault on agriculture that Perón directed through IAPI, the state agency used to transfer the economic surplus from agriculture to industry.

But even more important than just this play of structural interests in accounting for the Ecuadorean bourgeoisie's solid rejection of reformism was that there were no lower classes to stand behind reformist state managers capable of forcing dominant-class capitulation and some level of "reactive participation." In Argentina, Juan Perón successfully courted the Argentine working class in his quest for political power. He was able to mobilize and channel popular pressures for change through the Peronist labor unions he created. Ties between the Popular Front parties and the Chilean working class gave the program of Aguirre Cerda a strong popular base, as did the party-mass nexus in Uruguay. The electoral victories of the Southern Cone populists legitimized these regimes and underscored the breadth of mass support for reform.

The military-technocratic coalition that produced the reformist project in Ecuador had no equivalent popular base. The absence of an organized constituency was related both to the character of popular organizations and to the limited political vision of the leadership. The military in Ecuador never attempted to organize a popular base of support. Its reluctance to do so stemmed from innate institutional fears within the military regarding popular mobilization as well as ideological disagreements within the armed forces. At the same time, there was no independent popular organization or party that commanded a national following capable of sustaining the regime when it came under attack from dominant-class organizations. It was the military's coolness on the question of popular mobilization that denied the reformers a powerful lever with which to squeeze compromises from those at the top of Ecuadorean society. In Argentina, Chile, and Uruguay, the civilian leaders of populism were not reluctant to reach out to popular classes. Indeed, they had no alternative route to power but through the masses.

Civilian populism of the 1940s differs from the military reformism of the 1970s in another important way. In Ecuador, the military's ban on party activities and the closing of the Congress made the bourgeoisie's prospects for penetrating the regime in order to temper its "distributivist excesses" haphazard and irregular. If industrialists had a chronic complaint during the Rodríguez Lara years, it was the regime's failure to consult with them on a regular basis. In contrast, the electoral installations of the Radical government in Chile and Batllismo in Uruguay left representative institutions intact and available as political tools to influence the policy process. How industrialists perceive the prospects for access to and influence over regimes affects their political strategies and tactics. Without recourse to the normal channels of influence available in democracy, Ecuadorean industrialists publicly hounded and privately lobbied in frustrating attempts to gain regularized access to the regime. In this process, they became everything but a tolerant opposition.

It was the bourgeoisie's rancor over the lack of access that led dominant-class organizations to join in the calls for a *retorno constitucional*. Despite the dangers implicit in a return to competitive politics, the reestablishment of electoral politics seemed preferable to a continuation of political skirmishes with the military. The exclusionary ideological tendencies of the bourgeoisie by no means contradicted bourgeois participation in the *retorno*. If anything, such behavior testifies to dominant-class confidence in its ability to control political outcomes. In ideological terms, the upper stratum of Ecuadorean industrialists clearly reject standard populist formulas. The ideology of productivism, with its stress on ubridled economic growth rather than distribution or participation, is embraced by the majority of industrialists. In their perspective, Ecuador's economic afflictions are rooted in a scarcity of resources, an unskilled and undisciplined labor force, and irrational state interventions that interrupt the operation of the market. The absence of resources, not their distribution, is the key to the bourgeoisie's perspective on development problems.

In addition to divergent structural situations, the early industrial classes of the Southern Cone and the late-developing industrial bourgeoisie of Ecuador responded differently to the challenge of reformism because of different political memories. Even as industrialists themselves were emerging as a class in the Southern Cone, they were forced to confront demands from growing middle and working classes for political participation and an increased share in economic growth. Middle-class reformism initiated the rupture of the oligarchic state that was completed by populism; leaders "learned" the politics of compromise through small defeats and accommodations. Yrigoyen, Alessandri, and José Batlle paved the way for Perón, Aguirre Cerda, and Luis Batlle. In Ecuador, the slow growth of middle- and working-class groups meant that there was no early constituency for democratization and reform. Traditional parties remained in place and maneuvered within a limited electoral universe created by restrictions on the suffrage. The two "populist" parties—the Velasquistas and the CFP—wheeled and dealed with these traditional rivals, often allying with them, and rarely making serious redistributive demands. In short, oligarchic politics demonstrated a tenacity in Ecuador that was perhaps rivaled only by the experience of Central America. Until the 1970s, Ecuador's elite, closely tied by family connections and economic interests, ruled over a country in which the social order had never been seriously threatened by popular movements. As such, they were unprepared for and resistant to the calls for change from the military and allied technocrats. Moreover, in the thirty years that separate these two sets of experiences, the agenda of reform itself had expanded—waving the banner of reform in the Latin America of the 1970s entailed much more than it had in the 1940s. The appearance of revolutionary movements (Bolivia, Cuba) and socialist experiments (Cuba, Chile) and the promotion of "developmentalist" ideology through institutions such as ECLA all worked in the direction of expanding the concept of what constituted "reform." Suddenly, reformism was much more than rehashed Keynesianism. In the lexicon of the 1970s it included restructuring capital and redefining property relations. Policy measures to improve distribution (such as wage increases, social security benefits) were superseded by policies that adjusted authority relations (such as agrarian reform, proposals to "democratize" capital).

In short, the pursuit of reformist policies in the 1970s posed a role for the state that violated the normative vision of a still conservative and parochial bourgeoisie in Ecuador. With little concern for the legitimating and rationalizing character of state intervention in a capitalist economy, Ecuadorean industrialists demanded a return to a state that would provide the simple order and vigilance that was the hallmark of the old oligarchic order. When the military proved to be less than complaint, the bourgeoisie turned to democracy, looking to its revival as a means to reoccupy the state.

Democracy and the Right

The irony of the return to democracy in Ecuador is that it reflected not the strength and pervasive demands of popular-class organizations and political parties, but was contingent on their weakness.[6] For Ecuador's dominant classes, still caught up in oligarchic manners and untouched by serious reform, democratization was a look to the past—a search to recreate the "democratic parenthesis" of the 1950s that was dominated by the likes of Galo Plaza and Camilo Ponce, men of privilege with clear ties to others of the same rank. The acceptability of democracy as a political option was built on the bourgeoisie's belief that it would control the executive and legislative branches once more. For the Ecuadorean bourgeoisie, no forced demobilization or depoliticization of the popular classes was required to restructure their domination. The lack of a concerted threat from below through militant trade unionism or peasant organizations made a highly repressive regime unnecessary. Whereas bureaucratic authoritarianism became the response of the Southern Cone bourgeoisie in the aftermath of populism, the Ecuadorean bourgeoisie's overwhelming resistance to reformism had stymied the development of political forces on the left so successfully that democracy could reemerge easily as an acceptable political option for dominant classes. The potential threat of democratic institutions, given the disorganization and fragmentation of the anti-right forces, was low.

So far, the political forces on the right have proved to be quite effective in their penetration of the democratic state. During the Roldós-Hurtado administration, pressure from right-wing parties and dominant-class associations defused the promises for change. The revitalization of the right culminated in the Febres-Cordero election of 1984 that unequivocally opened the doors of the state to business elites.

The striking feature of the bourgeoisie's behavior in the 1979–1984 period is its continuing inability to cope with and accept the uncertainties in access and outcomes that are part of democratic politics. Whenever defeat seemed imminent, groups representing the political and economic right questioned the legitimacy of democratic institutions and procedures as well as the integrity of their rivals. Belligerence and bullying defined the political style of the right—and it was partially this style that escalated conflict into systemic crises. The right was able to force capitulation on issues by threatening the life of democracy itself. Given the weak mobilization capacity of popular-class organizations and the conflicts among center-left parties, leaders to the center and left of the political spectrum have been so far been unable to act effectively as counterweights to the right. This kind of interplay takes its toll on the institutionalization of a democratic regime; procedure dissolves into constant improvisations and ad hoc, transitory resolutions to crises take the place of clear-cut rules on how to solve conflict within the institutional framework.

The hyperdefensive character of the industrial bourgeoisie and its dislike of competition and opposition raise serious questions about the depth of dominant-class commitment to maintaining democratic forms. As Albert Hirschman and others have recently argued, the consolidation of democracy in Latin America is contingent on innovations in existing political culture. Democracy requires tolerant players and "good" losers.[7] Groups in civil society must be ready to accept the uncertainties and possible losses that are a part of democratic politics. So far, there is little to indicate that such a transformation is taking place within elite political culture in Ecuador. Dominant-class ideology expressed during the military-reformist interregnum and thereafter was still permeated by the old fears—the incompetence of the masses and their political representatives, the illegitimacy of the state outside of direct elite control, and the irrationality of state intervention into the social and economic order.

Yet the tenacious and enduring character of upper-class conservatism in Ecuador does not necessarily imply some future turn toward highly repressive authoritarianism even if the right should lose future electoral contests. As the Roldós-Hurtado period illustrates, the right can mount successful oppositions from within the state through the legislature; and, as always in capitalist economies, business associations can restrict the alternatives available to policymakers by questioning the "investment climate" and threatening capital flight.[8] Moreover, as other Latin American countries such as Venezuela and Mexico clearly demonstrate, corporatist structures of representation that set up clear channels between business organizations and the executive branch can be constructed so as to shield certain dimensions of economic policymaking from the vagaries of electoral politics.[9] This wedding of democratic and corporatist types of representation is, of course, not unique to Latin America. Western Europe offers a number of examples of such blended institutional arrangements characterized by weak legislatures and powerful executive bureaucracies tied to key groups in civil society.[10]

The political future of Ecuador and much of the rest of Latin America depends to a great degree on how long the domestic bourgeoisie will continue to see democracy as the "best possible shell" for capitalism.[11] Clearly, electoral successes for the right and the construction of corporatist modes of policymaking that guarantee access to the state for the private sector may do much to quell the anxieties of dominant classes and lessen the uncertainties generated by democratic politics. Such arrangements may form the basis of a new regime type—a "democratic-authoritarian" hybrid that combines electioneering in a public sphere with a privatization of economic policymaking.

The question of how much democracy versus how much authoritarianism will be mixed in these regimes brings us back to the importance of the bourgeoisie's perceptions of the political processes around them. These perceptions are not just the product of cool reflections on the profit and loss columns, but are shaped by collective political memories as well as the desire to ensure "future certainty." The variations in the industrialization process and its superimposition on different class structures in Latin America has produced a collection of dominant classes with marked differences in their political capacity to ally, coopt, and make accommodations to other social groups. In Ecuador, industrialists and their fellow elites have yet to be socialized into the politics of compromise. As such, they continue to act as an intolerant right—one that acquiesces to democracy because its institutions remain weak, tentative, and easily twisted.

Appendix: Methods and Field Research

The scarcity of published information on the operations of industrial firms in Ecuador makes research on this topic extremely difficult. Much of the data for this analysis came from personal interviews. Most of the interviews took place between July 1979 and August 1980 in Quito and Guayaquil. Over all, I spoke with eighty top executives. This group included domestic industrialists and both domestic and foreign managers of multinational corporations. These interviews provided the background materials on the history of industrial firms that is used throughout the book.

The formal survey of Ecuadorean industrialists that is presented in chapter 3 is based on interviews conducted with executives who preside over the largest industrial firms in the country. Because systematic information on assets, stockholding, and other facts about individual firms was not available in public sources, I relied on partial information for 1977–1978 provided by the Superintendencia de Compañías to draw up a list of the largest industrial firms as defined by sales. With this information I was able to compile a list of "sales leaders" (that is, firms registering sales of S/ 99 million or more in 1977 or 1978). Of the 586 firms registering sales information for these two years, 94 fell into this category. Once the list was completed, I was able to compile a list of the firms' executives using commercial industrial directories and informants familiar with the companies. With this information, I chose firms randomly from the sales leader list and attempted to make contact with their executives. Access to these individuals was often difficult to obtain, but I was able to complete personal interviews with top executives heading forty-three of the ninety-four leading firms. It is important to note that the data provided by the Superintendencia was incomplete for several reasons. At the time of my research, industrial firms were not reporting all data to the Superintendencia and those firms not incorporated as *sociedades anonómias* were not required to report at all. As a result, some large family-owned companies not registered in the stock market may have been omitted. Moreover, it was impossible to verify the accuracy of the data collected by the Superintendencia.

The characteristics of the firms headed by these forty-three executives throw some light on the structural position of capitalists standing at the "commanding heights" of Ecuadorean industry. Sixteen (or 37 percent) of the executives headed firms producing traditional consumer nondurables (food, beverages, cigarettes, textiles), while agro-export industrial firms accounted for nine executives (21 percent) in the sample. The eighteen remaining executives (42 percent) headed firms that produced more sophisticated consumer products and intermediate and capital goods. This last category included manufacturers of pharmaceuticals, household appliances, metal products, cartons, plastic products, paper, animal feed, and cement, and a vehicle assembly operation. The location of these firms reflected the regional concentration of Ecuadorean industry; only two of them were located outside the provinces of Pichincha and Guayas. Executives reported important associations with foreign capital. Significant stockholding (defined as 10 percent or more of the company's stock) by foreign capital was reported in twenty-two of the forty-tree firms. Transfer-of-technology agreements with foreign firms were reported by twenty-three firms and twenty-five reported utilizing credit from foreign banks.

The majority of the interviews were conducted in Spanish. No tape recordings of the conversations were made; I relied on notes taken during the interviews. Many of the questions in the closed-ended portion of the interview schedule were based on the format used by Fernando Henrique Cardoso in *Ideologías de la burgesía industrial en sociedades dependientes*. I incorporated more open-ended questions into the schedule after several preliminary interviews in which informants expressed dissatisfaction with a completely closed format.

To maintain the anonymity of the informants, I give no names in the text. Interviews are referred to in the notes by the date and location of the interview. References to specific individuals occur only in those cases where an event or the opinion of an individual was already a matter of public record.

A number of background interviews were also carried out with policy-makers in government agencies and interest groups. Within the public sector, I conducted interviews in the Ministries of Industry, Agriculture, and CONADE (formerly JUNAPLA), Banco Central del Ecuador, the Corporación Financiera Nacional, Programa Nacional de Café, and the Programa Nacional de Cacao. Among the interest-group leaders inter-viewed were officials from the Cámara de Industriales de Pichincha, the Cámara de Industrias de Guayaquil, the Asociación Nacional de Empre-sarios, the Asociación Ecuatoriana de Industrias de Cacao, Asociación de Productores Farmacéuticos, Cámara de Pequeños Industriales del Guayas, Cámara de Pequeños Industriales de Pichincha, Asociación Industrias Conserveras Agropecuarias del Ecuador, Asociación de Industriales de Productos Lácteos del Ecuador, and the Ecuadorean–North American Chamber of Commerce.

Much of the material in chapter 6 concerning the transition to democ-racy is taken from my interviews with politicians and party activists on several trips to Ecuador from 1983 to 1987. As with the industrialists, names of individual informants are cited in the text only when the informa-tion given or the opinion presented was already a matter of public record.

Notes

Introduction

1 For an excellent collection of essays, see Claudio Veliz, ed., *Obstacles to Change in Latin America* (New York: Oxford University Press, 1966).

2 James Weinstein, *The Corporate Ideal in the Liberal State, 1900–1918* (Boston: Beacon Press, 1968); Gabriel Kolko, *The Triumph of Conservatism: A Re-Interpretation of American History 1900–1916* (New York: Free Press of Glencoe, 1963).

3 Theda Skocpol, "Political Responses to Capitalist Crisis: Neo-Marxist Theories of the State and the Case of the New Deal," *Politics and Society* 10, no. 2 (1980): 157–201.

4 Notwithstanding the controversy raging between Henry Turner and David Abraham over the role of business in the fascist rise to power in Germany, it is clear that after fascist regimes came to power, the business community was reconciled with the regimes and benefited from certain aspects of fascist economic policy. See David Abraham, *The Collapse of the Weimar Republic: Political Economy and Crisis* (Princeton, N.J.: Princeton University Press, 1981). For the Italian case, see Roland Sarti, *Fascism and the Industrial Leadership in Italy 1919–1940* (Berkeley and Los Angeles: University of California Press, 1971). For a comparative discussion, see Daniel Guerin, *Fascism and Big Business* (New York: Monad Press, 1979).

5 For a discussion and statistical breakdown of class composition in Latin America, see Alejandro Portes, "Latin American Class Structures: Their Composition and Change during the Last Decade," *Latin American Research Review* 20, no. 3 (1985): 7–40.

6 This definition of reform is based on discussions by Fred Block and Alain de Janvry. See Fred Block, "The Ruling Class Does Not Rule," *Socialist Revolution*, no. 33 (May–June 1977), 6–28. Alain de Janvry, *The Agrarian Question and Reformism in Latin America* (Baltimore, Md.: Johns Hopkins University Press, 1981), p. 194.

7 See Block, "The Ruling Class Does Not Rule." For further elaboration of his ideas, see

151

Block, "Beyond Corporate Liberalism," *Social Problems* 24, no. 3 (February 1977): 352–61, "Class Consciousness and Capitalist Rationalization: A Reply to Critics," *Socialist Review*, nos. 40–41 (July–October 1978): 212–20, "Beyond Relative Autonomy: State Managers as Historical Subjects," *New Political Science* 2, no. 7 (Fall 1981): 33–49. Nicos Poulantzas linked the relative autonomy of the state to the fractionalization of the bourgeoisie in a number of his works: *Political Power and Social Classes*, trans. Timothy O'Hagan (London: New Left Books, 1973), *Fascism and Dictatorship* trans. Timothy O'Hagan (London: New Left Books, 1975), *Classes in Contemporary Capitalism*, trans. David Fernbach (London: New Left Books, 1975). For David Vogel's argument, see "Why Businessmen Distrust Their State: The Political Consciousness of American Corporate Executives," *British Journal of Political Science* 8, no. 1 (January 1978): 169–73.

8 Charles Lindblom, "The Market as Prison," in *The Political Economy: Readings in the Politics and Economics of American Public Policy*, ed. Thomas Ferguson and Joel Rogers (Armonk, N.Y.: M. E. Sharpe, 1984), p. 4. For Lindblom's argument on the "privileged position" of business in capitalist economies, see *Politics and Market: The World's Political-Economic Systems* (New York: Basic Books, 1977), pp. 170–200.

9 In relation to peasants, James Scott defines the concept of moral economy as "their notion of economic justice . . . their view of which claims on their product were tolerable and which intolerable." See *The Moral Economy of the Peasant: Rebellion and Subsistence in Southeast Asia* (New Haven, Conn.: Yale University Press, 1976), p. 3.

10 John M. Merriman, "Introduction," in *Consciousness and Class Experience in Nineteenth Century Europe*, ed. John Merriman (New York: Holmes & Meier, 1979), p. 8.

11 Goran Therborn poses a similar sounding question regarding the relationship between the state and "ruling classes." See *What Does the Ruling Class Do When It Rules?* (London: New Left Books, 1978).

12 For a discussion of these "situations of dependency" and the distinction between enclave and national economies, see Fernando Henrique Cardoso and Enzo Faletto, *Dependency and Development in Latin America*, trans. Marjory Mattingly Urquidi (Berkeley and Los Angeles: University of California Press, 1979), pp. 66–73.

13 In his reflections on European industrialization, Alexander Gerschenkron emphasized the importance of the timing of the process and how that affected the employment of technology and the role of the state. See his *Economic Backwardness in Historical Perspective* (Cambridge, Mass.: Harvard University Press, 1962), pp. 5–30.

14 The distinctions between the "early" populism practiced by middle-class reformers and the later "classic" populist movements that espoused more explicit economic development goals is made by Michael Conniff, "Introduction: Toward a Comparative Definition of Populism," in *Latin American Populism in Comparative Perspective*, ed. Michael Conniff (Albuquerque: University of New Mexico Press, 1987), p. 7.

1. Industrialists and Reform in Comparative Perspective

1 The most colorful denunciations of the Latin American bourgeoisie can be found in the work of André Gunder Frank. See *Lumpenbourgeoisie: Lumpendevelopment, Depen-*

dence, Class, and Politics in Latin America (New York: Monthly Review Press, 1972).

2 See the discussion of the English case by Christopher Hill, "A Bourgeois Revolution?" in *Three British Revolutions: 1641, 1688, 1776,* ed. J.G.A. Pocock (Princeton, N.J.: Princeton University Press, 1980), pp. 109–39. For the classic argument on the reactionary consequences of certain types of upper-class alliances, see Barrington Moore, Jr., *Social Origins of Dictatorship and Democracy: Lord and Peasant in the Making of the Modern World* (Boston: Beacon Press, 1966), pp. 433–452.

3 Joseph Schumpeter, *Imperialism and Social Classes,* trans. Heinz Norden (New York: Augustus M. Kelley, 1951), p. 220.

4 Guillermo O'Donnell, "Notas para el estudio de la burgesía local, con especial referencia a sus vinculaciones con el capital transnacional y el aparato estatal," *Estudios Sociales,* no. 12 (July 1978).

5 Warren Dean, *The Industrialization of São Paulo, 1880–1945* (Austin: University of Texas Press, 1969), pp. 65–80; Joseph Love, *São Paulo in the Brazilian Federation, 1887–1937* (Stanford, Calif.: Stanford University Press, 1980), pp. 53–61; Henry Kirsch, *Industrial Development in a Traditional Society: The Conflict of Entrepreneurship and Modernization in Chile* (Gainesville: University Presses of Florida, 1977), pp. 64–95.

6 Maurice Zeitlin and Richard Ratcliff, "Research Methods for the Analysis of the Internal Structure of Dominant Classes: The Case of Landlords and Capitalists in Chile," *Latin American Research Review* 10, no. 3 (Fall 1975): 5–62.

7 Miguel Murmis and Juan Carlos Portantiero, "Crecimiento industrial y alianza de clases en la Argentina 1930–1940," in *Estudios sobre los origenes del Peronismo,* ed. Miguel Murmis (Buenos Aires: Siglo Veintiuno, 1972), pp. 11–12.

8 Raúl Jacob describes the tensions between industrial and agricultural capital in *Breve historia de la industria en Uruguay* (Montevideo: Fundación de Cultura Universitaria, n.d.), pp. 124–29. For a discussion of the role of immigrants in the industrialization process, see José Barran and Benjamín Nahum, *Batlle, los estancieros, y el imperio británico,* Tomo I: *El Urugay del novecientos* (Montevideo: Ediciones de la Banda Oriental), pp. 93–100.

9 For further discussion of the divisions among economic elites in Argentina, see José Luiz de Imaz, *Los que mandan (Those Who Rule),* trans. Carlos A. Astiz (Albany: State University of New York Press, 1970); Eugene Guiness Sharkey, "Unión Industrial Argentina 1887–1920: Problems of Industrial Development," Ph.D. diss., Rutgers University, 1977.

10 Florestan Ferandes, *Reflections on the Brazilian Counter-Revolution: Essays by Florestan Fernandes,* trans. Michael Vale, ed. Warren Dean (Armonk, N.Y.: M.E. Sharpe, 1981), p. 66.

11 Peter Evans, *Dependent Development: The Alliance of Multinational, State and Local Capital in Brazil* (Princeton, N.J.: Princeton University Press, 1979). The transformation of the local bourgeoisie through their new associations with multinationals has also been suggested by other writers. See Osvaldo Sunkel, "Transnational Capitalism and National Disintegration in Latin America," *Social and Economic Studies* 22, no. 1

(March 1973): 132–76. Also see Luciano Martins, "The Politics of U.S. Multinational Corporations," in *Latin America and the United States: The Changing Political Realities,* ed. Julio Cotler and Richard Fagen (Stanford, Calif.: Stanford University Press, 1974).

12   Guillermo O'Donnell first formulated the argument in *Modernization and Bureaucratic-Authoritarianism: Studies in South American Politics* (Berkeley and Los Angeles: University of California Press, 1973). For a later elaboration, see "Reflections on the Patterns of Change in the Bureaucratic-Authoritarian State," *Latin American Research Review* 12, no. 1 (Winter 1978): 3–38. O'Donnell's analysis of the Argentine case is *1966–1973 El estado burocrático autoritario* (Buenos Aires: Editorial de Belgrano, 1983). Cardoso and Faletto make a similar argument in *Dependency and Development,* pp. 149–71.

13   For a discussion of similar strains in American business ideology, see James Prothro, *Dollar Decade: Business Ideas in the 1920s* (Baton Rouge: Louisiana State University Press, 1954); Francis Sutton et al., *The American Business Creed* (New York: Schocken Books, 1956); Robert Heilbroner, "The View from the Top: Reflections on a Changing Business Ideology," in *The Business Establishment,* ed. Frank Cheit (New York: Wiley, 1964); Theodore leavitt, "Why Business Always Loses," *Harvard Business Review* 46, no. 2 (March–April 1968): 81–89.

14   This discussion of populism is informed by a number of important works on the subject. For a analysis of the key characteristics of populism see James M. Malloy, "Authoritarianism and Corporatism in Latin America: The Modal Pattern," in *Authoritarianism and Corporatism in Latin America,* ed. James M. Malloy (Pittsburgh: University of Pittsburgh Press, 1977), pp. 3–22; Gino Germani, *Authoritarianism, Fascism and National Populism* (New Brunswick, N.J.: Transaction Books, 1978); Octavio Ianni, *La formación del estado populista* (Mexico City: Ediciones ERA, 1975); Paul Drake, "Conclusion: Requiem for Populism?" in *Latin American Populism in Comparative Perspective,* ed. Michael L. Conniff (Albuquerque: University of New Mexico Press, 1982), pp. 217–246.

15   For an overview of economic development in the period, see Carlos F. Díaz-Alejandro, "Latin America in the 1930s," in *Latin America in the 1930s: The Role of the Periphery in World Crisis,* ed. Rosemary Thorp (London: Macmillan, 1984), pp. 17–49. In the same volume, see Gabriel Palma, "From Export-led to an Import-substituting Economy: Chile 1914–1939," pp. 50–80. More detailed data on the industrialization process can be found in Carlos F. Díaz-Alejandro, *Essays on the Economic History of the Argentine Republic* (New Haven, Conn.: Yale University Press, 1970); Markos Mamalakis and Clark Winton Reynolds, *Essays on the Chilean Economy* (Homewood, Ill.: Richard D. Irwin, 1965); Oscar Muñoz, *Crecimiento industrial de Chile: 1914–1965* (Santiago: Insituto de Economia, 1968). For an overview of industrialization in Latin America, see Frederick Stirton Weaver, *Class, State, and Industrial Structure: The Historical Process of South American Industrial Growth* (Westport, Conn.: Greenwood Press, 1980).

16   This interpretation of populism as a multiclass alliance is a theme in numerous country case studies of the phenomenon. In addition to the works already cited, see Juan Corradi, "Argentina," in *Latin America: The Struggle with Dependency and Beyond* (Cambridge, Mass.: Schenkman, 1974), pp. 356–57; Mónica Peralta Ramos, *Etapas de*

acumulación y alianzas de clases en la Argentina, 1930–1970 (Buenos Aires: Siglo Veintiuno, 1972).

17   Martin Weinstein, *Uruguay: The Politics of Failure* (Westport, Conn.: Greenwood Press, 1975), p. 80.

18   M.J.H. Finch, *A Political Economy of Uruguay Since 1870* (New York: St. Martin's Press, 1981), p. 176.

19   Eldon Kenworthy, "The Formation of the Peronist Coalition," Ph.D. diss., Yale University, 1970, p. 184.

20   Judith Teichman, "Interest Conflict and Entrepreneurial Support for Perón," *Latin American Research Review* 16, no. 1 (1981): 144–55.

21   William Ascher, *Scheming for the Poor: The Politics of Redistribution in Latin America* (Cambridge, Mass.: Harvard University Press, 1984), p. 57.

22   Dardo Cúneo, *Comportamiento y crisis de la clase empresaria* (Buenos Aires: Editorial Pleamar, 1967).

23   David Rock, "The Survival and Restoration of Peronism," in *Argentina in the Twentieth Century*, ed. David Rock (Pittsburgh, Pa.: University of Pittsburgh Press, 1975), p. 189.

24   Raúl Jacob, *Breve historia*, p. 121.

25   Marcello Carmagnani, *Estado y sociedad en América Latina 1850–1930* (Barcelona: Editorial Critica, 1984), pp. 226–52.

26   David Rock, *Politics in Argentina 1890–1930: The Rise and Fall of Radicalism* (Cambridge: Cambridge University Press, 1975), pp. 214–17.

27   For a discussion of the development of the left in Chile, see Paul Drake, *Socialism and Populism in Chile, 1932–1952* (Urbana: University of Illinois Press, 1978). For a discussion of the polarization in the Chilean party system, see Arturo Valenzuela, *The Breakdown of Democratic Regimes: Chile* (Baltimore, Md.: Johns Hopkins University Press, 1978).

28   José P. Barran and Benjamín Nahum, *El Nacimiento del Batllismo*, vol. 3 of *Batlle, Los estancieros y el imperio británico* (Montevideo: Ediciones de la Banda Oriental, 1982), pp. 62–83.

29   Paul Drake, "The Political Response of the Chilean Upper Class to the Great Depression and the Threat of Socialism," in *The Rich, the Well Born and the Powerful: Elites and Upper Classes in History*, ed. Frederic Cople Jaher (Urbana: University of Illinois Press, 1973), pp. 304–37. In his study of the Sociedad Nacional de Agricultura in Chile, Thomas Wright also points to the cooptive and conciliatory political strategies sometimes employed by the organization. See *Landowners and Reform in Chile: The Sociedad Nacional de Agricultura 1919–1940* (Urbana: University of Illinois Press, 1982).

30   Rock, *Politics in Argentina*, p. 266; Carmagnani, *Estado*, p. 251.

31   The notion of "reactive participation" is taken from Cesar Guimarães, "Businessmen, Types of Capitalism and Political Order," delivered at the annual meeting of the International Political Science Association, Edinburgh, Scotland, August, 1976.

32   Fernando Henrique Cardoso, *Ideologías de la burguesía industrial en sociedades dependientes (Argentina y Brasil)* (Mexico City: Siglo Veintiuno, 1971), p. 17.

33 Guillermo O'Donnell, "Estado y alianzas en la Argentina 1956–1976" (Documento CEDES/G. E. CLACSO/5/Buenos Aires, 1976), 31–32.

34 Marcelo Cavarozzi, "The Government and the Industrial Bourgeoisie in Chile: 1938–1964," Ph.D. diss., University of California, Berkeley, 1975, p. 162.

35 Rock, "The Survival," p. 191.

36 The works cited above by Cardoso, O'Donnell, and Cavarozzi contain these arguments. Also see Luciano Martins, *Industrialização, burgesia nacional e desenvolvimento* (Rio de Janeiro: Editora Saga, 1968); Vilmar Faria, "Desenvolvimento e hegemonia burgesa," *Boletín de ELAS* 1, no. 2 (1968): 23–45; and "Dépendance et ídeologie des dirigeants industriels brésiliens," *Sociologie du Travail* no. 3 (July–September 1971): 264–81.

37 For important empirical critiques of the O'Donnell argument, see José Serra, "Three Mistaken Theses Regarding Connections Between Industrialization and Authoritarian Regimes," in *The New Authoritariansim in Latin America*, ed. David Collier (Princeton, N.J.: Princeton University Press, 1979), pp. 99–164; and in the same volume see Robert R. Kaufman, "Industrial Change and Authoritarian Rule in Latin America: A Concrete Review of the Bureaucratic-Authoritarian Model," pp. 165–254. For a critique of the functionalist thrust of O'Donnell's argument, see Michael Wallerstein, "The Collapse of Democracy In Brazil: Its Economic Determinants," *Latin American Research Review* 15, no. 3 (1980): 3–40. See also Karen L. Remmer and Gilbert W. Merkx, "Bureaucratic-Authoritarianism Revisited," *Latin American Research Review* 17, no. 2 (1982): 3–40.

2 The Making of the Industrial Bourgeoisie

1 For biographies of these two entrepeneurs, see José de Souza Martins, *Conde Matarazzo, O empresário e a empresa* (São Paulo: HUCITEC, 1976); Thomas C. Cochran and Ruben E. Reina, *Capitalism in Argentine Culture: A Study of Torcuato di Tella and S.I.A.M.* (Philadelphia: University of Pennsylvania Press, 1962).

2 Luis Noboa has kept a very low public profile; as a result, there is very little written concerning his career. One of the few written accounts is "Luis Noboa: Perfil del hombre más rico del país," *Vistazo*, 16 February 1979. My observations on the development of the Noboa group enterprises are taken from discussions with managers in the Noboa group firms and other individuals with ties to the Noboa family.

3 Alexander Gerschenkron, *Economic Backwardness in Historical Perspective* (Cambridge, Mass.: Harvard University Press, 1962), pp. 5–30.

4 Much has been written on the hacienda as the pivotal institution of the sierra. See Andrés Guerrero, *La hacienda precapitalista y la clase terrateniente en América Latina y su inserción en el modo de producción capitalista: El caso ecuatoriano* (Quito: Escuela de Sociología, 1975). For a further analysis of traditional agricultural organization, see Jaime Galarza, *El yugo feudal* (Quito: Ediciones Solitierra, 1973). For a modern novelist's portrayal of a traditional hacienda see Jorge Icaza, *Huasipungo (The Villagers: A Novel)*, trans. Bernard M. Dulsey (Carbondale: Southern Illinois University Press, 1964).

5 For a detailed description of the cacao boom, see Louis Weinman Johnson, "Ecuador

and Cacao: Domestic Responses to the Boom-Collapse Mono-export Cycle," Ph.D. diss., University of California, Los Angeles, 1970; Andrés Guerrero, *Los Oligarcas del cacao* (Quito: Editorial El Conejo, 1980); Manuel Chiriboga, "Emergencia y consolidación de la burgesía agro-exportadora en el Ecuador," *Revista Ciencias Sociales* 3, nos. 10–11 (1979): 35–45.

6 Mario Rosales, "Crecimiento económico, urbanización, y pobreza," in *Ecuador: El mito del desarrollo,* ed. Alberto Acosta et al. (Quito: Editorial El Conejo, 1982), p. 133.

7 Rafael Guerrero, "La formación del capital industrial en la provincia del Guayas, 1900–1925," *Revista Ciencias Sociales* 3, nos. 10–11 (1979): 62–64.

8 Weinman Johnson, "Ecuador and Cacao," p. 76.

9 The first systematic analysis of the Ecuadorean economy was undertaken by the United Nations Economic Commission for Latin America (ECLA). In its 1953 study, the commission noted the "rigorous parallelism" with which local investments in industry adjusted to the curve of exports. See Comisión Económica para América Latina, *El desarrollo económico del Ecuador* (Mexico: CEPAL, 1954), p. 142.

10 Galo Plaza described the meeting in his book, *Problems of Democracy in Latin America* (Chapel Hill: University of North Carolina Press, 1955), p. 59. Plaza later went on to praise the contributions of the United Fruit Company in a subsequent book. See Stacy May and Galo Plaza, *The United Fruit Company in Latin America* (Washington, D.C.: National Planning Association, 1958). For a further discussion of the Ecuadorean banana trade, see J. F. Sandoval-Moreano, "Commodities, International Trade and Dependent Economic Growth," M. Phil. diss., University of Sussex, 1977; and Jaime Cueva Silva, *Comercialización del banano ecuatoriano* (Quito: AECA, 1964).

11 CEPAL. *El desarrollo económico,* pp. 168–69. The sucre is the monetary unit of Ecuador, hereafter designated by S/.

12 Charles B. Gibson, "The Role of Foreign Trade in Ecuadorian Development," Ph.D. diss., University of Pennsylvania, 1968, p. 406.

13 James J. Parsons, "Bananas in Ecuador: A New Chapter in the History of Tropical Agriculture," *Economic Geography* 33, no. 3 (July 1957): 201.

14 For a discussion of the organization of banana production see Junta Nacional de Planificación Económica (JUNAPLA), *Programa nacional del banano* (Quito: JUNAPLA, n.d.), pp. 35–56.

15 Ibid., pp. 33–34.

16 William Black (general manager, Molinos del Ecuador), interview, Guayaquil, 6 March 1980. See the appendix for details about my interview procedure.

17 CEPAL, *El desarrollo económico,* 115. Jaime Nebot Velasco (minister of the economy, 1953–1954), interview, Guayaquil, 8 March 1980.

18 Ricardo Muñoz, (president, Compañía Ecuatoriana de Caucho), interview, Quito, 15 August 1980; Robert Crosley (Compañía Ecuatoriana de Caucho), interview, Quito, 20 August 1980.

19 For a discussion of the role of landowners in this agricultural modernization, see the definitive work on agrarian reform, Osvaldo Barsky, *La reforma agraria ecuatoriana* (Quito: Corporación Editora Nacional, 1984), pp. 55–167. For analyses that emphasize

the role of class conflict in the process, see Fernando Velasco, *Reforma agraria y movimiento campesino indígena de la sierra* (Quito: Editorial El Conejo, 1979); and Andrés Guerrero, *Haciendas, capital y lucha de clases andinas* (Quito: Editorial El Conejo, 1983).

20 This figure is taken from Fabio Villalobos et al., *Ecuador: Situación y perspectivas de la agroindustria* (Quito: CEPLAES, 1978), p. 22.

21 Jorge Salcedo (president, Solubles Instántaneos, C.A.), interview, Guayaquil, 6 March 1980.

22 For a review of the literature on the development and operation of "economic groups" in developing countries, see Nathaniel H. Leff, "Industrial Organization and Entrepreneurship in Developing Countries: The Economic Groups," *Economic Development and Cultural Change* 26, no. 4 (July 1978): 661–75. For a fascinating study of economic groups in prerevolutionary Nicaragua, see Harry Strachan, *The Role of Family and Other Groups in Economic Development: The Case of Nicaragua* (New York: Praeger, 1976).

23 For a further discussion of the July Revolution of 1925, see Oswaldo Albornoz, *Del crimen de El Ejido a la revolución del 9 del julio de 1925* (Guayaquil: Editorial Claridad, 1969), pp. 139–57; Luis Robalino Davila, *El 9 de julio de 1925* (Quito: Editorial "La Unica," 1973); Linda Alexander Rodríguez, *The Search for Public Policy: Regional Politics and Government Finances in Ecuador, 1830–1940* (Berkeley and Los Angeles: University of California Press, 1985), pp. 126–62.

24 Germánico Salgado, "Lo que fuimos and lo que somos," in Gerhard Drekonja et al., *Ecuador Hoy* (Colombia: Siglo Veintiuno, 1978), p. 40.

25 This reference to the 1948–1961 period as a "democratic parenthesis" comes from Agustín Cueva, *El proceso de dominación política en el Ecuador* (Quito: Ediciones Solitierra, 1973), p. 53.

26 For further discussion of the development of JUNAPLA, see José Moncada Sánchez, *La evolución de la planificación en el Ecuador* (Quito: JUNAPLA, 1964); R. J. Bromley, *Development and Planning in Ecuador* (Sussex: Latin American Publications Fund, 1977); Clarence Zuvekas, "Economic Planning in Ecuador: An Evaluation," *Inter-American Economic Affairs* 25, no. 4 (Spring 1972): 3–69.

27 This is the previously cited ECLA (CEPAL) study, *El desarrollo económico*.

28 The contribution by ECLA technocrats in the formulation of the first plan is acknowledged in the document itself. See JUNAPLA, *Bases y directivas para programar el desarrollo económico del Ecuador* (Quito: JUNAPLA, 1958), pp. 11–12.

29 Ibid., p. 29.

30 David Parker Hanson, "Political Decision-Making in Ecuador: The Influence of Business Groups," Ph.D. diss., University of Florida, 1971, p. 325.

31 JUNAPLA, *Evolución histórica del comercio exterior ecuatoriano, 1950–1970* (Quito: JUNAPLA, 1975), pp. 8–9.

32 Hernan A. Aulestia and Nilo Idrobo, "La inversión extranjera en el Ecuador," thesis, Facultad de Ciencias Económicas, Universidad Central del Ecuador, Quito, 1979, p. 220.

33 The list of firms was compiled from interviews and written sources: Juvenal Angel,

Dictionary of American Firms Operating in Foreign Countries, Encyclopedia of International Information, vol. 2 (New York: Simon & Schuster, 1975), pp. 737–47; "U.S. Firms and Businessmen," photocopy, U.S. Embassy, Quito, April 1978.

34 My survey is explained in the appendix on methods and field research. Guillermo Navarro Jiménez, in an earlier study based on data from the Superintendencia de Compañías, also pointed to the presence of *grupos económicos* with greatly diversified portfolios; see *La concentración de capitales en el Ecuador* (Quito: Universidad Central, 1975).

35 Figures are taken from Galo Montaño and Eduardo Wygard, *Visión sobre la industria ecuatoriana* (Quito: COFIEC, 1975), pp. 215, 218, 221.

36 Reinaldo Torres Caicedo, *Los estratos socioeconómicos del Ecuador: Ensayos de cuantificación,* photocopy, JUNAPLA, Quito, 1960, pp. 28–31.

37 ECIEL refers to the Program of Joint Studies on Latin American Economic Integration. Under the coordination of the Brookings Institution, ECIEL undertook a six-nation study of consumption patterns in Latin America in the late 1960s. The results of this study are analyzed in Philip Musgrove, *Consumer Behavior in Latin America: Income and Spending in Ten Andean Cities* (Washington, D.C.: Brookings, 1978). For the figures on Ecuador, see pp. 310–11.

38 James Wilkie and Stephen Haber, eds., *Statistical Abstract of Latin America,* vol. 21 (Los Angeles: UCLA Latin American Center Publications, 1981), p. 312. For further discussion of the transformation of the state's role in the economy during the 1970s, see Arnaldo M. Bocco, "Políticas estatales y ciclo económico," in *Economía política del Ecuador: Campo, región, nación,* ed. Louis Lefeber (Quito: Corporación Editora Nacional, 1985): pp. 369–404.

39 For an excellent discussion on the evolution of public expenditures, see David Schodt, "Indicators of Budgetary Policy under Military and Civilian Governments during the Petroleum Period: Ecuador 1972–1984," delivered at the Latin American Studies Association meeting, Albuquerque, N.M., April 1985, pp. 25–33.

40 World Bank, *Ecuador: Development Problems and Prospects* (Washington, D.C.: World Bank, 1979), p. 642.

41 Ibid., pp. 2–3.

42 Ibid., p. 360.

43 Important work on the growth of the informal sector of the Ecuadorean economy has been done by Gilda Farrell. See "Los microcomerciantes del sector informal urbano: Los casos de Quito y Guayaquil," in *El Sector informal urbano en los países andinos,* ed. Daniel Carbonetto et al. (Quito: ILDIS, CEPESIU, 1985), pp. 139–78; and "Migración temporal y articulación al mercado urbano de trabajo," in *Economía política del Ecuador,* pp. 179–96. Also see the excellent study dealing with the participation of formal-sector workers in the informal economy by Juan Pablo Pérez Saínz, *Entre la fábrica y la ciudad* (Quito: Editorial El Conejo, 1985).

44 World Bank, *Ecuador: Development,* p. 14. The figures on income are taken from Junta Nacional de Planificación y Coordinación Económica, *Indicadores socio-económicos* (Quito: JUNAPLA, April 1978), p. 67.

45 *Business Latin America*, 12 December 1973, pp. 411–13. *Business Latin America*, 19 December 1979, pp. 403–05.

46 World Bank, *Ecuador*, p. 19.

47 Roelf Smit, "El mercado de frutas y hortalizas y sus perspectivas para la producción ecuatoriana," photocopy, Ministerio de Agricultura y Ganadería, Proyecto PNUD/ FAO-ECU/72/018 Agroindustrias, Quito, November 1977.

48 The notion of "industrial development in breadth" in contrast to "industrial development in depth" is developed in Economic Commission for Latin America, *The Process of Industrial Development in Latin America* (New York: United Nations, 1966), p. 31.

49 For a critique of Ecuador's Andean Pact assignments, see José Moncada Sánchez, *Integración andina y desarrollo económico: El caso ecuatoriano* (Caracas: ILDIS, 1975).

50 Aulestia and Idrobo, "La inversión extranjera," p. 220.

51 This figure was obtained from information provided by the Junta Nacional de Planificación, Quito, 1979.

52 For a discussion of how the Industrial Development Law has encouraged the development of capital-intensive industries, see Manuel R. Agosín, "Analysis of Ecuador's Industrial Development Law," *Journal of Developing Areas* 13, no. 3 (April 1979): 273. Also see Jorge Fernández, "Un decenio de industrialización en el Ecuador: Un balance crítico" in *El proceso de industrialización ecuatoriano*, ed. Cristian Sepúlveda (Quito: Pontificia Universidad Católica del Ecuador, 1983), pp. 87–88.

53 Figures are taken from Instituto de Investigaciones Económicas y Políticas, *El capitalismo ecuatoriano contemporáneo: Su funcionamiento* (Guayaquil: Facultad de Ciencias Económicas, Universidad de Guayaquil, n.d.), p. 140.

54 World Bank, *Ecuador*, p. 228.

55 For a discussion of how capitalists collect "collusive quasi-rents" through the state, see Guido di Tella, "Rents, Quasi-Rents, Normal Profits and Growth: Argentina and the Areas of Recent Settlement," in *Argentina, Australia, and Canada: Studies in Comparative Development, 1870–1965*, ed. D.C.M. Platt and Guido di Tella (London: Macmillan 1985), pp. 37–53.

56 Fondo de Promoción de Exportaciones (FOPEX), "Comercialización interna y externa del cacao y semi-elaborados de cacao," photocopy, Información Técnica, Serie: Perfiles por Productos, no. 1, Quito, November 1978, p. 42.

57 For a further discussion of the development of the semi-elaborates industry, see the following issues of Walter Spurrier's *Weekly Analysis of Ecuadorean Issues:* "Cacao: A Budding Industry, A Declining Crop," 15 October 1976; "Cacao Industry: Good Times," 2 September 1977; "Policy Changes May Affect Cacao Industry," 21 September 1979. Also see Asociación Ecuatoriana de Industrias del Cacao, "La industria de elaborados de cacao," photocopy, Guayaquil, 1979; "Ecuadorean Cocoa Industry," in *The Manufacturing Confectioner* (May 1977); "Ecuador's Cocoa Processors Reach for New Levels of Quality Control," *Candy and Snack Industry* (June 1979): 41–47.

58 These figures were provided by the Corporación Financiera Nacional, Quito, 1979.

59   The Salcedo group enterprises led the struggle for the protection of the cacao industry. Guillermo Arosemena, general manager of Salco, S.A., published this defense of the industry in *El Comercio*, 14 March 1972.

60   Figures taken from "Grupo Salcedo/Salcedo Group," promotional pamphlet distributed by Salcedo group firms, Guayaquil, 1979).

61   Figures based on information provided by the Superintendencia de Compañías, Quito, 1979.

62   Junta Nacional de Planificación, *Ecuador: Estrategia de desarrollo (Lineamientos)* (Quito: JUNAPLA, 1979).

63   Henry Kirsch, *Industrial Development in a Traditional Society: The Conflict of Entrepreneurship and Modernization in Chile* (Gainesville: University Presses of Florida, 1977), pp. 64–95.

64   For a detailed examination of the behavior of multinational corporations in Latin America, see Mira Wilkins, *The Maturing of Multinational Enterprise: American Business Abroad from 1914 to 1970* (Cambridge, Mass.: Harvard University Press, 1974).

65   Jorge Fernández, "Un decenio de industrialización," p. 103.

66   Carlos F. Díaz-Alejandro, "Latin America in the 1930s," in *Latin America in the 1930s: The Role of the Periphery in World Crisis*, ed. Rosemary Thorp (London: Macmillan, 1984), p. 42.

67   David Rock, *Politics in Argentina 1890–1930: The Rise and Fall of Radicalism* (Cambridge: Cambridge University Press, 1975), p. 10; M.J.H. Finch, *A Political Economy of Uruguay Since 1870* (New York: St. Martin's Press, 1981), p. 29.

68   These factors are discussed in Brian Loveman, *Chile: The Legacy of Hispanic Capitalism* (New York: Oxford University Press, 1979), pp. 150–212.

69   Paul Drake, *Socialism and Populism in Chile, 1932–52* (Urbana: University of Illinois Press, 1978), p. 21.

3 The Conservative Class: Ideology, Alliances, and State Power

1   The conservative character of the industrial elite was confirmed in the early empirical studies of the topic done by the United Nations Economic Commission for Latin America. See Guillermo Briones, *El empresario industrial en América Latina: Chile* (Santiago: Comisión Económica para América Latina, 1963); Eduardo Zalduendo, *El empresario industrial en América Latina: Argentina* (Santiago: Comisión Económica para América Latina, 1963). For country studies, see Albert Lauterbach, *Enterprise in Latin America* (Ithaca, N.Y.: Cornell University Press, 1966); Dale Johnson, "Industry and Industrialists in Chile," Ph.D. diss., Stanford University, 1967; Aaron Lipman, *The Colombian Entrepreneur in Bogota* (Coral Gables, Fla.: University of Miami Press, 1969); Flavia DeRossi, *The Mexican Entrepreneur* (Paris: OECD, 1971); Frits Wils, *Industrialization, Industrialists and the Nation-State in Peru* (Berkeley and Los Angeles: University of California Press, 1977). Many of my observations about the ideological posture of the industrial bourgeoisie in Ecuador are similar to the conclusions drawn by

Renato Boschi in his study of Brazilian industrialists; see "National Industrial Elites and the State in Post-1964 Brazil: Institutional Mediations and Political Change," Ph.D. diss., University of Michigan, 1978.

2   For a complete discussion of the survey sample and methods employed, see the appendix.

3   The separation of ownership and control in advanced capitalist countries has raised serious controversies concerning the identity of the capitalist classes and the class identity of managers. For an excellent discussion of these issues, see Maurice Zeitlin, "Corporate Ownership and Control: The Large Corporation and the Capitalist Class," *American Journal of Sociology* 79, no. 5 (March 1974): 1073–1119. Also see Erik O. Wright, *Class, Crisis and the State* (London: New Left Books, 1978), pp. 59–96.

4   G. William Domhoff argues that the social cohesion created by elite social clubs is an important vehicle for creating "policy cohesion" within a bourgeoisie; see "Social Clubs, Policy-Planning Groups and Corporations," *Insurgent Sociologist* 5, no. 3 (Spring 1975): 173–95, and *The Bohemian Grove and Other Retreats* (New York: Harper and Row, 1974).

5   Guillermo O'Donnell, *Modernization and Bureaucratic-Authoritarianism: Studies in South American Politics* (Berkeley and Los Angeles: University of California Press, 1973), p. 81.

6   The notion of productivism as an ideological position is taken from Roland Sarti's study of the industrial bourgeoisie of Italy: *Fascism and Industrial Leadership in Italy, 1919–1940* (Berkeley and Los Angeles: University of California Press, 1971), pp. 22–23.

7   The idea that ideological commitments to abstract principles tend to break down when abstractions are translated into concrete policy proposals was first elaborated in the classic article by James W. Prothro and Charles M. Griggs, "Fundamental Principles of Democracy: Bases of Agreement and Disagreement," *Journal of Politics* 22, no. 2 (May 1960): 276–94. Also on this point see Herbert McClosky, "Consensus and Ideology in American Politics," *American Political Science Review* 58, no. 2 (June 1964): 361–82.

8   Eric Hobsbawm has referred to this phenomenon as the "blind alley class consciousness" of the bourgeoisie—its tendency to cling to classical liberal economic thought even though its principles are increasingly irrelevant to the running of modern capitalist economies; see "Notes on Class Consciousness," in *Workers: Worlds of Labor* (New York: Pantheon Books, 1985), pp. 13–32.

9   Frits Wils, *Industrialization, Industrialists*, p. 161.

10 Fernando Henrique Cardoso, *Ideologías de la burgesía industrial en sociedades dependientes (Argentina y Brasil)* (Mexico: Siglo Veintiuno, 1971); Luciano Martins, *Industrialização, burgesia nacional e desenvolvimento* (Rio de Janeiro: Editora Saga, 1968); Vilmar Faria, "Desenvolvimento economico e hegemonia burgesa," *Boletin de ELAS* 1, no. 2 (1968): 23–45; and "Dépendance et idéologie des dirigeants industriels brésiliens," *Sociologie du Travail*, no. 3 (July–September 1971): 264–81.

11 Cardoso, *Ideologías*, 188–214.

12 Warren Dean, *The Industrialization of São Paulo, 1880–1945* (Austin: University of Texas Press, 1969), p. 180.

13 Eldon Kenworthy, "The Formation of the Peronist Coalition," Ph.D. diss., Yale University, 1970, pp. 180.

14 Gabriel Kolko, *The Triumph of Conservatism: A Reinterpretation of American History 1900–1916* (New York: Free Press of Glencoe, 1963); James Weinstein, *The Corporate Ideal in the Liberal State* (Boston: Beacon Press, 1968).

15 The classic statement of the genre is, of course, found in C. Wright Mills, *The Power Elite* (New York: Oxford University Press, 1956). The position has been echoed in the work of G. William Domhoff, *The Higher Circles: The Governing Class in America* (New York: Random House, 1970).

16 Fred Block, "The Ruling Class Does Not Rule," *Socialist Revolution*, no. 33 (May–June 1977): 6–28.

17 David Vogel, "Why Businessmen Distrust Their State: The Political Consciousness of American Corporate Executives," *British Journal of Political Science* 8, no. 1 (January 1978): 169–73.

18 The idea of a "historic negativism" toward reform operating in the American business community is taken from Theodore Leavitt, "Why Business Always Loses," *Harvard Business Review* 46, no. 2 (March–April 1968): 81–89. The conservative character of American industrialists is the subject of much of the literature. See, for example, Edward Kirkland, *Dream and Thought in the Business Community* (Chicago: Quadrangle Books, 1956); James Prothro, *Dollar Decade: Business Ideas in the 1920s* (Baton Rouge: Louisiana State University Press, 1954); Robert McCloskey, *American Conservatism in the Age of Enterprise: 1865–1910* (New York: Harper & Row, 1951); Francis X. Sutton et al., *The American Business Creed* (New York: Schocken Books, 1956); Robert Heilbroner, "The View from the Top: Reflections on a Changing Business Ideology," in *The Business Establishment*, ed. Frank Cheit (New York: Wiley, 1964). For a more recent treatment of the subject, see Leonard Silk and David Vogel, *Ethics and Profits: The Crisis of Confidence in American Business* (New York: Simon & Schuster, 1976).

19 For an excellent discussion of the contradictions between accumulation and legitimation functions in advanced capitalism see James O'Connor, *The Fiscal Crisis of the State* (New York: St. Martin's Press, 1973).

20 Joseph Schumpeter, *Capitalism, Socialism and Democracy* (New York: Harper & Row, 1942), pp. 137–38.

21 Theda Skocpol, "Political Response to Capitalist Crisis: Neo-Marxist Theories of the State and the Case of the New Deal," *Politics and Society* 10, no. 2 (1980): 157–201.

22 Angela Maria de Castro Gomes, *Burgesia e trabalho: Política e legislação social no Brasil, 1917–1937* (Rio de Janeiro: Editora Campus, 1979), pp. 307–12; James M. Malloy, *The Politics of Social Security in Brazil* (Pittsburgh, Pa.: University of Pittsburgh Press, 1979). For a comprehensive comparative study of the evolution of social security in Latin America see Carmelo Meso-Lago, *Social Security in Latin America: Pressure Groups, Stratification, and Inequality* (Pittsburgh, Pa.: University of Pittsburgh Press, 1978).

23 Nora Hamilton, *The Limits of State Autonomy: Post-Revolutionary Mexico* (Princeton, N.J.: Princeton University Press, 1982), pp. 280–86.

4 Policy Wars: Industrialists versus the State, 1972–1975

1 See the interview with Noboa in *Vistazo*, 16 February 1979.

2 Ecuador was one of the fastest growing markets in Latin America during the 1970s. For a comparative look at market indicators for the region during the period, see *Business Latin America*, 12 December 1973, pp. 411–13 and 19 December 1979, pp. 403–05. For statistics on the growth of government expenditures in the same period, see James Wilkie and Stephen Haber, eds., *Statistical Abstract of Latin America*, vol. 21 (Los Angeles: UCLA Latin American Center Publications, University of California Press, 1981), p. 312.

3 John S. Fitch, *The Military Coup d'Etat as Political Process: Ecuador, 1948–1966* (Baltimore, Md.: Johns Hopkins University Press, 1977), p. 136.

4 For a discussion of the numerous scandals surrounding natural resource policy, see Jaime Galarza, *El festín del petróleo* (Quito: Ediciones Solitierra, 1972).

5 Fitch, *The Military Coup*, p. 181.

6 On the CFP and the development of the party system, see John Martz, "Populist Leadership and the Party Caudillo: Ecuador and the CFP," *Studies in Comparative International Development*, no. 3 (Fall 1983): 22–50; John D. Martz, *Ecuador: Conflicting Political Culture and the Quest for Progress* (Boston: Allyn & Bacon, 1972), pp. 108–45; Robert J. Alexander, *Political Parties of the Americas* (Westport, Conn.: Greenwood Press, 1982), pp. 374–83.

7 For a discussion of Velasco Ibarra's cabinet appointments see, David Parker Hanson, "Political Decision-Making in Ecuador: The Influence of Business Groups," Ph.D. diss., University of Florida, 1971, p. 325. For an analysis of his early links to dominant economic groups, see Rafael Quintero, *El mito del populismo en el Ecuador* (Quito: FLACSO, 1980). For a discussion of Velasco's political discourse, see George I. Blanksten, *Ecuador: Constitutions and Caudillos* (Berkeley and Los Angeles: University of California Press, 1951), pp. 42–51.

8 The July document was published by the Junta Nacional de Planificación, *Lineamientos fundamentales del Plan integral de transformación y desarrollo* (Quito: JUNAPLA, 1972). Also see *Plan integral de transformación y desarrollo 1973–1977: Resumen general* (Quito: JUNAPLA, 1972).

9 The contrasts between "state capitalist" and "national capitalist" models are developed at length by Helio Jaguaribe in *Political Development: A General Theory and a Latin American Case Study* (New York: Harper & Row, 1973), pp. 290–97, 513–27.

10 There is a voluminous literature on the Peruvian revolution. The basic policies of the Peruvian model are contained in the document by the Instituto Nacional de Planificación, *Plan nacional de desarrollo 1971–1975*, vol. 1: *Plan global* (Lima: Instituto Nacional de Planificación, 1971). For further discussions of the economic policies of the regime, see George Philip, *The Rise and Fall of the Peruvian Military Radicals 1968–*

1976 (London: Athlone Press, 1978); Alfred Stepan, *The State and Society: Peru in Comparative Perspective* (Princeton, N.J.: Princeton University Press, 1978); Abraham Lowenthal, ed., *The Peruvian Experiment: Continuity and Change Under Military Rule* (Princeton, N.J.: Princeton University Press, 1975); Abraham Lowenthal and Cynthia McClintock, eds., *The Peruvian Experiment Reconsidered* (Princeton, N.J.: Princeton University Press, 1983); Rosemary Thorp and Geoffrey Bertram, *Peru 1890–1977: Growth and Policy in an Open Economy* (New York: Columbia University Press, 1978).

11   Galo Salvador, "Planificación, desarrollo y sector industrial," *Planificación*, no. 7 (November 1976): 70–71. Similar views were expressed by Galo Montaño, who served as Ecuador's chief industrial planner at the Junta del Acuerdo de Cartagena 1970–1974. Montaño later served as minister of industry in the Poveda Burbano government. Interview, 16 July 1980, Quito.

12   Secretaría General de la Administración Pública, *Las empresas públicas en el desarrollo nacional* (Quito: Dirección Nacional de Personal, 1977), p. 22.

13   World Bank, *Ecuador: Development Problems and Prospects* (Washington, D.C.: World Bank, 1979), p. 483.

14   *Weekly Analysis of Ecuadorean Issues*, 16 February 1971.

15   Ibid., 27 April 1973.

16   *Latin American Weekly Reports*, 12 January 1973; *Weekly Analysis*, 5 January 1973.

17   The Chamber of Industry was created by an executive decree in 1936 and membership was mandatory. See Cámara de Industriales de Pichincha, *Regimen legal: Estatutos y reglamento* (Quito: Cámara de Industriales de Pichincha, 1981), pp. 7–11.

18   List of investments compiled from Comisíon de Valores y Corporación Financiera Nacional, *Memoria* (annual volumes from 1968 through 1974).

19   Investments by these agencies are discussed in Alan Middleton, "Proyecto: El gasto público y las migraciones internas en el Ecuador," photocopy, FLACSO-PISPAL, Quito, n.d.

20   Interview, Corporación Financiera Nacional, Quito, July 1977.

21   *El Comercio*, 5 May 1975. For further information on the creation of DINE, see *Weekly Analysis*, 14 September 1973.

22   *Weekly Analysis*, 13 April 1973.

23   *Weekly Analysis*, 14 September 1973.

24   León Febres-Cordero, "Guayaquil frente al futuro en el campo desarrollo industrial," in *Guayaquil frente al futuro*, ed. Banco de Guayaquil (Guayaquil: Banco de Guayaquil, 1973), p. 128.

25   Ernesto Jouvín Cisneros, "Guayaqil frente a los mercados comunes y la integración," in *Guayaquil frente*, p. 273.

26   *Ficha de información socio-política*, 12 October 1974.

27   *Ficha*, 13 November 1974.

28   *Weekly Analysis*, 24 January 1975.

29   Marco Antonio Guzmán, interview, 12 August 1980, Quito.

30   *Ficha*, 15 January 1975.

31   Ibid.

32   Ibid.

33   Lynn Mytelka, *Regional Development in a Global Economy* (New Haven, Conn.: Yale University Press, 1979), p. 34. For further discussion of the political processes surrounding the enactment of the code, see Frances Armstrong, "Political Components and Practical Effects of the Andean Foreign Investment Code," *Stanford Law Review* 27 (July 1975): 1597–1628.

34   *Weekly Analysis*, 18 May 1971; *El Comercio*, 16 June 1971.

35   *El Universo*, 17 July 1971.

36   *El Tiempo*, 23 July 1971.

37   *El Tiempo*, 24 December 1972.

38   *Weekly Analysis*, 25 January 1974.

39   *El Comercio*, 13 February 1974.

40   *El Comercio*, 31 August 1974.

41   *El Comercio*, 2 December 1974.

42   *El Comercio*, 31 December 1974 and 2 January 1975.

43   *El Comercio*, 9 January 1975.

44   *El Comercio*, 6 February 1975.

45   *Ficha*, 21 July 1975.

46   *Weekly Analysis*, 15 August 1975.

47   *Ficha*, 22 August 1975.

48   For the literature on changes in agricultural organization during the 1960s, see notes to chapter 2.

49   M. R. Redclift, *Agrarian Reform and Peasant Organization on the Ecuadorian Coast* (London: Althone Press, 1978), p. 33.

50   Ibid., pp. 94–120.

51   For figures on food production, see the statistical tables in Wilkie and Haber, *Statistical Abstract of Latin America*, vol. 21, p. 10.

52   Banco Central del Ecuador, *Boletín Anuario*, no. 2 (1979): 89.

53   World Bank, *Ecuador*, p. 389.

54   Ibid., p. 140.

55   Quoted in Jorge Hidrobo, "Acción política de las clases sociales y las políticas agraria e industrial, 1972–79," photocopy, Center for Latin American Studies, University of Pittsburgh, August 1981, p. 34.

56   Quoted in Victor Alvarado et al., "Los gobiernos, las leyes, y las cámaras de producción: 1970–1975," *Difusión Económica* 15, no. 1 (April 1977): 160.

57   For Maldonado's observations on the experience, see the interview in Jorge Silva Luvecce, *Nacionalismo y petróleo en el Ecuador actual* (Quito: Universidad Central del Ecuador, n.d.), pp. 89–104.

58   See speech by Febres-Codero cited above in *Guayaquil frente*, p. 130.

59   SINAMOS (Sistema Nacional de Apoyo a la Movilización Social) was founded by the Peruvian junta as an umbrella organization to act as a conduit for state-sponsored political participation. SINAMOS proved to be one of the most controversial and problematic institutional innovations attempted by the Peruvian military. It was dis-

mantled after 1975 under Morales Bermúdez. For a discussion of this attempt at the installation of a corporatist political structure, see Sandra L. Woy, "Infrastructure of Participation in Peru: SINAMOS" in *Political Participation in Latin America*, ed. John D. Booth and Mitchell Seligson (New York: Holmes & Meier, 1978), pp. 189–208.

60 Osvaldo Hurtado and Joachim Herudek, *La organización popular en el Ecuador* (Quito: IEDES, 1974), p. 89.

61 Amparo Menéndez-Carrión, "The 1952–1978 Presidential Elections and Guayaquil's *Suburbio:* A Micro-Analysis of Voting Behavior in a Context of Social Control," Ph.D. diss., Johns Hopkins University, 1985, published in Spanish as *La conquista del voto: De Velasco a Roldós* (Quito: Corporación Editora Nacional, 1986).

62 For a further discussion of the trade union movement during the military regimes, see Nick D. Mills, *Crisis, conflicto y consenso: Ecuador 1979–1984* (Quito: Corporación Editora Nacional, 1984), pp. 127–42. For discussions of the movement during the democratic period, see Juan Pablo Pérez Saínz, *Clase obrera y democracia en Ecuador* (Quito: Editorial El Conejo, 1985); Jorge León and Juan Pablo Pérez, "Crisis y movimiento sindical en Ecuador: Las huelgas nacionales del FUT (1981–1983)," in *Movimientos sociales en el Ecuador*, ed. Manuel Chiriboga et al. (Quito: CLACSO, 1986), pp. 93–150.

63 The level of domestic violence and armed conflict was substantially higher in Peru than in Ecuador during 1960–1967. For the statistics and a discussion, see Manuel Moreno Ibáñez, "On Measuring Political Conflict in Latin America, 1948–1967," in *Statistical Abstract of Latin America*, vol. 20, ed. James Wilkie and Peter Reich (Los Angeles: UCLA Center for Latin American Studies Publication, University of California, 1980), p. 556.

5 The Crisis of Representation and the End of Reform, 1976–1979

1 *Ficha de Información Socio-Política*, 23 September 1975.

2 Nicos Poulantzas, *The Crisis of the Dictatorship*, trans. David Fernbach (London: New Left Books, 1976), p. 49.

3 Ibid., p. 50.

4 Guillermo O'Donnell, "Reflections on the Patterns of Change in the Bureaucratic-Authoritarian State," *Latin American Research Review* 13, no. 1 (1978): 17–18.

5 Jorge Hidrobo, "Acción política de las clases sociales y las políticas agraria e industrial 1972–1975," photocopy, Center for Latin American Studies, University of Pittsburgh, August 1981.

6 Junta Nacional de Planificación y Coordinación Económica, *Guia institucional del sector público* (Quito: JUNAPLA, 1976), pp. 376, 395.

7 See the speech by León Febres-Cordero in *Guayaquil frente al futuro*, ed. Banco de Guayaquil (Guayaquil: Banco de Guayaquil, 1973), p. 129.

8 For a discussion of the social estrangement of regime policymakers and business leaders, see *Weekly Analysis of Ecuadorean Issues*, 15 August 1975. Fitch reports that by the mid-1960s, over 80 percent of all cadets entering the Army Academy were from middle-

or lower-class backgrounds. See John S. Fitch, *The Military Coup d'Etat as Political Process: Ecuador, 1948–1966* (Baltimore, Md.: Johns Hopkins University Press, 1977), p. 26. The point concerning the social estangement of military officers and businessmen is taken from a discussion in David Schodt, *Ecuador: An Andean Enigma* (Boulder, Colo.: Westview Press, 1987), p. 192.

9   Poulantzas, *The Crisis*, p. 50.

10 *Weekly Analysis*, 25 January 1974.

11 *Ficha*, 12 October 1974.

12 *Ficha*, 19 May 1975.

13 *Ficha*, 20 June 1975.

14 Ibid.; *Ficha*, 21 July 1975.

15 George Philip, "Oil and Politics in Ecuador," University of London, Institute of Latin American Studies, Working Papers no. 1, p. 15.

16 *Weekly Analysis*, 21 November 1975.

17 Banco Central, *Boletín del Banco Central* 48, no. 563 (August–September 1975).

18 Banco Central, *Boletín Anuario*, no. 33 (1980): 138–39.

19 *Weekly Analysis*, 29 August 1975.

20 *Weekly Analysis*, 19 June 1975.

21 *Weekly Analysis*, 29 August 1975.

22 For interpretations in this vein, see Patricio Moncayo, *Ecuador: Grietas en la dominación* (Quito: Escuela de Ciencias de la Información de La Universidad Central del Ecuador, 1977); Instituto de Investigaciones Económicas y Políticas, *El capitalismo ecuatoriano contemporáneo: Su funcionamiento* (Guayaquil: Facultad de Ciencias Económicas, Universidad de Guayaquil, n.d.); Augusto Varas and Fernando Bustamante, *Fuerzas armadas y política en Ecuador* (Quito: Ediciones Latinoamerica, 1978); Luis Verdesoto, "Representación gremial y política de la burgesía industrial ecuatoriana: 1972–1976," M.A. thesis, Pontífica Universidad Católica del Peru, 1978.

23 *Ficha*, 22 August 1975.

24 Ibid.

25 Ibid.

26 *Ficha*, 23 September 1975.

27 *Ficha*, 25 November 1975.

28 While the Communist party never participated directly in the Rodríguez Lara government, the party maintained a sympathetic posture toward the regime, particularly with regard to its oil policies. For a discussion of the historical development of the party, see John Martz, "Marxism in Ecuador," *Inter-American Economic Affairs* 33, no. 1 (Summer 1979): 3–28.

29 *Ficha*, 22 August 1975.

30 *Ficha*, 25 November 1975.

31 Ibid.

32 Ibid.

33 *Ficha*, 27 January 1976.

34 Luis Salazar (Director, FEDEXPOR), interview, Quito, 23 July 1979; Alberto Ledesma (member of the board, FEDEXPOR), interview, Quito, 3 August 1979.

35 See the following FEDEXPOR position papers: "El comercio exterior del Ecuador y su política de promoción de exportaciones," photocopy, Quito, March 1977; "Informe anual 1978," photocopy, Quito, 1977; "Política de fomento y diversificación de las exportaciones ecuatorianas," photocopy, Quito, 1977.

36 *El Comercio*, 10 May 1977.

37 *Weekly Analysis*, 17 March 1978.

38 *Weekly Analysis*, 6 January 1978.

39 *El Comercio*, 5 November 1978.

40 *Weekly Analysis*, 19 November 1978.

41 Banco Central del Ecuador, *Invest in Ecuador* (Quito: Banco Central, 1979); Centro de Desarrollo Industrial, *The Investment Climate in Ecuador* (Quito: CENDES, 1977).

42 *Weekly Analysis*, 20 August 1976.

43 *Weekly Analysis*, 21 October 1977.

44 Galo Montaño, interview, Quito, 16 July 1980.

45 See the following documents by the Cámara de Industriales de Pichincha, *Informe anual 1976–1977*, p. 8; *Carta Industrial*, no. 31 (January–February 1978): 6.

46 *El Comercio*, 8 May 1977.

47 For a review of the events of the *retorno*, see John Martz, "The Quest for Popular Democracy in Ecuador," *Current History* 78, no. 454 (February 1980): 66–70.

48 See "El Plan de reestructuración jurídica del estado y el destino nacional," in Cámara de Industrias de Guayaquil, *Boletín Informativo* 4, no. 46 (September 1976).

49 See "Informe anual de labores del Presidente de la Cámara," in Cámara de Industriales de Pichincha, *Boletín*, no. 31 (January–February 1978).

6 Restructuring Domination Through Democratization, 1979–1984

1 Febres-Cordero's inaugural address appears in María Arboleda et al., *Mi poder en la oposición* (Quito: Editorial El Conejo, 1985): 207–213.

2 For Febres-Codero's attacks on the government during this period, see the interviews in *Vistazo*, 9 March and 6 August 1982; *Impacto*, no. 44 (1983).

3 There is a growing literature on the transition in Ecuador. See Howard Handelman and Thomas Sanders, *Military Government and the Movement toward Democracy in South America* (Bloomington: Indiana University Press, 1981), pp. 3–74; John Martz, "The Quest for Popular Democracy in Ecuador," *Current History* 78, no. 454 (February 1980): 66–70; Patricio Moncayo, *Reforma o democracia? Alternativas del sistema político ecuatoriano* (Quito: Editorial El Conejo, 1982); Luis Orleans Calle Vargas, *La constitución de 1978 y el proceso de reestructuración jurídica del estado 1976–1978* (Guayaquil: Universidad de Guayaquil, 1978); Marcelo Ortiz Villacís, *El control del poder, 1966–1984* (Quito: Editorial Oveja Negra, 1983). For an analysis of electoral returns, see FLACSO, *Elecciones en el Ecuador 1978–1980* (Quito: Editorial Oveja

Negra, 1983). For a discussion of the first round electoral returns of 1984, see Alberto Acosta et al., *1984: Ecuador en las urnas* (Quito: Editorial El Conejo, 1984).

4   A number of authors have examined types of transition to democracy in Latin America and elsewhere. See, for example, Donald Share, "Transitions to Democracy and Transition Through Transaction," delivered at the annual meeting of the American Political Science Association, New Orleans, August 1985. Also see Silvio Duncan Baretta and John Markoff, "Brazil's *Abertura:* A Transition from What to What?" in *Authoritarians and Democrats* ed. James Malloy and Mitchell Seligson (Pittsburgh, Pa.: University of Pittsburgh Press, 1987); Scott Mainwaring and Eduardo J. Viola, "Transitions to Democracy: Brazil and Argentina in the 1980s," *Journal of International Affairs* 38, (1985): 193–219.

5   The candidacy of Raúl Clemente Huerta was the outcome of an internal struggle within the Radical Liberal party. Francisco Huerta Montalvo, nephew of Clemente Huerta, was the original nominee of the party who was forced to resign in the wake of a legal case before the Tribunal Supremo Electoral. Huerta Montalvo then left the Liberal party to form the Partido Democrata.

6   The Tribunal Supremo Electoral annulled 71,500 of the votes cast for the Roldós-Hurtado ticket in the first. This narrowed their lead in the round from 31 percent of the vote to 27.7 percent of the vote. These figures are taken from Howard Handelman, "A New Political Direction?" in *Military Governments and the Movement*, p. 49.

7   The original twenty-one-point program can be found in *Democracia y crisis: Osvaldo Hurtado, Vicepresidente, 1979–1981*, ed. CORDES (Quito: CORDES, 1984), pp. 11–49.

8   Roldós's economic team included such notable businessmen as Rodrigo Paz and Roberto Dunn as well as his brother, León Roldós, who had close connections with *guayaquileño* financial circles.

9   For Raúl Baca Carbo's views, see "Las dudas del Convergencia," *Nueva* (August 1981): 42–47. In an interview December 6, 1984, Borja characterized the Convergencia as one of the causes of his defeat because it associated the ID with an unpopular government.

10   For a more extensive discussion of the campaign of the Chambers against the Hurtado government, see Nick D. Mills, *Crisis, conflicto y consenso: Ecuador 1979–1984* (Quito: Corporation Editora Nacional, 1984), pp. 83–102.

11   In an interview (Quito, 20 January 1987), Pedro Kohn (president of the Cámara de Industriales de Pichincha, 1984–86) pointed to business disatisfaction with the Hurtado government in regard to its style and tone. According to Kohn, the business community was particularly upset with Hurtado's characterization of them as "Miami boys"—that is, as investors who took their profits out of Ecuador and spend them in Miami.

12   Osvaldo Hurtado, interview, Quito, 10 December 1984. For an examination of the stylistic tensions between the Hurtado government and the private sector, see Howard Handelman, "Elite Interest Groups under Military and Democratic Regimes: Ecuador, 1972–1984," delivered at the annual meeting of the Latin American Studies Association, Albuquerque, New Mexico, April 17–20, 1985.

13   *Hoy,* 23 October 1982.

14   Benjamín Ortiz's interview with Hurtado appears in *Democracia y crisis: Diálogos del Presidente Osvaldo Hurtado con la prensa 1981–1984,* Vb, ed. CORDES (Quito: CORDES, 1984), p. 240.

15   The divisions within the business community became visible when a leading conservative businessman of Quito, Carlos Ponce Martínez, denounced the actions of the Chambers (*Hoy,* 21 November 1982). For the legislators' rejection of the calls for a *golpe,* see *Hoy,* 16 November 1982.

16   For an examination of the phenomenon of retrospective voting see Morris Fiorina, *Retrospective Voting in American National Elections* (New Haven, Conn.: Yale University Press, 1981)

17   Sixto Durán Ballén, interview, Quito, 2 September 1983.

18   The Febres-Cordero campaign hired a Colombian publicity consultant, Oscar Lombana. Lombana had served as a strategist on the successful presidential campaign of Colombia's Belisario Betancur. For a discussion of the changes in strategy between the first and second rounds of the elections, see Walter Spurrier, "Febres-Cordero Pulls the Election," in *Weekly Analysis of Ecuadorean Issues,* 11 May 1984.

19   Rodrigo Borja, intervew, Quito, 6 December 1984.

20   *El Comercio,* 6 April 1984; *Weekly Analysis of Ecuadorean Issues,* 12 April 1984.

21   *Hoy,* 23 August 1984; *El Universo,* 15 August 1984. For a list of the party and interest group ties of the members of the Febres-Cordero cabinet, see *Respuesta* 2 (November 1984): 8.

22   The pressures on ID congressmen to desert were intense. For denunciations of FRN maneuvers by the ID, see *El Comercio,* 11 August 1984, 21 September 1984, 16 December 1984.

23   See "Cronología de la crisis política," in *El Comercio,* 16 December 1984.

24   Fernando Larrea (congressional leader of ID), interview, Quito, 12 December 1984; Jorge Moreno (congressional leader of MPD), interview, Quito, 11 December 1984; Carlos Feraud Blum (congressional leader of PD), Quito, 20 December 1984; Roberto Dunn (congressional leader of PRE), interview, Quito, 19 December 1984.

25   Figures on the petroleum sector were taken from the World Bank, *Ecuador: An Agenda for Recovery and Sustained Growth* (Washington, D.C.: World Bank, 1984), pp. 89–107.

26   Figures on the debt were taken from Cornelio Marchán, "Ecuador: Crisis y opciones de desarrollo," delivered at the seminar on the Grupo Andino, 17–19 September 1985, Junta del Acuerdo de Cartagena.

7 From Military Reformism to Democratic Authoritarianism

1   For an examination of the central themes in the debate over Latin American authoritarianism in the 1970s, see James M. Malloy, ed., *Authoritarianism and Corporatism in Latin America* (Pittsburgh, Pa.: University of Pittsburgh Press, 1977); David Collier, ed., *The*

New Authoritarianism in Latin America (Princeton, N.J.: Princeton University Press, 1979); Alfred Stepan, *Authoritarian Brazil: Origins, Policies and Future* (New Haven, Conn.: Yale University Press, 1973).

2   Julio Cotler, "State and Regime: Comparative Notes on the Southern Cone and Enclave Economies," in *The New Authoritarianism*, ed. Collier, pp. 281–82.

3   Marcelo Cavarozzi, "The Government and the Industrial Bourgeoisie in Chile: 1938–1945," Ph.D. diss., University of California, Berkeley, 1975, pp. 415–16.

4   Florestan Fernandes, *A Revolucão burgesa no Brasil* (Rio de Janeiro: Zahar Editores, 1975), p. 221.

5   For further discussion of the emergence of these types of regimes in the region, see the essays by James Malloy and Eduardo Gamarra, Luis Abugattas, and Catherine Conaghan in *Authoritarians and Democrats: Regime Transition in Latin America*, ed. James M. Malloy and Mitchell Seligson (Pittsburgh, Pa.: University of Pittsburgh Press, 1987).

6   Therborn suggests that democratization in Western Europe was contingent upon the constant push of working classes for the extension of rights. See "The Rule of Capital and the Rise of Democracy," in *States and Societies*, ed. David Held (Oxford: Martin Robertson, 1983), pp. 261–71.

7   Albert O. Hirschman, "On Democracy in Latin America," *New York Review of Books*, no. 6, April 10, 1986. For an examination of requisites of democracy that stresses the importance of elite perceptions and a consensus on the "rules of the game," see the classic piece by Robert Dahl, *Polyarchy: Participation and Opposition* (New Haven, Conn.: Yale University Press, 1971).

8   O'Donnell and Schmitter have suggested that, at least at the beginning of a democratic period, electoral rules should be structured to "help" the right in order to assure their representation and their loyalty to the new democratic arrangements. See Guillermo O'Donnell and Philippe C. Schmitter, *Transitions from Authoritarian Rule: Tentative Conclusions about Uncertain Democracies* (Baltimore, Md.: Johns Hopkins University Press, 1986), pp. 61–64.

9   For discussions of corporatist structures in these cases, see Terry Karl, "The Political Economy of Petrodollars: Oil and Democracy in Venezuela," Ph.D. diss., Stanford University, 1982, pp. 622–24; José Luis Reyna and Richard Weinert, eds., *Authoritarianism in Mexico* (Philadelphia: Institute for the Study of Human Issues, 1977).

10 For a further discussion of corporatism in Western Europe, see Suzanne Berger, ed., *Organizing Interests in Western Europe* (Cambridge: Cambridge University Press, 1981); Philippe Schmitter and Gerhard Lembruch, eds., *Trends toward Corporatist Intermediation* (London: Sage Publications, 1982).

11 See Bob Jessop, "Capitalism and Democracy: The Best Possible Political Shell?" in *States and Societies*, ed. David Held et al. (New York: New York University Press, 1983), pp. 272–89.

Bibliography

Books and Articles

Abraham, David. *The Collapse of the Weimar Republic: Political Economy and Crisis*. Princeton, N.J.: Princeton University Press, 1981.

Acosta, Alberto, et al. *1984: Ecuador en las urnas*. Quito: Editorial El Conejo, 1984.

Agosín, Manuel R. "An Analysis of Ecuador's Industrial Development Law." *Journal of Developing Areas* 13, no. 3 (April 1979): 263–74.

Albornoz, Oswaldo. *Del crimen de El Ejido a la revolución del 9 de julio de 1925*. Guayaquil: Editorial Claridad, 1969.

Alexander, Robert J. *Political Parties of the Americas*. Westport, Conn: Greenwood Press, 1982.

Alvarado, Victor, et al. "Los gobiernos, las leyes y las cámaras de producción: 1970–1979." *Difusión Económica* 15, no. 1 (April 1977): 149–66.

Angel, Juvenal. *Directory of American Firms Operating in Foreign Countries*. Vol. 2 of *Encyclopedia of International Information*. New York: Simon and Schuster, 1975.

Arboleda, María, et al. *Mi poder en la oposición*. Quito: Editorial El Conejo, 1985.

Armstrong, Frances. "Political Components and Practical Effects of the Andean Foreign Investment Code," *Stanford Law Review* 27, (July 1975): 1597–1628.

Ascher, William. *Scheming for the Poor: The Politics of Redistribution in Latin America* Cambridge, Mass.: Harvard University Press, 1984.

Asociación Ecuatoriana de Industrias del Cacao (ASEICA). "La industria de elaborados de cacao." Guayaquil, 1979. Photocopy.

Aulestia, Hernan A., and Nilo Idrobo. "La inversión extranjera en el Ecuador." Thesis, Facultad de Ciencias Económicas, Universidad Central del Ecuador, Quito, 1979.

Banco Central del Ecuador. *Invest in Ecuador*. Quito: Banco Central del Ecuador, 1977.

Baretta, Silvio Duncan, and John Markoff. "Brazil's *Abertura*: A Transition from What to

173

174   Bibliography

What?" In *Authoritarians and Democrats: Regime Transition in Latin America*, ed. James M. Malloy and Mitchell Seligson. Pittsburgh, Pa.: University of Pittsburgh Press, 1987.

Barran, José P., and Benjamín Nahum. *El nacimiento del Batllismo*. Vol. 3 of *Batlle, los estancieros y el imperio británico*. Montevideo: Ediciones de la Banda Oriental, 1982.

Barsky, Osvaldo. *La reforma agraria ecuatoriana*. Quito: Corporación Editora Nacional, 1984.

Berger, Suzanne, ed. *Organizing Interests in Western Europe*. Cambridge: Cambridge University Press, 1981.

Blanksten, George I. *Ecuador: Constitutions and Caudillos*. Berkeley and Los Angeles: University of California Press, 1951.

Block, Fred. "Beyond Corporate Liberalism." *Social Problems* 24, no. 3 (February 1977): 352–61.

———. "The Ruling Class Does Not Rule." *Socialist Revolution*, no. 3 (May–June 1977): 6–28.

———. "Class Consciousness and Capitalist Rationalization: A Reply to Critics." *Socialist Review*, nos. 40–41 (July–October 1978): 212–20.

———. "Beyond Relative Autonomy: State Managers as Historical Subjects." *New Political Science* 2, no. 7 (Fall 1981): 33–49.

Bocco, Arnaldo M. "Políticas estatales y ciclo económico." In *Economia política del Ecuador: Campo, región, nación*, ed. Louis Lefeber. Quito: Corporación Editora Nacional, 1985.

Boschi, Renato R. "National Industrial Elites and the State in Post-1964 Brazil: Institutional Mediations and Political Change." Ph.D. diss., University of Michigan, 1978.

Briones, Guillermo. *El empresario industrial en América Latina: Chile*. Santiago: CEPAL, 1963.

Bromley, R. J. *Development Planning in Ecuador*. Sussex: Latin American Publications Fund, 1977.

Calle Vargas, Luis Orleans. *La constitución de 1978 y el proceso de reestructuración jurídica del estado 1976–1978*. Guayaquil: Universidad de Guayaquil, 1978.

Cámara de Industriales de Pichincha. *Regimen legal: Estatuos y reglamento*. Quito: Cámara de Industriales de Pichincha, 1981.

Cardoso, Fernando Henrique. *Ideologías de la burgesía industrial en sociedades dependientes (Argentina y Brasil)*. Mexico City: Siglo Veintiuno, 1971.

Cardoso, Fernando Henrique, and Enzo Faletto. *Dependency and Development in Latin America*. Trans. Marjory Mattingly Urquidi. Berkeley and Los Angeles: University of California Press, 1979.

Carmagnani, Marcello. *Estado y sociedad en América Latina 1850–1930*. Barcelona: Editorial Critica, 1984.

Castro Gomes, Angela Maria de. *Burgesia e trabalho: Política e legislação social no Brasil: 1917–1937*. Rio de Janeiro: Editora Campus, 1979.

Cavarozzi, Marcelo. "The Government and the Industrial Bourgeoisie in Chile: 1938–1964." Ph.D. diss., University of California, Berkeley, 1975.

Centro de Desarrollo Industrial. *The Investment Climate in Ecuador*. Quito: Centro de Desarrollo Industrial, n.d.

Chiriboga, Manuel. "Emergencia y consolidación de la burgesía agro-exportadora en el Ecuador durante el período cacaotero." *Revista Ciencias Sociales* 3, nos. 10–11 (1979): 28–57.

Cochran, Thomas, and Ruben E. Reina. *Capitalism in Argentine Culture: A Study of Torcuato di Tella and S.I.A.M.* Philadelphia: University of Pennsylvania Press, 1962.

Collier, David, ed. *The New Authoritarianism in Latin America.* Princeton, N.J.: Princeton University Press, 1979.

Conaghan, Catherine M. "Industrialists and the Reformist Interregnum: Dominant Class Behavior and Ideology in Ecuador, 1972–1979." Ph.D. diss., Yale University, 1983.

Coniff, Michael L., ed. *Latin American Populism in Comparative Perspective.* Albuquerque: University of New Mexico Press, 1982.

CORDES, comp. *Democracia y crisis: Diálogos del Presidente Osvaldo Hurtado con la prensa 1981–1984,* Vb. Quito: CORDES, 1984.

———. *Democracia y crisis: Osvaldo Hurtado, Vicepresidente, 1979–1981.* Quito: CORDES, 1984.

Corradi, Juan Eugenio. "Argentina." In *Latin America: The Struggle with Dependency and Beyond,* ed. Ronald H. Chilcote and Joel Edelstein. Cambridge, Mass.: Schenkman, 1974.

Cotler, Julio. "State and Regime: Comparative Notes on the Southern Cone and Enclave Economies." In *The New Authoritarianism in Latin America,* ed. David Collier. Princeton, N.J.: Princeton University Press, 1979.

Cueva, Agustín. *El proceso de dominación política en el Ecuador.* Quito: Ediciones Solitierra, 1973.

Cueva Silva, Jaime. *Comercialización del banano ecuatoriano.* Quito: AECA, 1964.

Cúneo, Dardo. *Comportamiento y crisis de la clase empresaria.* Buenos Aires: Editorial Pleamar, 1967.

Dahl, Robert A. *Polyarchy: Participation and Opposition.* New Haven, Conn.: Yale University Press, 1971.

Dean, Warren. *The Industrialization of São Paulo, 1880–1945.* Austin: University of Texas Press, 1969.

DeRossi, Flavia. *The Mexican Enterpreneur.* Paris: OECD, 1971.

Díaz-Alejandro, Carlos F. *Essays on the Economic History of the Argentine Republic.* New Haven, Conn.: Yale University Press, 1970.

———. "Latin America in the 1930s." In *Latin America in the 1930s: The Role of the Periphery in World Crisis,* edited by Rosemary Thorp. London: Macmillan, 1984.

di Tella, Guido. "Rents, Quasi-Rents, Normal Profits and Growth: Argentina and the Areas of Recent Settlement." In *Argentina, Australia and Canada: Studies in Comparative Development 1870–1965,* ed. D.C.M. Platt and Guido di Tella. London: Macmillan, 1985.

Domhoff, G. William. *The Higher Circles: The Governing Class in America.* New York: Random House, 1970.

———. *The Bohemian Grove and Other Retreats.* New York: Harper and Row, 1974.

———. "Social Clubs, Policy-Planning Groups and Corporations." *Insurgent Sociologist,* no. 3 (Spring 1975): 173–95.

Drake, Paul. "The Political Response of the Chilean Upper Class to the Great Depression and the Threat of Socialism." In *The Rich, the Well Born and the Powerful: Elites and Upper Classes in History*, ed. Frederic Cople Jaher. Urbana: University of Illinois Press, 1973.

———. *Socialism and Populism in Chile, 1932–1952.* Urbana: University of Illinois Press, 1978.

———. "Conclusion: Requiem for Populism?" In *Latin American Populism in Comparative Perspective*, edited by Michael L. Conniff. Albuquerque: University of New Mexico Press, 1982.

"Ecuador's Cocoa Processors Reach for New Levels of Quality Control." *Candy and Snack Industry* (June 1979): 41–47.

"Ecuadorean Cocoa Industry." *Manufacturing Confectioner* (May 1977): 22–26.

Evans, Peter. *Dependent Development: The Alliance of Multinational, State and Local Capital in Brazil.* Princeton, N.J.: Princeton University Press, 1979.

Faria, Vilmar. "Desenvolvimento e hegemonia burgesa." *Boletín de ELAS* 1, no. 2 (1968): 23–45.

———. "Dépendance et idéologie des dirigeants industriels brésiliens." *Sociologie du Travail*, no. 3 (July–September 1971): 264–81.

Farrell, Gilda. "Migración temporal y articulación al mercado urbano de trabajo." In *Economia política del Ecuador: Campo, región, nación*, ed. Louis Lefeber. Quito: Corporación Editora Nacional, 1985.

———. "Los microcomerciantes del sector informal urbano: Los casos de Quito y Guayaquil." In *El sector informal urbano en los paises andinos*, ed. Daniel Carbonetto. Quito: ILDIS, CEPESIU, 1985.

Febres-Cordero, León. "Guayaquil frente al futuro en el campo desarrollo industrial." In *Guayaquil frente al futuro*, comp. Banco de Guayaquil. Guayaquil: Banco de Guayaquil, 1973.

Ferguson, Thomas, and Joel Rogers, eds. *The Political Economy: Readings in the Politics and Economics of American Public Policy.* Armonk, N.Y.: M.E. Sharpe, 1981.

Fernandes, Florestan. *A revolução burgesa no Brasil: Ensaio de interpretação.* Rio de Janeiro: Zahar Editores, 1975.

———. *Reflections on the Brazilian Counter-Revolution: Essays by Florestan Fernandes.* Edited by Warren Dean. Trans. Michel Vale. Armonk, N.Y.: M.E. Sharpe, 1981.

Fernández, Jorge. "Un decenio de industrialización en el Ecuador: Un balance crítico." In *El proceso de industrialización ecuatoriana*, ed. Cristian Sepúlveda. Quito: Pontificia Universidad Católica del Ecuador, 1983.

Finch, M.J.H. *A Political Economy of Uruguay Since 1870.* New York: St. Martin's Press, 1981.

Fiorina, Morris. *Retrospective Voting in American National Elections.* New Haven, Conn.: Yale University Press, 1981.

Fitch, John S. *The Military Coup D'Etat as a Political Process: Ecuador 1948–1966.* Baltimore, Md.: Johns Hopkins University Press, 1977.

FLASCO, comp. *Elecciones en el Ecuador 1978–1980.* Quito: Editorial Oveja Negra, 1983.

Fondo de Promoción de Exportaciones (FOPEX). Corporación Financiera Nacional. "Comercialización interna y externa del cacao y semi-elaborados de cacao." Información Técnica, Serie: Perfiles por productos, no. 1, November 1978. Photocopy.

Galarza, Jaime. *El festín del petróleo.* Quito: Cicetronia Cia., 1972.

————. *El yugo feudal.* Quito: Ediciones Soliteirra, 1973.

Germani, Gino. *Authoritarianism, Fascism and National Populism.* New Brunswick, N.J.: Transaction Books, 1978.

Gerschenkron, Alexander. *Economic Backwardness in Historical Perspective.* Cambridge, Mass.: Harvard University Press, 1962.

Gibson, Charles R. "The Role of Foreign Trade in Ecuadorian Development." Ph.D. diss., University of Pennsylvania, 1968.

Guerin, Daniel. *Fascism and Big Business.* New York: Monad Press, 1973.

Guerrero, Andrés. *La hacienda precapitalista y la clase terrateniente en América Latina y su inserción en el modo de producción capitalista: El caso ecuatoriano.* Quito: Escuela de Sociología, Universidad Central del Ecuador, 1975.

————. *Los oligarcas del cacao.* Quito: Editorial El Conejo, 1980.

————. *Haciendas, capital y lucha de clases andinas.* Quito: Editorial El Conejo, 1983.

Guerrero, Rafael. "La formación del capital industrial en la provincia del Guayas, 1900–1925." *Revista Ciencias Sociales* 3, nos. 10–11 (1979): 58–88.

Guimarães, Cesar. "Businessmen, Types of Capitalism and Political Order." Delivered at the International Political Science Association Congress, Edinburgh, Scotland, August 1976.

Gunder Frank, André. *Lumpenbourgeoisie: Lumpendevelopment, Dependence, Class and Politics in Latin America.* New York: Monthly Review Press, 1972.

Hamilton, Nora. *The Limits of State Autonomy: Post-Revolutionary Mexico.* Princeton, N.J.: Princeton University Press, 1982.

Handelman, Howard. "Elite Interest Groups under Military and Democratic Regimes: Ecuador, 1972–1984." Delivered at the Latin American Studies Association Meeting, Albuquerque, New Mexico, April 1985.

Handelman, Howard, and Thomas Sanders. *Military Government and the Movement toward Democracy in South America.* Bloomington: Indiana University Press, 1981.

Hanson, David Parker. "Political Decision-Making in Ecuador: The Influence of Business Groups." Ph.D. diss., University of Florida, 1971.

Heilbroner, Robert. "The View from the Top: Reflections on a Changing Business Ideology." In *The Business Establishment*, ed. Frank Cheit. New York: Wiley, 1964.

Hidrobo, Jorge. "Acción política de las clases sociales y las políticas agraria e industrial, Ecuador 1972–1970." Center for Latin American Studies, University of Pittsburgh, August 1981. Photocopy.

Hirschman, Albert. "The Political Economy of Import-Substituting Industrialization in Latin America." In *A Bias for Hope: Essays on Development and Latin America.* New Haven, Conn.: Yale University Press, 1971.

————. "On Democracy in Latin America." *New York Review of Books*, no. 6, April 10, 1986.

Hobsbawm, Eric. *Workers: Worlds of Labor.* New York: Pantheon Books, 1985.

Hurtado, Osvaldo. *Political Power in Ecuador.* Trans. Nick M. Mills. Albuquerque: University of New Mexico Press, 1980.

Hurtado, Osvaldo, and Joachim Herudek. *La organización popular en el Ecuador.* Quito: IEDES, 1974.

Ianni, Octavio. *La formación del estado populista.* Mexico: Ediciones Era, 1975.

Icaza, Jorge. *Huasipungo (The Villagers: A Novel).* Trans. Bernard M. Dulsey. Carbondale: Southern Illinois University Press, 1964.

Imaz, José Luis de. *Los que mandan (Those Who Rule).* Trans. Carlos A. Astiz. Albany: State University of New York Press, 1970.

Instituto de Investigaciones Económicas y Políticas. Universidad de Guayaquil. *El capitalismo ecuatoriano contemporáneo: Su funcionamiento.* Guayaquil: Universidad de Guayaquil, n.d.

Instituto Nacional de Planificación. *Plan nacional de desarrollo 1971–1975.* Vol. 1: *Plan global.* Lima: Instituto Nacional de Planificación, 1971.

Jacob, Raúl. *Breve historia de la industria uruguaya.* Montevideo: Fundación de Cultura Universitaria, n.d.

Jaguaribe, Helio. *Political Development: A General Theory and a Latin American Case Study.* New York: Harper and Row, 1973.

Janvry, Alain de. *The Agrarian Question and Reformism in Latin America.* Baltimore, Md.: Johns Hopkins University Press, 1981.

Jessop, Bob. "Capitalism and Democracy: The Best Possible Political Shell?" In *States and Societies,* ed. David Held. New York: New York University Press, 1983.

Johnson, Dale. "Industry and Industrialists in Chile." Ph.D. diss., Stanford University, 1967.

Jouvín Cisneros, Ernesto. "Guayaquil frente a los mercados comunes y la integración." In *Guayaquil frente al futuro,* comp. Banco de Guayaquil. Guayaquil: Banco de Guayaquil, 1973.

Junta Nacional de Planificación y Coordinación Económica. "Antedecentes y perspectivas de la industria ecuatoriana." Quito, n.d. Photocopy.

———. *Programa del banano.* Quito: JUNAPLA, n.d.

———. *Bases y directivas para programar el desarrollo económico del Ecuador.* Quito: JUNAPLA, 1958.

———. *Lineamientos fundamentales del Plan integral de transformación y desarrollo.* Quito: JUNAPLA, 1972.

———. *Evolución histórica del comercio exterior ecuatoriano 1950–1970.* Quito: JUNAPLA, 1975.

———. *Desarrollo y educación en el Ecuador.* Quito: JUNAPLA, 1979.

———. *Ecuador: Estrategia de desarrollo (Lineamientos).* Quito: JUNAPLA, 1979.

Karl, Terry Lynn. "The Political Economy of Petrodollars: Oil and Democracy in Venezuela." Ph.D. diss., Stanford University, 1982.

Kaufman, Robert R. "Industrial Change and Authoritarian Rule in Latin America: A Concrete Review of the Bureaucratic-Authoritarian Model." In *The New Authoritarianism in Latin America,* ed. David Collier. Princeton, N.J.: Princeton University Press, 1979.

Kenworthy, Eldon. "The Formation of the Peronist Coalition." Ph.D. diss., Yale University, 1970.

Kirkland, Edward. *Dream and Thought in the Business Community.* Chicago: Quadrangle Books, 1956.

Kirsch, Henry. *Industrial Development in a Traditional Society: The Conflict of Entrepreneurship and Modernization in Chile.* Gainesville: University Presses of Florida, 1980.

Kolko, Gabriel. *The Triumph of Conservatism: A Reinterpretation of American History 1900–1916.* New York: Free Press of Glencoe, 1963.

Lauterbach, Albert. *Enterprise in Latin America.* Ithaca, N.Y.: Cornell University Press, 1966.

Leavitt, Theodore. "Why Business Always Loses." *Harvard Business Review* 46, no. 2 (March–April 1968): 81–89.

Lefeber, Louis, ed. *Economia política del Ecuador: Campo, región, nación.* Quito: Corporación Editora Nacional, 1985.

Leff, Nathaniel H. "Industrial Organization and Entrepreneurship in the Developing Countries: The Economic Groups." *Economic Development and Cultural Change* 26, no. 4 (July 1978): 661–75.

León, Jorge, and Juan Pablo Pérez Saínz, "Crisis y movimiento sindical en Ecuador: Las huelgas nacionales del FUT (1981–1983)." In *Movimientos sociales en el Ecuador*, ed. Manuel Chiriboga et al. Quito: CLACSO, 1986.

Levy, James. "The Artisans of Quito: 1890–1920." Delivered at Latin American Studies Association Meeting, Albuquerque, New Mexico, April 1985.

Lindblom, Charles E. *Politics and Markets.* New York: Basic Books, 1977.

———. "The Market as Prison." In *The Political Economy: Readings in the Politics and Economics of American Public Policy*, ed. Thomas Ferguson and Joel Rogers. Armonk, N.Y.: M.E. Sharpe, 1981.

Love, Joseph. *São Paulo in the Brazilian Federation, 1887–1937.* Stanford, Calif.: Stanford University Press, 1980.

Loveman, Brian. *Chile: The Legacy of Hispanic Capitalism.* New York: Oxford University Press, 1979.

Lowenthal, Abraham, ed. *The Peruvian Experiment: Continuity and Change Under Military Rule.* Princeton, N.J.: Princeton University Press, 1975.

Lowenthal Abraham and Cynthia McClintock, eds. *The Peruvian Experiment Reconsidered.* Princeton, N.J.: Princeton University Press, 1983.

Mainwaring, Scott, and Eduardo J. Viola. "Transition to Democracy: Brazil and Argentina in the 1980s." *Journal of International Affairs* 30 (1985): 193–219.

Malloy, James M. "Authoritarianism and Corporatism in Latin America: The Modal Pattern." In *Authoritarianism and Corporatism in Latin America*, ed. James M. Malloy. Pittsburgh, Pa.: University of Pittsburgh Press, 1977.

———. *The Politics of Social Security in Brazil.* Pittsburgh, Pa.: University of Pittsburgh Press, 1979.

Malloy, James M., and Mitchell A. Seligson. *Authoritarians and Democrats: Regime Transition in Latin America.* Pittsburgh, Pa.: University of Pittsburgh Press, 1987.

Mamalakis, Markos, and Clark Winton Reynolds. *Essays on the Chilean Economy.* Homewood, Ill.: Richard D. Irwin, 1965.

Marchán, Cornelio. "Ecuador: Crisis y opciones de desarrollo." Seminar on the Grupo Andino, September 1985, Junta del Acuerdo de Cartagena. Photocopy.

Martins, Luciano. *Industrialização, burgesia nacional e desenvolvimento.* Rio de Janeiro: Editorial Saga, 1968.

———. "The Politics of U.S. Multinational Corporations." In *Latin America and the United States: The Changing Political Realities,* ed. Julio Cotler and Richard Fagen. Stanford, Calif.: Stanford University Press, 1974.

Martz, John D. *Petroleum and Politics in Ecuador.* New Brunswick, N.J.: Transaction Books, 1987.

———. *Ecuador: Conflicting Political Culture and the Quest for Progress.* Boston: Allyn & Bacon, 1972.

———. "Marxism in Ecuador." *Inter-American Economic Affairs* 33, no. 1 (Summer 1979): 3–28.

———. "The Quest for Popular Democracy in Ecuador." *Current History* 78, no. 454 (February 1980): 66–70.

———. "Populist Leadership and the Party Caudillo: Ecuador and the CFP." *Studies in Comparative International Development,* no. 3 (Fall 1983): 22–50.

May, Stacy, and Galo Plaza. *The United Fruit Company in Latin America.* Washington, D.C.: National Planning Association, 1958.

McClosky, Herbert. "Consensus and Ideology in American Politics." *American Political Science Review* 58, no. 2 (June 1964): 361–82.

McCloskey, Robert. *American Conservatism in the Age of Enterprise 1865–1910.* New York: Harper and Row, 1951.

Menéndez-Carrión, Amparo. "The 1952–1978 Presidential Elections and Guayaquil's Suburbio: A Micro-Analysis of Voting Behavior in a Context of Social Control." Ph.D. diss., Johns Hopkins University, 1985.

———. *La conquista del voto: De Velasco a Roldós.* Quito: Corporación Editora Nacional, 1986.

Merriman, John, ed. *Consciousness and Class Experience in Nineteenth-Century Europe.* New York: Holmes & Meier, 1979.

Mesa-Lago, Carmelo. *Social Security in Latin America: Pressure Groups, Stratification, and Inequality.* Pittsburgh, Pa.: University of Pittsburgh Press, 1978.

Middleton, Alan. "Proyecto: El gasto público y las migraciones internas en el Ecuador." FLACSO-PISPAL, Quito, n.d. Photocopy.

———. "Division and Cohesion in the Working Class: Artisans and Wage Labourers in Ecuador." *Journal of Latin American Studies* 14, no. 1 (1982): 171–97.

Mills, C. Wright. *The Power Elite.* New York: Oxford University Press, 1956.

Mills, Nick D. *Crisis, conflicto y consenso: Ecuador 1979–1984.* Quito: Corporación Editora Nacional, 1984.

Moncada Sánchez, José. *La evolución de la planificación en el Ecuador.* Quito: JUNAPLA, 1964.

———. *Integración andina y desarrollo económico: El caso ecuatoriano.* Caracas: ILDIS, 1975.

Moncayo, Patricio. *Ecuador: Grietas en la dominación*. Quito: Escuela de Ciencias de la Información de la Universidad Central del Ecuador, 1977.

―――. *Reforma o democracia? Alternativas del sistema político ecuatoriano*. Quito: Editorial El Conejo, 1982.

Montaño Pérez, Galo, and Eduardo Wygard. *Visión sobre la industria ecuatoriana*. Quito: COFIEC, 1978.

Moore, Barrington, Jr. *Social Origins of Dictatorship and Democracy: Lord and Peasant in the Making of the Modern World* Boston: Beacon Press, 1966.

Moreno Ibáñez, Manuel. "On Measuring Political Conflict in Latin America." In *Statistical Abstract of Latin America*, vol. 20, ed. James Wilkie and Peter Reich. Los Angeles: UCLA Center for Latin American Studies, University of California Press, 1980.

Muñoz, Oscar. *Crecimiento industrial de Chile: 1914–1965*. Santiago: Instituto de Economia, 1968.

Murmis, Miguel, and Juan Carlos Portantiero. "Crecimiento industrial y alianza de clases en la Argentina 1930–1940." In *Estudios sobre los origenes del Peronismo*, ed. Miguel Murmis. Buenos Aires: Siglo Vientiuno, 1972.

Musgrove, Philip. *Consumer Behavior in Latin America: Income and Spending in Ten Andean Cities*. Washington, D.C.: The Brookings Institution, 1978.

Mytelka, Lynn. *Regional Development in a Global Economy*. New Haven, Conn.: Yale University Press, 1979.

O'Connor, James. *The Fiscal Crisis of the State*. New York: St. Martin's Press, 1973.

O'Donnell, Guillermo. *Modernization and Bureaucratic-Authoritarianism: Studies in South American Politics*. Berkeley: University of California Press, 1973.

―――. "Estado y alianzas en la Argentina 1956–1976." Documento CEDES/G.E. CLACSO/5/Buenos Aires, 1976.

―――. "Reflections on the Patterns of Change in the Bureaucratic-Authoritarian State." *Latin American Research Review* 12, no. 1 (Winter 1978): 3–38.

―――. "Notas para el estudio de la burgesía local, con especial referencia a sus vinculaciones con el capital transnacional y el aparato estatal." *Estudios Sociales*, no. 12 CEDES, Buenos Aires, July 1978.

―――. *1966–1973 El estado burocrático-autoritario*. Buenos Aires: Editorial de Belgrano, 1983.

O'Donnell, Guillermo, and Philippe C. Schmitter. *Transitions from Authoritarian Rule: Tentative Conclusions about Uncertain Democracies*. Baltimore: Johns Hopkins University Press, 1986.

Ortiz Villacís, Marcelo. *El control del poder, 1966–1974*. Quito: Editorial Oveja Negra, 1983.

Palma, Gabriel. "From Export-led to an Import-substituting Economy: Chile 1914–1939." In *Latin America in the 1930s: The Role of the Periphery in World Crisis*, ed. Rosemary Thorp. London: Macmillan, 1984.

Parsons, James J. "Bananas in Ecuador: A New Chapter in the History of Tropical Agriculture." *Economic Geography* 33, no. 30 (July 1957): 201–16.

Peralta Ramos, Mónica. *Etapas de acumulación y alianzas de clases en la Argentina 1930–1970*. Buenos Aires: Siglo XXI, 1972.

Pérez Sáinz, Juan Pablo. *Clase obrera y democracia en Ecuador* Quito: Editorial El Conejo, 1985.

———. *Entre la fábrica y la ciudad.* Quito: Editorial El Conejo, 1986.

Philip, George. "Oil and Politics in Ecuador." University of London, Institute of Latin American Studies, Working Papers no. 1.

———. *The Rise and Fall of the Peruvian Military Radicals 1968–1976.* London: Athlone Press, 1978.

Plaza, Galo. *Problems of Democracy in Latin America.* Chapel Hill: University of North Carolina Press, 1955.

Pocock, J.G.A., ed. *Three British Revolutions: 1641, 1688, 1776.* Princeton, N.J.: Princeton University Press, 1980.

Portes, Alejandro. "Latin American Class Structures: Their Composition and Change during the Last Decade." *Latin American Research Review* 20, no. 3 (1985): 7–40.

Poulantzas, Nicos. *Political Power and Social Classes.* Trans. Timothy O'Hagan. London: New Left Books, 1973.

———. *Classes in Contemporary Capitalism.* Trans. David Fernbach. London: New Left Books, 1975.

———. *Fascism and Dictatorship.* Trans. Timothy O'Hagan. London: New Left Books, 1975.

———. *The Crisis of the Dictatorships.* Trans. David Fernbach. London: New Left Books, 1976.

Prothro, James. *Dollar Decade: Business Ideas in the 1920s.* Baton Rouge: Louisiana State University Press, 1954.

Prothro, James, and Charles Griggs. "Fundamental Principles of Democracy: Bases of Agreement and Disagreement." *Journal of Politics* 22, no. 2 (May 1960): 276–94.

Pyne, Peter. "Legislatures and Development: The Case of Ecuador 1960–1961." *Comparative Political Studies* 9, no. 1 (April 1976): 43–68.

Quintero, Rafael. *El mito del populismo en el Ecuador: Analisis de los fundamentos socioeconómicos del surgimiento del "Velasquismo" : 1895–1934.* Quito: FLACSO, 1980.

Redclift, Michael. *Agrarian Reform and Peasant Organization on the Ecuadorian Coast.* London: Althone Press, 1978.

Remmer, Karen L., and Gilbert W. Merkx. "Bureacratic-Authoritarianism Revisited." *Latin American Research Review* 17, no. 2 (1982): 3–40.

Reyna, José Luis, and Richard Weinert, eds. *Authoritarianism in Mexico.* Philadelphia: Institute for the Study of Human Issues, 1977.

Robalino Davila, Luis. *El 9 de julio de 1925.* Quito: Editorial "La Unica," 1973.

Rock, David. *Politics in Argentina 1890–1930: The Rise and Fall of Radicalism.* Cambridge: Cambridge University Press, 1975.

———. "The Survival and Restoration of Peronism." In *Argentina in the Twentieth Century,* ed. Rock. Pittsburgh, Pa.: University of Pittsburgh Press, 1975.

Rodríguez, Linda Alexander. *The Search for Public Policy: Regional Politics and Government Finances in Ecuador, 1830–1940.* Berkeley and Los Angeles: University of California Press, 1985.

Salcedo Group. "Grupo Salcedo/Salcedo Group." Guayaquil, 1979. Photocopy.

Salgado, Germáncio. "Lo que fuimos y lo que somos." In *Ecuador Hoy,* ed. Gerhard Drekonja et al., 1973.

Salvador, Galo. "Planificación, desarrollo y sector industrial." *Planificación,* no. 7 (November 1976).

Sandoval-Moreano, J. F. "Commodities, International Trade and Dependent Economic Growth." M. Phil. diss., University of Sussex, 1977.

Sarti, Roland. *Fascism and the Industrial Leadership in Italy 1919–1940.* Berkeley and Los Angeles: University of California Press, 1971.

Schmitter, Philippe, and Gerhard Lembruch, eds. *Trends toward Corporatist Intermediation.* London: Sage Publications, 1982.

Schodt, David. "Indicators of Budgetary Policy under Military and Civilian Governments during the Petroleum Period: Ecuador 1972–1984." Delivered at Latin American Studies Association, Meeting, Albuquerque, New Mexico, April 1985.

———. *Ecuador: An Andean Enigma.* Boulder, Colo.: Westview Press, 1987.

Schumpeter, Joseph. *Capitalism, Socialism, and Democracy.* New York: Harper and Row, 1942.

———. *Imperialism and Social Classes.* Trans. Heinz Norden. New York: Augustus M. Kelley, 1951.

Scott, James C. *The Moral Economy of the Peasant: Rebellion and Subsistence in Southeast Asia.* New Haven, Conn.: Yale University Press, 1976.

Secretaría General de la Administración Pública. *Las empresas públicas en el desarrollo nacional.* Quito: Dirección Nacional de Personal, 1977.

José Serra, "Three Mistaken Theses Regarding Connections between Industrialization and Authoritarian Regimes." In *The New Authoritarianism in Latin America,* ed. David Collier. Princeton, N.J.: Princeton University Press, 1979.

Share, Donald. "Transitions to Democracy and Transition Through Transaction." Delivered at the annual meeting of the American Political Science Association, New Orleans, August 1985.

Sharkey, Eugene G. "Unión Industrial Argentina 1887–1920: Problems of Industrial Development." Ph.D. diss., Rutgers University, 1977.

Silk, Leonard, and David Vogel. *Ethics and Profits: The Crisis of Confidence in American Business.* New York: Simon and Schuster, 1976.

Silva Luvecce, Jorge. *Nacionalismo y petróleo en el Ecuador actual.* Quito: Universidad Central del Ecuador, 1972.

Skocpol, Theda. "Political Response to Capitalist Crisis: Neo-Marxist Theories of the State and the Case of the New Deal." *Politics and Society* 10, no. 2 (1980): 157–201.

Smit, Roelf. "El mercado de frutas y hortalizas y sus perspectivas para la producción ecuatoriana." Ministerio de Agricultura y Ganadería, Proyecto PNUD/FAO-ECU/72/018, Agroindustrias, November 1977. Photocopy.

Souza Martins, José de. *Conde Matarazzo, O empresário e a empresa.* São Paulo: HUCITEC, 1976.

Stepan, Alfred C., ed. *Authoritarian Brazil: Origins, Policies and Future.* New Haven, Conn.: Yale University Press, 1973.

———. *The State and Society: Peru in Comparative Perspective*. Princeton, N.J.: Princeton University Press, 1978.

Strachan, Harry. *The Role of the Family and Other Groups in Nicaragua*. New York: Praeger, 1976.

Sunkel, Osvaldo. "Transnational Capitalism and National Disintegration in Latin America." *Social and Economic Studies* 22, no. 1 (March 1973): 132–76.

Sutton, Francis, et al. *The American Business Creed*. New York: Schocken Books, 1956.

Teichman, Judith. "Interest Conflict and Entrepreneurial Support for Perón." *Latin American Research Review* 16, no. 1 (1981): 144–55.

Therborn, Goran. *What Does the Ruling Class Do When It Rules?* London: New Left Books, 1978.

———. "The Rule of Capital and the Rise of Democracy." In *States and Societies*, ed. David Held. Oxford: Martin Robertson, 1983.

Thorp, Rosemary, ed. *Latin America in the 1930s: The Role of the Periphery in the World Crisis*. London: Macmillan, 1984.

Thorp, Rosemary, and Geoffrey Bertram. *Peru 1890–1977: Growth and Policy in an Open Economy*. New York: Columbia University Press, 1978.

Torres Caicedo, Reinaldo. *Los estratos socioeconómicos del Ecuador: Ensayos de cuantificación*. Quito: JUNAPLA, 1960.

United Nations. Comisión Económica para América Latina. *El dessarrollo económico del Ecuador*. Mexico City: CEPAL, 1954.

———. Economic Commission for Latin America. *The Process of Industrial Development in Latin America*. New York: United Nations, 1966.

United States Embassy, Quito. "U.S. Firms and Businessmen." Quito, 1978. Photocopy.

Valenzuela, Arturo. *The Breakdown of Democratic Regimes: Chile*. Baltimore, Md.: Johns Hopkins University Press, 1978.

Varas, Augusto, and Fernando Bustamante. *Fuerzas armadas y política en Ecuador*. Quito: Ediciones Latinoamerica, 1978.

Velasco, Fernando. *Reforma agraria y movimiento campesino indígena de la sierra*. Quito: Editorial El Conejo, 1979.

Veliz, Claudio, ed. *Obstacles to Change in Latin America*. New York: Oxford University Press, 1966.

Verdesoto, Luis. "Cámaras de Industria, estrategia reformista y política, 1972–1976." *Revista Ciencias Sociales* 2, nos. 7–8 (1978): 204–40.

———. "Representación gremial y política de la burgesía industrial ecuatoriana 1972–1976." M.A. thesis, Pontificia Universidad Católica del Peru, 1978.

Villalobos, Fabio, et al. *Ecuador: Situación y perspectivas de la agroindustria*. Quito: CEPLAES, 1978.

Vogel, David. "Why Businessmen Distrust Their State: The Political Consciousness of American Corporate Executives." *British Journal of Political Science* 8, no. 1 (January 1978): 169–73.

Wallerstein, Michael. "The Collapse of Democracy in Brazil: The Economic Determinants." *Latin American Research Review* 15, no. 3 (1980): 3–40.

Weaver, Frederick Stirton. *Class, State, and Industrial Structure: The Historical Process of South American Industrial Growth.* Westport, Conn.: Greenwood Press, 1980.

Weinman, Lois Johnson. "Ecuador and Cacao: Domestic Responses to the Boom-Collapse Mono-export Cycle." Ph.D. diss., University of California, Los Angeles, 1970.

Weinstein, James. *The Corporate Ideal in the Liberal State 1900–1918.* Boston: Beacon Press, 1968.

Weinstein, Martin. *Uruguay: The Politics of Failure.* Westport, Conn.: Greenwood Press, 1975.

Wilkie, James, and Stephen Haber, eds. *Statistical Abstract of Latin America,* Volume 21. Los Angeles: UCLA Latin American Center Publications, University of California Press, 1981.

Wilkins, Mira. *The Maturing of Multinational Enterprise: American Business Abroad from 1914 to 1970.* Cambridge, Mass.: Harvard University Press, 1974.

Wils, Frits. *Industrialization, Industrialists and the Nation-State in Peru.* Berkeley and Los Angeles: University of California Press, 1979.

World Bank. *Ecuador: Development Problems and Prospects.* Washington, D.C.: World Bank, 1979.

———. *Ecuador: An Agenda for Recovery and Sustained Growth.* Washington, D.C.: World Bank, 1984.

Woy, Sandra L. "Infrastructure of Participation in Peru: SINAMOS." In *Political Participation in Latin America,* ed. John D. Booth and Mitchell Seligson. New York: Holmes & Meier, 1978.

Wright, Erik Olin. *Class, Crisis and the State.* London: New Left Books, 1978.

Wright, Thomas C. *Landowners and Reform in Chile: The Sociedad Nacional de Agricultura 1919–1940.* Urbana: University of Illinois Press, 1982.

Zalduendo, Eduardo. *El empresario industrial en América Latina: Argentina.* Santiago: CEPAL, 1963.

Zeitlin, Maurice. "Corporate Ownership and Control: The Large Corporation and the Capitalist Class." *American Journal of Sociology* 79, no. 5 (March 1974): 1073–1119.

Zeitlin, Maurice, and Richard Ratcliff. "Research Methods for the the Analysis of the Internal Structure of Dominant Classes: The Case of Landlords and Capitalists in Chile." *Latin American Research Review* 10, no. 3 (Fall 1975): 5–62.

Zuvekas, Clarence. "Economic Planning in Ecuador: An Evaluation." *Inter-American Economic Affairs* 25, no. 4 (Spring 1972): 39–69.

Periodical Publications

Banco Central del Ecuador. *Boletín Anuario,* 1979–1982.

———. *Boletín del Banco Central del Ecuador,* 1970–1979.

———. *Memoria del Gerente General,* 1970–1979.

Banco Nacional de Fomento. *Informe de labores,* 1972–1979.

Business Latin America, 1971–1979.

Cámara de Industriales de Pichincha. *Carta Industrial,* 1976–1979.

————. *Informe Anual*, 1972–1986.

Cámara de Industrias de Guayaquil. *Boletín Informativo*, 1976–1979.

Centro de Desarrollo Industrial. *Informe de labores*, 1972–1979.

El Comercio, 1971–1986.

Corporación Financiera Nacional. *Boletín Informativo*, 1978–1979.

————. *Memoria*, 1970–1979.

Ficha de Información Socio-Política, 1974–1976.

Hoy, 1983–1987.

Latin America Weekly Reports, 1971–1979.

Nueva, 1979–1987.

Respuesta, 1984.

Superintendencia de Compañías. *Memoria*, 1972–1979.

El Telégrafo, 1971–1979.

El Tiempo, 1971–1979.

El Universo, 1971–1987.

Vistazo, 1972–1987.

Weekly Analysis of Ecuadorean Issues, 1971–1987.

Index